EMPIRES

EMPIRES
EUROPE AND GLOBALIZATION
1492–1788

GEORGE RAUDZENS

Foreword by Jeremy Black

SUTTON PUBLISHING

First published in the United Kingdom in 1999 by
Sutton Publishing Limited · Phoenix Mill
Thrupp · Stroud · Gloucestershire · GL5 2BU

British Library Cataloguing in Publication Data
A catalogue record for this book is available from the British Library

ISBN 0-7509-1986-8

 TM ALAN SUTTON™ and SUTTON™ are the
trade marks of Sutton Publishing Limited

Typeset in 11/12pt Ehrhardt.
Typesetting and origination by
Sutton Publishing Limited.
Printed in Great Britain by
WBC Limited, Bridgend.

Contents

Acknowledgements & Picture Credits

The author and publisher are grateful to the following for permission to reproduce text and illustrations.

Text: To Routledge Publishers, London, for quotes from F. Logan and P. Padfield; University of Hawaii Press, Honolulu, for quote from I. Elbl; University of California Press, Berkeley, for quotes from R. Hassig; Stanford University Press, Stanford, for quotes from J. Lockhart; Oxford University Press, Oxford, for quotes from Ian K. Steele; Harper & Row, New York, for quotes from W.J. Eccles. Full details are given in the Notes and Bibliography.

Illustrations: (numbers given are page references to this edition):
Courtesy of ADFA Library:
from Frank C. Bowen, *America Sails the Seas*, New York, 1938: pp. 88, 98, 155
from E.W. Lloyd and A.G. Hancock, *Artillery. Its Progress and Present Position*, Portsmouth, J. Griffin, 1893: pp. 13, 15

Courtesy of the Barry Scott Library, Macquarie University:
from Augustus Lynch Mason, *The Story of the Pioneers*, Cincinnati, 1899: pp. 100 (top and bottom), 132, 147, 148
from John Clark Ridpath, *Cyclopaedia of Universal History*, Cincinnati, 1885 (MU Lib D20 .R54, Vol. II, *The Modern World*): pp. 45, 53, 55, 59, 65, 87, 96, 106, 107, 109, 117, 125, 145, 150, 153
from Dr Sophus Ruge, *Geschichte des Zeitalters der Entdeckungen*, Berlin, 1881: pp. 9, 10, 11, 12, 28, 33, 44 (top and bottom), 64
from H.G. Wells, *The Outline of History*, rev. edn 1925 (MU Lib D21 .W39 1920, Vol. II), pp. 6, 63, 152

John Carter Brown Library, Providence, RI:
from Theodor de Bry, *America*, 1634: p. 102
from *Generall Historie of Virginia*, London, 1624: p. 99 (engraving by Robert Vaughan)

Courtesy of Dumbarton Oaks Research Library and Collection, Harvard University:
from Alfredo Chavero, *Lienzo de Tlaxcala*, Mexico, 1892: p. 57

Courtesy of the Houghton Library, Harvard University:
from Honorio Philopono, *Nova typis transacta navigatio*, Venice, 1621: p. 49 (original copy in Houghton Library)

Courtesy of the Macquarie University Library:
from The Author of 'Hochelaga', *The Conquest of Canada*, Vols. I and II, London, Richard Bentley, 1850: p. 121 (Vol. I; print by Th. Hamel); p. 149 (Vol. II; print by R. Houston)

Courtesy of the National Library of Australia: pp. 16, 34

All maps are provided by the author.

Foreword

The nature and impact of European warfare elsewhere in the world is the topic of George Raudzens' interesting work. Ranging widely from the Vikings to the close of the eighteenth century, Raudzens studies European maritime expansion. His individual chapters offer much of interest on particular periods and episodes of trade, colonialism and warfare. A mass of information is synthesized and Raudzens includes many insights of his own. Typical of his arresting approach is his emphasis on the limitations and failures of English colonization in the seventeenth century: 'Their government was largely uninterested in what their colonists were up to and largely unconscious of empire itself. When awareness finally came, with the necessary power, the colonists were already Americans and the French were in an excellent position to dominate all North America.'

Raudzens' emphasis is on sea power. In Asia it was sea transport not territorial control that was crucial, while in the New World the numerical argument about outnumbered Europeans is challenged by suggesting that the greater mobility of the invaders reversed the assumed numerical equation. Cortés benefited from seaborne reinforcements, while Pizarro was able to get within striking distance thanks to sea transport. Numbers were important in North America, ensuring that local populations were overwhelmed. Birchbark canoes provided an alternative mobility to the sea in North America, one that had to be taken into account, and was, most successfully, by the French. In conclusion, Raudzens argues that at the start of the globalization process, maritime and other technologies worked mainly to replace slower growth populations in the Americas and Australasia, without altering the demographies of Asia and Africa.

Naturally, such a bold scheme invites qualification and criticism, but Raudzens is to be congratulated on offering such an accessible and wide-ranging work. Whatever the limitations of European power, especially on land, the world was increasingly one where the crucial links between distant parts were controlled or created by Europeans. This helped to ensure that a 'world economy' developed, that distant regions traded, so that the British shipped Indian tea to North America or the Dutch moved Chinese porcelain to Europe. This trade was to the profit of the European maritime powers that controlled it, so that Britain was well placed for rapid economic growth in the eighteenth century.

An emphasis on European expansion might appear misplaced. Much of the world had never seen a European. European maps of central Asia or of inland Africa were either blank or full of errors and remained so until the nineteenth century. To talk of European power would have been curious in Tibet, conquered by China in 1720, or in Mombasa, whence the Omani Arabs had expelled the Portuguese in 1698, or in West Africa, where the Kingdom of Dahomey dominated European coastal trading posts from the 1720s, or in Angola and Mozambique, where Portuguese expansion was held in the sixteenth and seventeenth centuries.

Yet, however limited their political or military impact might have been, it was Europeans off the coast of Asia, not Asians off that of Europe. It was Europeans who charted the oceans, who explored their dark side of the world – the Pacific – and thus acquired the knowledge that helped them to profit from their strength. The world was increasingly re-named by the Europeans, its spaces organized in and by their maps and projections; although the consequences of this were not apparent in much of the world until the nineteenth century. European products became sought after and European self-confidence was enhanced. Many of the consequences of European ambition were unattractive, most obviously the slave trade, a process that reflected an ability to plan and execute long-range economic exchanges. We can now consider the rise of Europe without applauding its consequences. Yet, it is difficult to challenge its importance. The Europeans re-moulded the world, creating new political, economic, demographic, religious and cultural spaces and links that still greatly affect the world in which we live.

Only European powers had to decide how best to organize, control and support transoceanic land and sea operations, and these became more important in the mid-eighteenth century, as Britain and France developed *sepoy* forces in India that were larger, more effective and more dynamic than those of Portugal, and also sent appreciable numbers of regulars to North America. This led to a range of multiple military capabilities that no non-European power possessed, a range that was to be of great importance in helping to channel the products of nineteenth-century technological change and economic and demographic growth to European military and political advantage elsewhere in the world.

The unique European experience of creating a global network of empires and trade was based on an equally unique type of interaction between economy, technology and state formation. China, Korea and Japan were relatively centralized states; they knew how to build large ships and manufacture guns and their economies and levels of culture were not obviously below early modern European standards – they wished to import little from Europe. However, there was hardly any interaction between these three factors that might create development and change. Economic gain was a very important factor behind European maritime power projection: the possibility of profit acted as a powerful stimulus behind technological development and improved organization for war, trade and colonization. These were to frame the nineteenth-century world, and Raudzens' exciting book is a valuable introduction to its background.

Jeremy Black
University of Exeter

Introduction

Old Eurocentric certainties about the high importance of early modern oceanic expansion and colonization are now under interpretive assault. The civilizing mission becomes either marginal or a series of crimes against humanity. Dramatic changes become gradual shifts over long continuities. How much of the old version of expansion and colonization remains the same, and what needs to be changed? What old influences are still accepted and which ones have to be thrown out or substituted with others? There is no consensus but there are majority and minority interpretations, and what follows is an attempt to set out the main patterns of events and influences according to majority opinions.

What emerges is a more complex story than before but one with unifying themes that are more central than the old ethnic and national competitions among the empires of the Portuguese, Spanish, Dutch, English and French. During the 1490s, in the middle of the Renaissance and just before the Reformation, during the rise of national monarchies and commercial and military changes sometimes described as revolutionary, a few western Europeans suddenly set up the first rudimentary global seaborne transportation network and gained an unprecedented control over the links between previously separate or isolated communities. The trend in historiography is to play down the speed of these developments and argue for a more gradual evolution. It is also fashionable to stress intercultural accommodation rather than European superiority over non-Europeans. But intercontinental transportation links were largely blocked out between 1492 and 1498 by a few hundred Portuguese, Spanish and Italian sailors, and the ensuing long-range sailing ship network did become a Portuguese, Spanish, Dutch, English, French, and finally American monopoly for three centuries. This change began as suddenly as any big historical development in modern times. Even the Manhattan Project took four years. And the global transport monopoly, while fragmented by sometimes vicious competition among its small group of owners, did give these people great powers with which they could impinge on and influence much larger communities in Africa, Asia, the Americas and Australasia. The ocean transport monopolists took over more than half of Asia's external trades and an even larger part of Africa's external trade. They conquered or drove off all the original owners of both the Americas and Australasia, enslaving many, causing the death or cultural annihilation of most of the rest, and replacing Amerindians with European migrants and African slaves. What they destroyed and created up to the 1780s was indeed marginal to developments within Europe itself, as this energetic continent evolved nation states and developed industrialization, but it also ensured that many of these changes generated within Europe would be exported – forceably for the most part – to all other planetary communities. And by the 1780s it was already clear that the New World, to be followed later by a Europeanized Asia and Africa, could begin to shape the history of Europe itself by a growing feedback process.

The debate over the costs and benefits of this expansion and initial crude integration goes on. There are also large gaps in the record of events, whatever their meaning. Our early modern ancestors were not always proficient at statistics, paper records were seldom detailed but often lost or destroyed, and neither Africans, Amerindians nor Australasians left more than isolated fragments of their side of the story. So large uncertainties about the so-called facts, filled with diverse speculations, remain. But as this generation grows more conscious of its integration into a planetary community, the three centuries when a few Europeans opened up new avenues on the road to this integration are worth another re-examination. What follows is such an effort. It is not without its own peculiar slants and opinions, but hopefully it is both reasonably comprehensive and brief.

CHAPTER 1

The Vikings and Early Ocean Travel

VIKING EXPANSION IN EUROPE

Before the fifteenth century only two communities made regular long ocean voyages – the Polynesians and the Scandinavian Vikings. The former had no direct influence on early modern Europeans, and no indirect influence either. The latter probably had less impact than has been suggested by proud descendants and European North Americans. The Vikings clearly contributed more to the development of Europe itself than to the invention of long-range communication. They were the first to cross the Atlantic more regularly but nobody followed their lead for five centuries. The Viking transatlantic technology and methodology gave them links to Iceland and Greenland, which were revolutionary achievements, but their methods were too rigorous and their carrying capacity too restricted to suggest that they developed Atlantic routes in other directions. In about AD 1000 Leif the Lucky, son of Greenland colonizer Erik Raudsen, did reach the northern shores of North America but did not stay long. Why, then, was this such an isolated incident?

The Vikings' expansionist powers back in Europe were outstanding. In the 790s they began to push outward from present-day Sweden, Norway and Denmark in all directions except north, and for the next two centuries sent waves of raiders and migrants successfully into Atlantic Europe as far as the Mediterranean and into riverine Russia as far as the Black Sea. This complex story is impressive even when reduced to a bare chronological outline.[1] The Vikings began to raid weakly defended English and French coastal settlements, especially monasteries, in the 790s. They then raided and settled the Orkney and Shetland Islands and began to attack Ireland in the year 800. In 820 a thirteen-ship Viking fleet attacked Aquitaine in France and in the next decade similar fleets began the plundering of Ireland that was to last for some seventy years. Their attacks on England began in 835, and by 840 they were fighting large battles with Irish kings and setting up permanent settlements. In France they attacked up the Seine in 841, then at Nantes in 844, down to Seville in Spain in 844, and back up to Paris and Hamburg in 845. In the 850s they began to settle in England and also managed to loot Pisa in Italy. In 862 the Swedish

Vikings under Rurik took over as rulers of northern Russia and Estonia and in 865 3,000 Vikings began to conquer parts of England. In 874 they overran three out of the four English kingdoms, they burned Cologne and Trier in 882, and Oleg of the house of Rurik became king of Kiev and set up diplomatic relations with Byzantium. In 885 Vikings besieged Paris in their last main, weakly opposed, act of aggression. Between 890 and 892 a Viking army was driven out of the Netherlands and went to England instead, and between 911 and 918 Rollo the Viking won recognition as duke of Normandy. By about 920 or so Europeans had finally improved their fortifications against these attackers in the most exposed regions, and even had fortified bridges on rivers to stop the Viking ships sailing up them. In 937 the Vikings were expelled from Brittany and in 954 the last Viking king was driven from England, even though Viking migrants were now established settlers. From 980 they made one last big push against England. After discovering and settling Greenland in 985, in 991 they invaded England with a fleet of ninety-three ships, and again in 994 with ninety-four. A Danish army followed in 997 and, after some of them reached America in 1000, King Cnut won the battle of Ashington and became the ruler of all England in 1016. Between 1018 and 1042 England and Denmark were ruled by the same Danish king but in 1066 Harold, heir to Cnut the Viking, was defeated by William, heir to Rollo the Viking from Normandy: Viking expansion was over.

What did all this amount to and what were the causes? According to F. Donald Logan, this was spectacular expansion by a relatively small community but the record is just not complete enough to explain all the reasons and causes:

> The eruption of the Vikings out of their homelands in the late eighth and early ninth centuries remains a puzzling historical phenomenon. Without exaggerating the numbers involved we must say that it surely was more than an accident of history that in the 790s Norwegians were attacking the eastern and even the western coasts of Britain, the islands to the north and west, and Ireland; that the Danes between 800 and 810 repulsed the expansionist forces of Charlemagne and began to extend themselves along the Frisian coast; and that the Swedes had already crossed the Baltic into Latvia and by the early ninth century had travelled as far as Lake Ladoga. It was as if a fierce convulsion went through these northern lands, followed by other convulsions, and for nearly two centuries Scandinavia sent streams of emigrants to the west and south and east, first as seasonal raiders, then as more permanently situated raiders, and, finally, as settlers. How does one explain this phenomenon? The historian faces here an historical problem beyond the power of his sources and his talents to provide an absolute answer. He is thrown into the penumbra where partial evidence and assumption meet to produce conclusions far from certain, conclusions which must be couched in subjunctive moods, and where we are, unhappily, never free from nagging doubt. Some might call this an uncharacteristically humble position for the historian. So be it.
>
> The word 'cause' at this stage must be stricken from the historian's vocabulary and replaced by the more convenient 'factor'. That there was a

population factor involved in the Viking explosion has been the view of many historians since the late nineteenth century.[2]

So, along with other authorities, Logan speculates about Scandinavian population pressures in a region of limited farming land and about opportunities to the south in an as yet sparsely settled and weakly governed Europe. He then turns to the very important causal factor of the unique Viking specialty of deep-sea navigation capabilities. They had the best ships and were the best sailors of their time and place:

> Without ships the Viking expansion would have been unimaginable; without a knowledge of navigation their ships would have been of limited use. The Scandinavians were people who lived near and by the sea. The very name Viking, although meaning raider or adventurer during this period, probably has its root in the word *vik*, meaning inlet; they were the 'inlet folk'. The boat was their natural companion and ally: with it they could fish, trade, and communicate with their neighbours, and without it they could not survive.[3]

Else Roesdahl also agrees that the Viking ships were an indispensable prerequisite to the overall Viking impact.[4] So it becomes clear that the Vikings had the excess population and the means for transportation, and Atlantic Europe presented the opportunities.

But there were actually never very many Viking raiders and migrants. The records of their victims suggest tens of thousands of fearsome invaders descending out of hundreds of ships. In fact, their largest vessels carried about 70 men at the most and their fleets seldom had more than 100 ships. Units they called 'armies' had 200 men or less. Sometimes the 'armies' joined up into army groups, especially during their later invasion campaigns, but such forces never exceeded the very low thousands.[5] With these they effectively colonized the best part of the British Isles, key parts of France, Russia, the Netherlands and Germany, and left an imprint on medieval Europe entirely disproportionate to their human resources. It still seems quite heroic, even though by AD 1000 their influence was just about completely over.

THE VIKINGS GO TO AMERICA – VERY BRIEFLY

At the end of their greatness the Vikings made it all the way to Canada. While the sagas that record those voyages to America are factually dubious and unverifiable, it is at least clear that a few of them crossed the whole north Atlantic. The total number of colonists attempting to settle Newfoundland in about 1010 under Thorfinn Karlsefni and Freydis Eriksdotter – the main effort – was sixty, mostly men, in one ship. The local Amerindian Skraelings had them thoroughly outnumbered, especially after Freydis started a blood feud among her own people and organized the killing of a number of her fellow Vikings. As was to be the case in every subsequent European settlement among Amerindians, antagonisms developed into hostilities. In the greater European invasion from 1493 onwards, the Amerindians sometimes won the odd fight but never the whole war. In this first incursion it was different. They decisively drove the invaders into the sea. According to the Vinland Saga the highly unpleasant Freydis was probably the best defensive advantage the Vikings had but the Skraelings triumphed, despite her fearful tactics:

> Freydis came out and saw the retreat. She shouted, 'Why do you flee from such pitiful wretches, brave men like you? You should be able to slaughter them like cattle. If I had weapons, I am sure I could fight better than any of you.'
>
> The men paid no attention to what she was saying. Freydis tried to join them but she could not keep up with them because she was pregnant. She was following them into the woods when the Skraelings closed in on her. In front of her lay a dead man, Thorbrand Snorrason, with a flintstone buried in his head, and his sword beside him. She snatched up the sword and prepared to defend herself. When the Skraelings came rushing towards her she pulled one of her breasts out of her bodice and slapped it with the sword. The Skraelings were terrified at the sight of this and fled back to their boats and hastened away.
>
> Karlsefni and his men came over to her and praised her courage. Two of their men had been killed, and four of the Skraelings, even though Karlsefni and his men had been fighting against heavy odds.[6]

As the Saga concludes, 'Karlsefni and his men had realized by now that although the land was excellent they could never live there in safety or freedom from fear, because of the native inhabitants'.[7]

This may or may not actually have happened. However, despite a Yale University Press decision in 1966 to print a possible forgery as the authentic Vinland map proving the Viking discovery of America, later justified, such proof is provided by archaeological evidence. Vikings did live for a time at L'Anse aux Meadows on the island of Newfoundland[8] but the Vinland voyages to America were too difficult to be kept up. The limits of westward Viking migration in the Atlantic were at Greenland. Their routes to Iceland and Greenland were humanity's first long-term and long-range ocean communications. In the Greenland case these travels were still continuing – if only just – into the decade of Columbus and Vasco da Gama. This impressive pioneering effort was at the same time also very marginal, and can be adequately summed up in outline.

In about 860 the Vikings discovered Iceland and began to settle it in 870. In about 900 Gunnbjorn Ulfsson discovered Greenland and in 930 Iceland became an independent republic. Erik the Red – Raudsen – emigrated from Scandinavia to Iceland in 960 and then colonized Greenland between 985 and 986. At about this time either Bjarni Herjolfsson or Erik's son, Leif the Lucky, discovered the coast of North America, and in 1001, a year after the Icelanders were first converted to Christianity, Leif explored Vinland, which was probably the island of Newfoundland. Thorfinn Karlsefni unsuccessfully attempted to colonize Vinland in 1010 and in 1121 Bishop Erik tried to find Vinland again in order to bring the gospel to the Skraelings: he also failed. In 1126 a bishopric was set up on Greenland and to that extent it was part of Europe's medieval Christendom.

In 1261 it came under Norwegian rule. Things began to go wrong as the climate got colder early in the fourteenth century. Perhaps Inuit people, formerly called Eskimos, wiped out the Norse settlements in western Greenland in 1345. In 1347 some Greenlanders made another visit to present-day Canada but the last regular ship from Greenland seems to have arrived in Iceland in 1410. In 1492 the papacy was still worried about the souls of the Christians on Greenland but by then, or shortly after, the last Europeans out there had probably all died.

The Vikings were soon outstripped in population, wealth and power by southern neighbours in Europe – who were partly composed of their own relations – and too isolated in the north Atlantic to create a widespread cultural or transportation revolution in their own time: theirs was a unique minority *tour de force*. They had a big impact on ship technology, however. The Atlantic sailing ships of the fifteenth century evolved from Viking designs, which made ocean navigation permanently global.

VIKING SHIPS

In classical times Mediterranean ships were already capable of navigating along Europe's Atlantic coast. Even though the demise of the Romans arrested technological and navigational development, there were nevertheless ship design continuities that were carried over from the ancient era to the Vikings. Nor were the Vikings alone in reviving long-range navigation techniques. Among other contributors to the ongoing development of ships were the old Irish folk. According to G.J. Marcus, the real pioneers of deep-water Atlantic navigation in the early Middle Ages were Irish sailors who used skin-covered rowboats called curachs. With these craft they actually beat the Vikings to Iceland but did not follow up this achievement effectively with colonists.[9] But Marcus does concede that Norse equipment was a great improvement over curachs:

> It was Norse mastery of ship design and construction which made possible the first Viking raids toward the close of the eighth century. It was in the course of that century, probably by the middle decades, that the true sailing ship had been evolved.[10]

Other experts generally agree. This ship gave Vikings transportation and communication superiority everywhere in European waters, and beyond. Such superiority translates into increased energy. As Dennis O. Flynn puts it, 'Transportation is not something that happens after production; *transportation is production*'.[11] In other words, better shipping facilities made more goods and services available more quickly, which in turn led to more wealth and power. The Viking ships brought military advantage first, followed by enhanced conquest, commercial and migration capabilities.

These vessels were essentially large plank canoes with one mast for one sail. There were two basic types, the *langskip* or longship and the *knorr* or *knarr*. The first was a troop carrier and assault ship driven both by muscle power, through oars, and wind power via the single sail. It carried a large crew proportional to its

A Viking longship of the type used to cross the North Atlantic c. *AD 1000.*

carrying capacity. The *knorr* was beamier, partly decked and mainly wind-driven, with a relatively small crew. It was chiefly a cargo carrier or a transporter for migrant and civilian passengers. Else Roesdahl calls longships 'war-and-travel-ships' and points to the reconstructed example of the Gokstad ship, 23.3 metres long and 5.25 metres broad, with a crew of 70 rowing in shifts; she also cites the archeologically investigated Skuldelev 5 ship, 17.4 metres by 2.6 metres, with a crew between 40 and 50, which was the more typical type.[12] The cargo-carrying *knorrs* averaged 16 to 20 metres in length, were much wider than the war ships, and could hold about 40 tons of goods additional to operating crew. A smaller version, 13.8 metres by 3.4 metres, with a crew of 5, could carry 4.6 tons, according to one recent calculation. Propulsion was entirely by wind power.[13] Archaeologically exact reconstructions of *knorrs*, such as the Saga Siglar, have sustained average speeds of 6 to 8 knots per hour, which, among other things, allowed them to make the crossing from Denmark to England in 36 hours.[14] There were wide variations on these specifications and F. Donald Logan warns that from surviving evidence '. . . *the* typical Viking ship did not exist'.[15] But it is nevertheless clear that Viking ships were small wooden boats with very rudimentary sailing systems and entirely open to the elements at all times. The fact that they crossed the Atlantic was no doubt due more to the heroic fortitude of their crews than excellence of design, and they only completed their journeys by braving the open ocean for relatively short bursts between the landing places of Iceland, Greenland and Vinland. From the first Vinland crossing it took over four centuries to improve on Viking designs sufficiently to cross an entire ocean in a single stage.

CHAPTER 2

Ships: Creating Europe's Ocean Transports, 1000–1630

CARAVELS, CARRACKS, AND GALLEONS

A variety of south-western Europeans contributed to the perfection of the 'full-rigged' ocean ship designs of the fifteenth century but the Portuguese and Spanish mariners were the first to put them into regular service. The sea trade and travel facilities of Europe expanded almost continuously from the eighth century, pushed along most strongly by the Vikings and then further stimulated by the Crusades and general population growth. This was all coastal navigation. In the Mediterranean it remained muscle powered; the galleys, for trade but even more for war, continued to dominate there into the fifteenth century, especially in the fleets of Venice and Genoa and later on in those of the Ottoman Turks and the Spanish

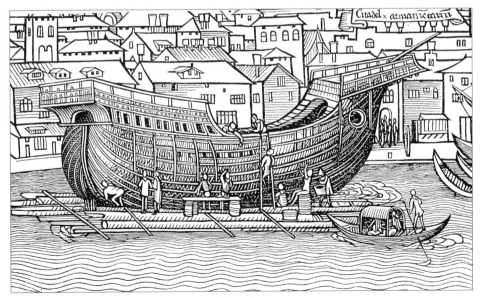

Sailing ship hull, typical of carracks, late fifteenth century.

kings. But the essential evolution occurred in sailing ships through an amalgamation of multi-masted Baltic and German medieval types with Mediterranean and Iberian sailing designs. The results began to crystallize in the 1430s with the appearance of the Portuguese caravel, the first of five main types – along with the carrack (also the *nau* or *nao*), the galleon, the *fluyt* and the war-service-only man-of-war – that comprised the oceanic 'full-rigged ship' by about 1630. These were the essential designs that enabled the creation of the first intercontinental connections. They carried commercial goods, migrants, conquerors, and armed and violent competitors. This basic ship technology remained largely unchanged until the advent of steam-powered vessels in the 1830s. For four centuries these full-rigged ships were the sole physical means of moving people and goods among the main continents and their maritime communities.

The development process has been assessed by a variety of scholars, especially and most recently by Richard W. Unger.[1] Briefer up-to-date assessments are presented by Carla Rahn Phillips[2] and Oscar H.K. Spate,[3] among others. The full-rigged sailing ship was developed from northern and southern European designs during the fourteenth and fifteenth centuries. Northern ships called cogs, with large square sails on single masts, had followed Viking hull designs of overlapping or clapboard planking. Southern designs had two or three masts

East Indian galley, sixteenth century.

A full-rigged European sailing ship, late fifteenth century.

carrying triangular sails and their hulls were made of planking attached edge to edge to structural timber ribs. The southern hulls were stronger but there were advantages to northern square sails. In the middle of the thirteenth century sea travel between the Mediterranean and northern Atlantic Europe had increased a great deal, partly because of the Portuguese and Spanish 'reconquests', that removed much of the previous Muslim interference with Christian traffic. As ship designs blended, by the fifteenth century cogs evolved into caravels and into carracks shortly afterward. The latter were fully developed in the first instance in Spain, especially by the Basques, and also by the Portuguese. Caravels already had ocean-crossing capabilities but were small ships with limited carrying capacity. Carracks were the first true long-range ocean transports, with three masts, a set of square and also triangular sails and the strongest timber hull structures at that time. They could carry very heavy cargoes almost indefinitely, or as long as food and water lasted for the crew. They could sail non-stop for many months at a time. The Portuguese called their carracks *naus* and developed the first big fleet early in the sixteenth century. The Spanish called them *naos* and built the biggest fleet in the second half of the sixteenth century, by which time most of the rest of Atlantic Europe and some of Mediterranean Europe were commonly using them.

The smaller and quicker caravels also stayed in service. They found the new ocean routes while the carracks carried the heavy loads. In the 1430s the Portuguese used caravels for trade and colonization down the African coast and to

East Indian merchant ship, sixteenth century.

the Atlantic islands of the Azores, Cape Verdes and Madeira. In 1492 Columbus had two caravels, the *Nina* and *Pinta*, while the *Santa Maria* was a small carrack, or *nao*. Bartolome Dias and Vasco da Gama used caravels to round the Cape of Good Hope and get to India between 1488 and 1498. Caravels usually weighed about 50 tons; carracks were between 300 and 500 tons on average, with a few weighing as much as 1,500 tons. After the discoveries the caravels were used as auxiliary and minor role vessels, for things like communication and emergency reinforcement. The carracks became the mainstay of ocean transport in the early overseas empires. According to Unger, manning levels ranged from between 3 to 10 tons of ship weight per sailor, which gave a 500-ton carrack a working crew of about 50, not counting passengers.[4]

During the sixteenth century the one major variation on caravels and carracks was the galleon. This ship appeared in the 1510s and developed such romantic connotations that a variety of competing national historians have attempted to claim exclusive invention credit for their particular ancestors. Thus the first galleons might have been created either by the Portuguese, the Venetians, the Castilians, the English or perhaps the Serbs. In any case, the same mariners who used carracks as heavy transports used galleons as somewhat smaller but faster –

and invariably more heavily armed – versions. Galleons were more streamlined, for their age anyhow, and the English called them 'race-built', for raiding and combat. Average weight was around 300 tons or a bit more. They carried the more elite passengers and the less bulky but more expensive cargoes.

ARTILLERY

While galleons were heavily armed, caravels and carracks also carried weapons and armed personnel. To Europeans the ocean was hostile territory, a continual combat zone. A few of all three armed types were directly owned by governments and used mainly as warships. Most were private but could be hired or impressed by governments for war purposes for short periods of time. In all cases guns and fighting personnel were integral. There were as yet no distinct ship designs for war service only, no pure battleships. All ships carried cargo, all ships fought, and almost all were privately constructed and owned. By the 1450s, at about the same time as the advent of caravels, sea service artillery or ship's guns – introduced in rudimentary form as early as the 1380s – were in full working order and in general European service.[5] Standard weapons were a variety of bronze muzzle-loading cannon, the biggest of which fired iron balls weighing 50 lbs or more and had an overall weight of over 4 tons each. They were very expensive, very durable – lasting hundreds of years if looked after properly – and already about as accurate as artillery got before industrialization.

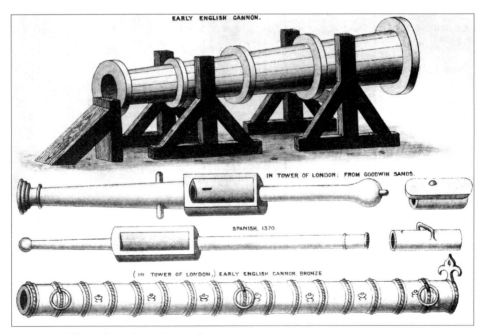

Early English artillery pieces, sixteenth century.

They could regularly hit small targets beyond 500 metres, though at very modest reloading rates.[6]

Such guns, especially the smaller types, were also mounted on Mediterranean galleys, which continued to make up the bulk of the local fighting ship types. But there was little room for them on galleys teeming with oars and crowded with rowers and soldiers. On these ships the main attacking strategy continued to be marine infantry boarding tactics. It was on carracks and galleons that the guns sprouted in increasing numbers. On land an 8,000-lb full cannon required huge amounts of muscle power – oxen, horses and people – to move it anywhere at all on Europe's underdeveloped road network. Such big guns were increasingly used in land war, especially in sieges, but preference was for the smaller types. With the adoption of the ribbed frame heavy timber hulls of carracks, however, big cannon in large numbers could be readily carried, manoeuvred and discharged without undue fear of breaking up the ship from recoil forces. The high sides of these ocean ships, now bristling with gun barrels, formed floating fortifications. They became largely immune to boarding tactics and could be harmed only by other ships with guns. In about 1500 combat power was further improved by the invention of gun ports. Again there is dispute about who first had the idea and when it was implemented but there is no dispute that almost every shipbuilder adopted the design in the early sixteenth century. Holes were cut in rows, as low as possible along the sides of the ship, and fitted with hatches to keep out the waves. The gun muzzles protruded from these ports when ready to fire. The lowering of the gun decks moved the ship's centre of gravity closer to the waterline and so increased stability and seaworthiness. It was, however, essential to close the hatches in adverse weather conditions or when the ship heeled over under wind pressure. According to George Modelski and W.R. Thompson, in 1518 the standard armament of a Portuguese galleon consisted of thirty-five big guns.[7] According to Richard Unger, Portuguese carracks began to bombard Asian shipping in the Indian Ocean with gunfire from about 1500, although the first clear instance of a European ship sinking another ship with its guns was in 1513.[8] In the vigorous opinion of Carlo Cipolla, in a book entitled *Guns and Sails in the Early Phase of European Expansion 1400–1700*,[9] it was this unrivalled European superiority in long-range transportation, combined with firepower, that directly accounts for European imperial domination in Africa, Asia and America. William H. McNeill, who describes the rise of a series of gunpowder empires at the start of the early modern period, agrees with Cipolla.[10] J.F. Guilmartin joins in as follows:

> The Portuguese could have reached India without gunpowder; but they could never have maintained themselves there or brought their cargoes back. The same general considerations apply to the Spanish in the New World. There was a great deal more to it than just gunpowder; but without gunpowder Cortés and Pizarro would have been doomed to failure from the start and the Spanish would hardly have left more of an imprint on the Western Hemisphere than the Vikings.[11]

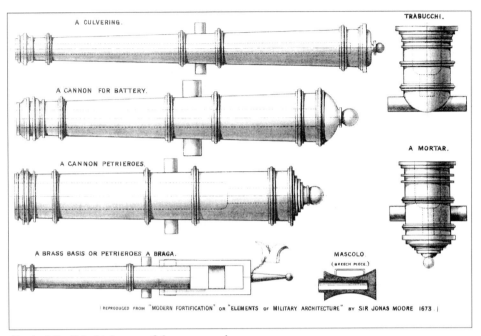

Typical English ship's guns of the seventeenth century.

Maybe so but maybe not.[12] The Spanish, for a start, had a lot more ships and people than the Vikings, and there were other big differences. Still, for most historians who take the broad rather than the specialist approach, the technological superiority argument lives on. Most recently it is again stressed by the followers of Geoffrey Parker's 'Military Revolution' thesis, which is partly a development from W.H. McNeill's arguments.[13] Parker emphasizes land warfare. Siege artillery was perfected by the 1440s and wiped out Constantinople and the medieval castles that were the bastions of feudal particularism and political fragmentation. Cannon dictated new and expensive fortifications, therefore favouring greater political centralization, under monarchs growing to national proportions, with greater tax revenues. In the 1490s the French pioneered the first effective field artillery. In about 1500 the Castilians began to adopt gunpowder infantry small arms, arquebuses and muskets. Others were forced to follow or suffer defeat. Monarchies and armies grew bigger. Frank Tallett, who actually argues that these types of changes were more gradual than revolutionary, nevertheless agrees that militarism expanded quickly. Thus there were 15,500 soldiers fighting in the battle of Ravenna in 1512 but at Malplaquet in 1709 there were 181,000 combatants. In 1494 Charles VIII of France initiated early modern warfare with his invasion of Italy with an army of 18,000 soldiers: in 1710 France had an army numbering 310,000 men.[14] And the start of this 'Military Revolution', whether revolutionary or evolutionary, coincided with the general European adoption of caravels, carracks and galleons. On both land and sea Europe launched an unprecedented spate of warfare, with more battles than in any other place or time. The frequency and intensity was less at sea and less overseas than near Europe. But there was a lot more combat than before.

Modelski and Thompson believe that sea power from this age of revolution and discovery to the present day is the main determinant of international power superiority, through a process and apparatus they call 'global reach'. They identify Portugal as the first world-class superpower because its gun-armed carracks and galleons gave it the first 'global reach'. Among their extensive supporting quantification they note that the Portuguese ran their overseas operations with 3 large ships in 1494, 112 ships in 1512, 300 in 1536 and 18 in 1580, with all sorts of variations. With numbers like these they led the world in the first half of the sixteenth century, though Spain soon caught up. Each carrack or galleon took two years to complete a round trip to India or beyond, lasted about eight years in operational service, and at least one ship a year sank, usually in bad weather.[15] Between 1492 and 1502 Spain sent 6 fleets totalling 62 big ships to the West Indies; in 1575 Queen Elizabeth I of England personally owned 24 ships, mostly for fighting, and England had another 135 privately owned ships weighing over 100 ton.[16] Carla Phillips adds that by 1583 Spain rose to top sea power with over 1,000 ships totalling 250,000 tons.[17] So Portugal had 'global reach' first, Spain second, and England was a long way behind.

But what about the ships and armaments of other cultures? Were they so much weaker? In the fifteenth century the Chinese had well-armed big ships too. Between 1405 and 1433 Chinese imperial admiral Cheng Ho, or Zheng He,

Chinese merchant ships at the time of first contacts with Europeans.

led most of seven great ocean-going junk fleets to India and Africa. His ships were at least much larger than contemporary European designs and perhaps more powerful in combat as well. He had no trouble with opposition and collected many accolades. But it seems he found nothing that China especially wanted, his fleets were cancelled, and the Chinese opted out of overseas operations.[18] Therefore, when the Portuguese arrived on the maritime scene, they had no Chinese opponents to worry about, not even seriously in the China Sea. M.N. Pearson argues that Asian shipping as a whole in the 1490s was of shorter range, lighter construction and without armaments. Muslim and Ottoman warships did operate in the Red Sea and Persian Gulf, and could navigate the Indian Ocean, but they were mostly galleys. Arab transports were dhows, excellent monsoon sailers and cargo carriers, but unarmed and lightly built. The discharging of heavy ordnance on a dhow could easily open up the hull and sink the vessel. So the Portuguese found no armed and dangerous competition in Asian waters.[19] Neither Africans nor Amerindians had armed long-range sea transports. Their Caribbean, riverine and coastal boats were relatively small and simple canoes driven almost entirely by muscle power and entirely without chemically propelled firepower devices. The Europeans had a sea power monopoly. Their biggest threat on the seas came from their own kind – other Europeans.

FLUYTS AND MEN-OF-WAR

These gun-armed full-rigged ships came in many varieties. They were, after all, built by craftsmen in many isolated shipyards, largely with hand tools. But there were only two main design variations from caravels, carracks and galleons until the steam age in the nineteenth century. Towards the end of the sixteenth century the Dutch developed a much more economical long-range bulk transport called the *fluyt*, later widely imitated by others. And in the 1630s, mostly led by the English, Atlantic European governments began to build ships for war only – true naval battleships like the *Sovereign of the Seas*, which had 100 guns in two rows of gunports – and were called men-of-war or 'ships of the line'. Almost all previous warships had also served as transports but these new designs were for fighting only. By 1653 the Dutch also created a first standing navy.[20] Conversely, *fluyts* sailed mostly or entirely without guns in order to be able to increase their loads.

These *fluyts* completed their evolutionary development in about 1595. They were larger, lower, shallower and cheaper than carracks, built by mass-production techniques and by wind- and water-powered saws and other machinery. They required less timber per ton than carracks, a great boon in a treeless country like the Netherlands, which imported all its building materials mostly from the Baltic region. The sail plan was simplified, with pulleys and tackles to reduce the work of sail control. *Fluyts* were slower than carracks and especially galleons but they were better sailers and required less crew. They delivered bulk cargoes at much reduced prices. Average sizes were in the 300 to 500 ton range. After 1600 the Dutch turned them out by the thousand, building the biggest ocean fleet in the world for themselves and also supplying the English, French and other European merchant marines. It took the English until well into the second half of the seventeenth century to build a bigger, though not more economical, deep-water transport service.[21]

The specialist battleships that the Dutch in turn copied from the English in the 1650s were also adopted by all the Atlantic European nations. These were galleon evolutions, had 'global reach', were immensely expensive and remained largely unchanged until the Crimean and American Civil Wars. Modelski and Thompson list in detail the number of warships each country had and at what date. The nation with over 50 per cent of all of them at any given time had sea power superiority. Thus in the pre-man-of-war era Portugal, with carracks and galleons only, was superior from 1502 to 1544, Spain from 1594 to 1597 (only), and the Netherlands from 1608 to 1642; in the man-of-war era Britain was the superior sea power from 1719 to the end of the age of sail.[22]

These are the bare outlines and only some of the opinions about this critical maritime technology. Much of the evidence is vague or missing. But there are surviving examples of these all-conquering ship types in famous museums, notably the carrack *Mary Rose* and the galleon transition to man-of-war, the *Vasa* or *Wasa*. Both sank fully loaded and manned, and were raised largely intact in our time. The *Mary Rose* belonged to Henry VIII. She was a 600-ton fighting warship with combat service against the French between 1512 and 1514 and again between 1522 and 1525. As a very old ship she was completely renovated in 1544. On 19 July 1545 she was sailing once more against the French in the English Channel, armed with 20 heavy cannon, 60 lighter guns and carrying a crew of 400 sailors and fighters. The lower gun ports had not been closed. A heavy sea poured in and she went down with heavy loss of life. The ship was discovered by skin divers in 1968 and is now a famous and sometimes travelling museum exhibit. E.D.S. Bradford, among others, has published the story of the *Mary Rose* in detail.[23] The *Vasa*, sixty-four guns and immensely expensive, was built for the Swedish king Gustavus Adolphus Vasa. On her sea trials on 10 August 1628, she went down in Stockholm harbour in full sight of numerous spectators, settling into deep mud. It seems once more that the lower gun ports had been left open. In 1961 the *Vasa* was dragged out of the mud and is now on display at the Vasa Museum in Stockholm.

These were the transport and war technologies pioneered and monopolized by a western European minority from the 1490s. The experts do not all agree about their importance in the global integration process; the relative power of the guns is most often disputed. Less frequently there are also ship technology minimizers. Philip D. Curtin insists that in practical terms the ships of other cultures were just as effective and that, in fact, 'The European "maritime revolution" of the fifteenth and sixteenth centuries was not so much a revolution in ship design as a discovery of the world wind systems'.[24] Perhaps, but his is a minority opinion so far. A larger group of experts prefer to ignore most of this technology entirely. But getting out to sea was by itself a story more than loaded with human drama. The ships were certainly central to contemporary expansionists. Among other things such as bloody battles and tragic shipwrecks, thousands died on these transports from malnutrition, overcrowding, exposure and gross sanitation inadequacies centred especially on the use of the hull as a toilet by both people and livestock. The Dutch, so long the dominant ocean carriers, paid a heavy price in sailor casualties. R.I. Rotberg and T.K. Rabb calculate that '. . . from 1602 to 1795, one million sailors embarked from Dutch ports in 4,700 sailings, of whom at least 660,000 never returned'.[25] They were killed on the job. Drama or no, did this technology drive expansion or was it itself a consequence? There were a multitude of other causes for expansion. The power of technology in generating changes for humanity remains in question. But the European ocean transport monopoly, whether cause, effect, or other, does seem to be a vital prerequisite or co-requisite for the trade links and conquests that began from the 1490s.

CHAPTER 3
The Sea Frontiers of Portugal

The Vikings, and probably the Spanish agent Columbus, crossed an entire ocean first, but the mariners of Portugal led humanity in long-range maritime travel. Between 1415 and 1488 they created a south-east Atlantic sea empire of African trading posts and offshore island colonies, with well-marked water routes right around the southern end of Africa itself. Four years before Columbus, Portuguese sailors were the first to reach an entirely new ocean on the other side of Africa. By then they had more of the most advanced caravels and carracks capable of transoceanic travel than any other unified group in Europe or beyond, with more of the latest bronze guns on board. Although Portugal had an excellent geographic position and political structure, the ships sailed from a base of limited human and natural resources. However, the sailors made up for their serious quantitative shortcomings and specialized in sea travel and combat particularly. From 1500, in half a century, they added to their Afro-Atlantic maritime empire a kingdom of armed trading posts from east Africa to India, Indonesia, China and Japan, linking all the richest communities of the Old World with the first lasting communications network. By the 1550s they extracted more wealth from African and Asian trade than anybody else and the Portuguese ruling elite was probably the richest in the world. There was even a developing colony in the New World – Brazil – promising more wealth still, and duly delivering it via slave-grown sugar plantations from the 1570s. By then, however, Spain was already both a wealthier and a bigger sea power than its small Lusitanian neighbour. The Portuguese showed the world how to build a maritime empire and make it pay but then froze their working formula into place and found better resourced imitators overtaking them. In Spain's case, riches went with power great enough to finish off Portuguese competition by seizing political control of the small country – and its vast but thinly manned sea frontiers – in 1580.

How did this epic demonstration of the triumph of specialist quality over resource quantity come about, and why did Portugal last for its particular time as leading world sea power? The experts now argue for evolutionary growth much assisted by initiatives from other European groups, and even more for African and Asian accommodation of the Lusitanians as generally useful suppliers of transport and commercial services. So the Portuguese more or less inherited the means to create an empire and they built that empire only because it was in African and Asian interests to let them. This sort of interpretive tendency, so completely opposite to older nationalistic and Eurocentric explanations, is not, however, fully documented. The surviving records are scanty, even from the Portuguese side; much was lost in the great earthquake and fires of Lisbon in 1755. Some Asian documentation is now being retrieved but little record-keeping took place in Africa in any case. The 'facts' are too few to prove either an overwhelming Portuguese proactivity or a basic Portuguese passivity. They do suggest that through imitation or not, and with African and Asian compliance or not, a very few Portuguese made some sort of memorable impact in a lot of places outside of Europe before anybody else did.

EARLY AFRICAN AND ATLANTIC EXPANSION

How did this Portuguese expansion process start? As in Spain, the Portuguese in the Middle Ages were preoccupied with reconquest, with land control wars against the Moors. They were quicker than the Spanish in driving these Muslim colonists out of Portugal itself. By 1249 reconquest was completed on the European side of the Pillars of Hercules. But the Moorish wars went on as the Portuguese crown and nobility sought to follow their old oppressors to North Africa. In 1415, under Joao I of the exceptionally talented and well-supported royal house of Aviz, the Portuguese captured Ceuta in present-day Morocco, the first European colony outside Europe itself since the Vikings in the north and the Crusader kingdoms of the Middle East. Prince Henrique, known later as Henry the Navigator for his sea expansion work, was knighted at Ceuta. For the next century Portuguese knights and more humble soldiers fought it out with the Moroccan Moors. They kept up their combat skills and developed a strong interest in the latest war techniques and technologies. The royal house of Aviz, in the continuing wartime emergency, kept the strong support from the leading citizenry, which was required to consolidate royal power, improve administrative efficiency and expand the tax base. By the 1480s the Portuguese monarchy was the strongest and most centralized government in Europe, with the best control over the aristocratic competitors for political authority and considerable power over the commercial groups in the country as well. The Moorish wars were mainly fought for religion but also for land and other resources. The trouble was that these wars were indecisive. In the words of B.W. Diffie and G.D. Winius, Ceuta had merely started '. . . a century of furious stalemate . . .'[1] which in itself was not much more than a school for soldiers. Instead of beating back Islam in Morocco, the Portuguese had trouble keeping Ceuta and had to watch as the Ottoman Turks, overrunning old Byzantium in 1453, pushed Muslim forces more strongly westward into the Mediterranean basin and eastern Europe with every decade after the 1450s.

So the Portuguese turned south and west, down the east coast of Africa, to advance by sea against the Moorish flank. It was here they built a unique new type of empire. They did have Italian models from the Mediterranean and some Italian precursors in the Atlantic also. In the late thirteenth century the pioneers of Atlantic coastal navigation were the Venetians and Genoese. They were using Mediterranean oar-propelled galleys but were beginning to rely increasingly on early models of sailing ships. Venice and Genoa led Europe in commercial enterprise and probably in per capita wealth at this time. In 1277 the Genoese were sending trading ships to northern Europe. In 1291 the Venetians came up with the very ambitious concept of sailing around Africa to Asia in order to get past the Muslims of the eastern Mediterranean who were controlling European access to spices and Chinese luxury manufactures. The ruling elite sent off a captain called Vivaldi or Vivaldo into the Atlantic to find a route to India. He disappeared. In 1315 his son went out to search for the father and the route. He also disappeared. Perhaps the technology as well as the geographic and navigational knowledge was still too primitive. Meanwhile, in 1312, the Genoese led the way to the offshore Atlantic islands. Lanzaroto Malocello discovered the Canary Islands south-west of the Pillars of Hercules in the open Atlantic. They were inhabited by native people of a unique culture called variously Canarians and Guanches. These new people were less warlike than the Europeans and, in 1335, Malocello took out colonizers both to take some of their land and to capture them as workers. By the 1340s French colonizers joined in and Spanish Catalans and some Portuguese traders began to trade and raid in the Canaries also. It was at this point that Portuguese Atlantic expansion slowly started, in company with the Italians, Spanish and French. Meanwhile, by 1341, Italians had also discovered the more southerly but totally uninhabited islands of Madeira and the Azores, which initially proved less attractive because they contained no native labour and would require more substantial migration to become economically attractive. The focus stayed on the Canaries. In 1402 the Castilians started a new colonization process there, in competition with French and especially Portuguese rivals. The Spanish effort won out but, through various conflicts, including a war with Portugal between 1474 and 1479, it took a big final effort between 1478 and 1496 to take over these islands completely, finishing after Columbus began the colonization of Hispaniola in the New World. The motives and methods of this Spanish colonization in the Canaries and West Indies were in fact linked. The Canaries were in many ways the proving grounds for the conquistadors of the Caribbean, Mexico and Peru.[2] But from the early fifteenth century the Spanish presence was too strong for the Portuguese and they turned to opportunities further south instead, though not without seriously upsetting the Spanish dominance.

A good part of the energy for this more long-range expansionist push by the Portuguese came from the crown after Ceuta in 1415, especially from Prince Henrique. 'Henry the Navigator' sponsored a growing number of southward voyages right up until his death in 1460. Traditionally he is regarded as a crusader against Muslims and a scientific geographer and patron of navigational sciences. M.N. Pearson and P.D. Curtin, among other recent historians, do not believe that spiritual and intellectual urges were primary.[3] Henry and his captains and noble allies were, according to Curtin, engaged in a '. . . mixture of feudal and commercial activity . . .'.[4] They were, like Spanish nobility, looking for new lands to conquer with food sources and workers, to expand their estates as they had done against the Moors in the reconquest. But unlike other European landed aristocrats, the Portuguese nobility were also more commercially minded. They were just as keen to capture or set up new trades as they were to seize estates and workers. At least this is the Curtin argument. There is, at any rate, little evidence that disputes the large involvement of the Portuguese nobility, and their 'fidalgo' relatives, in the creation of their full-sized maritime empires.

Under Henrique's patronage the expansion of both territories and trading posts became steady. In 1425 Portuguese settlers began to colonize Madeira, on which they grew sugar so successfully that by 1455 they began to export it to Europe. There was insatiable demand for it. The Madeira colonists, increasingly relying on African slave labour, were opening a sugar export business that was to dominate the Atlantic region until the start of the seventeenth century and which was to become one of the most economically influential of the new enterprises generated by overseas expansion. Meanwhile, by 1434, captain Gil Eannes sailed around Cape Bojador thus getting past the Sahara coast and down to the commercially attractive coasts of eastern Africa. In the 1440s, now equipped with the new caravels, Portuguese captains began to buy slaves from African traders for the Portuguese home market and, as importantly, they reached the Senegal coast where they could trade for gold from the inland sub-Saharan gold mines. In medieval times these mines supplied, via Arabs, most of the bullion required for high value coinage in Europe. Henrique's traders thus gained access to considerably cheaper gold bullion supplies. Expansion was beginning to pay off. By 1445 they built their first fortified African trading post, or *faetoria*, at Arguim. They also began to send settlers to the Azores and supply them with African slaves. By the 1460s the Portuguese had outposts in Sierra Leone, as the Henrique expansion gathered momentum and rolled on without him, and they colonized the Cape Verde Islands. In 1471 they reached present-day Ghana and, in 1472, they arrived at Benin and started to trade for malaguetta pepper, not as good as pepper from India, but still with a ready European market. They also colonized Sao Thomé Island that year. In 1482, when they built their main African *faetoria* at Sao Jorge de Mina – which meant 'St George of the (Gold) Mines' – on the Gold Coast, their first maritime empire was already in place, and it was an unprecedented achievement for Europeans.

The Portuguese Atlantic island empire now consisted of two groups, the Azores and Cape Verdes, and of two single islands, Madeira and Sao Thomé. All were originally uninhabited and settled by Portuguese land-seekers and a growing labour force of African slaves. M.N. Pearson argues that their colonization was a continuation of the Portuguese Lusitanian reconquest and a search for estates with more and better soils than were available at home. This was, in effect, an enlargement of Portuguese home territory.[5] Economically these acquisitions were modestly prosperous, supplying wheat, cattle products, wine, wax, honey, timber, dye stuffs and sugar. The most important export by far was sugar. But the population and output were still modest, despite the unprecedented width and extent of the sea transport net that held together this greater Atlantic Portugal.

Far more profitable and promising were the *faetorias* on the African coast, even though their viability depended heavily on African collaboration. This was still not the gunpowder age, just the dim dawning of it, and African rulers were too politically strong to be either conquered or even intimidated. From these outposts Portuguese traders and nobility investors, and the crown as investor and tax collector, received substantial amounts of gold, some pepper, but increasingly more and more slaves. Initially the slaves were for the Portuguese home or Atlantic labour market and the Mediterranean region. Later they would provide involuntary labour for more and more New World colonies, but by the 1480s they were already a substantial and profitable trade. Thus, while serfdom was dying out in western Europe (though actually growing in Poland, the Ukraine and Byelorussia), the Portuguese were now pushing involuntary labour against the social and economic trend of most of their own European hinterlands. How did this system develop?

John Thornton, in *Africa and Africans in the Making of the Atlantic World, 1400–1680,*[6] points out that this deplorable trade in humans was actually driven by African supplies rather than by either European or Portuguese markets, at least up until the opening of plantation types of colonies in the Americas. The Portuguese supplied the transport and marketing services but Africans supplied the slaves themselves. Only very early on are there a few instances of Portuguese crews kidnapping their own slaves forcibly. What drove the creation of slaves for sale were African laws and wars. Unlike other cultures, Africans below the Sahara held people as property, not land. Thus African rulers and nobles all owned masses of slaves while lands were held in common by any political grouping migrating into them. In warfare the object was to capture people rather than territory. There were many such rulers with huge numbers of slaves, and a small proportion of these slaves was always surplus to local labour requirements and so readily available for trade with outsiders for goods that were seen as exotic or luxurious. These marginal numbers of slaves came to hundreds of thousands – eventually to millions – for the Portuguese and other European traders.[7]

So the African elite was in control because it had the numbers and also the political cohesion and economic independence to accept or repel the Europeans along the coasts. The Portuguese had too few people or ships for territorial conquest. Later, between 1579 and 1591, they did fight for territory in Angola, and did make some gains, but only by becoming in effect auxiliaries to warring African kingdoms. In combat, high-sided Portuguese ships, especially when fully armed with guns in the sixteenth century, were reasonably safe from African assault but in most other ways the Africans, it is now believed, could outfight Europeans with little trouble. Ivana Elbl sums up the military balance as follows:

The Portuguese were well aware of the precariousness of their situation. Their technology – fortifications, weaponry, and sailing ships armed with artillery – was of little advantage in African conditions. In confined coastal waters and on rivers, the sailing ships were vulnerable to concentrated attacks by large war canoes and often fell prey to determined African parties. Metal armour was a torment in a tropical climate. The late fifteenth- and early sixteenth-century firearms were often too clumsy to have more than a psychological effect against small or moving targets.

While the Portuguese certainly could look after themselves militarily, African weaponry and tactics were still highly effective against them, and poisoned arrows usually caused horrible damage. The Portuguese outposts on the African mainland were small. The largest, Sao Jorge da Mina, was manned by only fifty to fifty-five people, only about one-third of whom were professional soldiers. The crown outposts lived in an all too justified fear of attack. Axim, a small Portuguese fortress near Cape Three Points on the Gold Coast, was overrun and looted in 1515 by the neighbouring Ahanta warriors lured by easy opportunity, and the Gwato factory was perennially at the mercy of the *oba* of Benin. Small size and distance from home made these installations quite susceptible to sustained attack. . . .

Assuring the goodwill of the African political elite was of key importance to the Portuguese.[8]

Although they were, to some extent, dependent on the Africans, it is still obvious that a transportation monopoly gave the trade initiatives to the Portuguese. However little they controlled interior Africa, Africans controlled their Atlantic trade no better, or even less than that. Furthermore, however limited Portuguese military advantages were, that they were able to maintain their *faetorias* in isolation for many months at a time against massive manpower odds does indicate a very impressive qualitative advantage over the Africans. These long-range transport monopoly and combat advantages did not bring Portugal or its ruling elite the kinds of vast riches they aspired to but they did bring steady and apparently growing profits with which, among other things such as improving the efficiencies of government and purchasing ever better ships, weapons and trade goods, they could fund further oceanic expansion in search of further profits. These advantages were also transferable to Asia, where they worked at least as well as in Africa, and perhaps better. Finally, this African trade empire was both a foundation for the later expansion of African commerce, especially of slaves, in which the Portuguese were joined by the Dutch and the English in the seventeenth century, and it was the model both for the later slave trade and especially for the Portuguese trading empire in Asia. That Asian empire was an outgrowth of this African experience.

EXPANSION INTO MARITIME ASIA

Carrying on from the west coast of Africa, but also looking to the old Venetian hope of a direct ocean route to Asian wealth, King Joao II and his merchant and noble advisers in 1487 collected a large quantity of seed money and sent off two expeditions to test the route to Asia by water theory. Bartolome Dias, an old Gold Coast veteran, received command of three specially funded extra long-range ships and proceeded to round the Cape of Good Hope, returning to Lisbon in 1488, four years before the Columbus Atlantic crossing, with the news that he had found the route into the Indian Ocean long but entirely practical. In 1487 Joao II had also sent Pedro de Covilha off overland to study the northern shores of the Indian Ocean from the African and Middle East landward sides. He was to report on the commercial and political situation. Land travel was slower than sea travel and it took Covilha until 1492 to get the information back to Lisbon. But, as

Columbus sailed off for Queen Isabella of Castile after failing to sell his idea that it was a lot quicker to get to India by going directly west across the Atlantic to Portugal, the Portuguese expansion lobby were already well supplied with accurate information about Indian Ocean access and opportunity. Thus, when Columbus fell into Portuguese hands on his way back from his discovery – he was forced by bad weather to put in to the Azores – the Portuguese accepted that he had found some more and very distant Atlantic islands but did not appear to believe these were just off the shores of the Asian mainland as Columbus insisted. They had the power to arrest him, and presumably to make him disappear, but they let him go to spread his wishful misinformation. The following year they observed the launching of the Hispaniola colonizing expedition by Isabella. This Spanish colony, according to Columbus, would not only produce gold but would be the bastion of transatlantic Asian trade. To make sure it was not instead another Spanish ploy to infiltrate Portuguese bases and routes on the eastern side of the southern Atlantic, the Portuguese agreed, via the Treaty of Tordesillas in 1494, to accept the Columbus islands as a Spanish zone. The treaty stipulated a line from pole to pole running just east of the West Indies. Everything to the west would be for Spanish exploitation as long as everything to the east – excepting only the Canaries, which were still being forcibly colonized at this time – was left to Portugal. The Portuguese already knew this included the real ocean route to Asia. They were reasonably certain that they had pulled off a very nice diplomatic coup against Castilian authorities who, they thought, were not nearly as knowledgeable about oceanic geography as was the experienced Portuguese maritime lobby.

This lobby required more time to complete the India project. Funds had to be raised and the Atlantic to the westward had to be checked just to make sure they were right about Columbus. In 1495 Joao Fernandez Lavrador sailed to Greenland to check the north and left his name on Canada's Labrador. There were other investigations. The new king, Dom Manoel, took office in 1495, bent on improving both government efficiency and overseas enterprise still further. In 1497 he was ready for India and selected Vasco da Gama, with four extra long-range ships, for the first voyage. There were no mistakes. On 20 May 1498 da Gama reached Calicut on the Malabar Coast, a main source of prime grade pepper, which had been brought to Europeans exclusively by Muslim or Muslim-controlled seaborne and landborne traders who also supplied Venice. Da Gama at once offered the Samorin, the local dictator, an alternative trade route at better prices. So far, so good. The Portuguese seemed on the brink of diverting the pepper trade right out of everybody else's control – especially religiously offensive Muslims – and cornering the market, which indeed was their objective.

But at this point things went wrong. The Portuguese found that their understanding of Asian conditions was still too lacking in detail, despite their fact-finding efforts. The Samorin's people were not, in fact, impressed with Portuguese prices, or Portuguese trade goods. European products and cloth turned out to be beneath Asian standards. Furthermore, the Muslim pepper traders did their best to drive these new competitors away. Thus da Gama's

Vasco da Gama (1460–1524), the first Portuguese to reach India by sea.

welcome was soon worn out, there were nasty incidents, and the Portuguese were lucky to collect a reasonable cargo of pepper before it was time to beat a hasty retreat. In 1499, after twenty-three months away, da Gama's four ships arrived back in Lisbon. The pepper brought 600 per cent profits. The only trouble was that it was going to be hard to get more, though in all other ways the expedition was an absolutely brilliant success. On Hispaniola, by contrast, the Spanish colonists were falling to pieces because of Amerindian resistance and dwindling gold supplies.

As the court of Isabella contemplated the growing disaster on Hispaniola, Dom Manoel, his nobles and his merchants organized a larger second expedition to Asia in 1500 under Pedro Cabral, with fourteen ships this time. On the way down the Atlantic the expedition discovered the coast of Brazil, found this new land to be on their side of the Treaty of Tordesillas line, and claimed it for Portugal, with small short-term but big long-term consequences – in many ways bigger than Asia. Arriving again in a hostile Calicut, Cabral's merchants attempted to set up a peaceful trade, only to be attacked by the locals and Muslim rivals. After sustaining heavy casualties, Cabral opened fire on a number of Arab vessels and retired to Cochin where, under arms, he managed to collect a pepper cargo with difficulty. Storms on the way home added to losses and costs. Again there were good profits but it was clear enough that the war against trade rivals in Indian waters was now on. The Portuguese would have to fight to trade, to conquer secure trading posts. The war costs would need to be carried as very hefty commercial overheads, materially reducing profitability. But if the Portuguese could gain a pepper – and other spices – monopoly in the European market, or at least get close, it would be worth the military outlays.

Thus, in 1503, Dom Manoel prepared ten large vessels with extra heavy armaments, especially large calibre artillery, and sent off expedition number three once again under da Gama. On the whole da Gama fought more than he traded, setting the pattern for commerce by conquest, or at least by military and naval intimidation. He had some important advantages. The same expert analysts who argue that Asian societies were far too strong to be pushed around by a few Europeans, and who point out that Asian trade continued on Asian rather than Portuguese terms because the latter made no impact on Asian land power at all, do concede Portuguese military superiority on the seas. According to Diffie and Winius the ships of Portugal's enemies in Asia, the Arabs, Egyptians and Gujaratis together, compared to Portuguese vessels were '. . . flimsily made and manned by demoralized crews . . .'.[9] M.N. Pearson states that most Asian ships were entirely unarmed and that those brought to fight the Portuguese were converted galleys or hastily improvised from merchant types. He believes the Asians did have the skills and resources to build combat ships equal to the Portuguese models but that Asian rulers did not bother to make the effort because external trade was so marginal to their power as to be almost irrelevant. Thus the Portuguese were also mostly irrelevant. The Asian focus was turned inland.[10]

Nevertheless, the Portuguese had to fight furiously, and against Asian fleets of great size as well, before they were allowed to do business even on Asian terms and to Asian advantage. Peter Padfield captures the dramatic details of da Gama's first big 1503 battle for control of Indian Ocean waters as well as any historian so far:

By this time the Calicut fleet had been reinforced by a fleet of Red Sea dhows, and the command had been taken by a warrior emissary from the Sultan of Egypt, Cojambar. Exactly how many large dhows and how many smaller sambuks, proas and rowing craft there were in the combined fleet is impossible to say; all Portuguese accounts differ and these are the only ones available. The King of Calicut apparently boasted he had 20 vessels for every one of the Portuguese – which would amount to a fleet of over 350. Cochin spies warned da Gama that the odds were ten to one against him – 180. Portuguese accounts vary from 29 to 70 vessels in the main squadron, with numerous smaller craft astern. Whatever the figures, the Portuguese must have been outnumbered, probably greatly, because of the resources available to the Muslim merchants and the known and feared strength of the Portuguese ships and guns; a small fleet would have been ludicrous for such an object. The dhows were equipped with guns of a sort but these were small and very weak compared with the Portuguese weapons, some indeed had wooden barrels, and 'threw their shot like bowl' – presumably in a lazy arc as in the game of *boule*. Their missile weapons were bows and arrows.

The Portuguese sighted their sails in the morning somewhere between Cochin and Calicut; they were heading southwards, arranged in a long line stretching back over the horizon 'for so the Captain Cojambar had ordered it that they might make more show'. Probably they were strung out because of their differing sizes, rigs and sailing speeds; large dhows of which the advanced squadron was formed are fast sailers. The wind was off the land – on the starboard hand of the northbound Portuguese – and directly Sodre saw the approaching fleet he hauled up as close to the wind as he could – again a highly significant move in any study of tactical development. It is possible, as one account has it, that the move was ordered by da Gama, or was the result of consensus in a council of war summoned on first sight of the enemy fleet; this would be more in keeping with battle conventions of the time.

The dhows and lesser craft which were hung with flags and banners of Islam wherever there were halyards to hoist them came on with a tumult of shouting and dinning gongs and horns. Sodre's caravels, cleared for action and without flags, sailing close-hauled 'one astern of the other in a line . . . under all the sail they could carry', raced for the windward position, leaving the few ships of the squadron astern and to leeward. As they reached the enemy main body which was probably bunched in lines abreast by this time, the line of caravels was well to windward; they opened fire, each with its two lee (port) side bombards, at Cojambar's flagship. The range was short enough for effective shooting and of these first ten shots, which may well have been directed so that they ricocheted over the calm surface, one or more hit Cojambar's mast and brought it down, another went through his poop timbers, and others hit three separate vessels low down, causing them to fill and sink. The gunners re-loaded and continued a rapid fire: 'they made such haste to load again that they loaded the guns with bags of powder which they had ready for this purpose made to measure so that they could load again very speedily'.

Very soon the dhows and smaller rowing craft became tangled in confusion as men from sinking craft leaped overboard and attempted to climb up the oars or sides of others; the caravels brailed up their sails and lay off, firing into the thick of them. 'It was not possible to miss . . . they shattered many [vessels] killing many people on account of which there were shrieks and cries among the Moors.' The wind completed the work, driving the Muslim vessels further seawards as da Gama's heavy ships reached the scene and joined in the work of destruction, also 'sailing in file one after the other as the Captain Major had ordered'.

The caravels and Sodre's light ships loosed their sails again as the second wave of the enemy, perhaps 70 to 100 sail, mostly light craft led by Coja Kassim, held on towards them, intending to close and board. The wind was freshening however, and the caravels, while not turning aside, were able to keep their distance and pour in a destructive fire from bombards and swivels, sweeping down the yelling, white-robed masses on Kassim's flagship – which did however manage to put one shot into a Portuguese vessel, killing the captain and wounding others with splinters. During this phase the caravels either could not keep to windward of all the enemy because Kassim's smaller craft were closer inshore and many were under oars, or they did not bother to try, but keeping steerage way, sailed amongst them all firing bombards from both sides into the enemy hulls between 'wind and water', and swivels at the men massed on deck, and in the process cutting rigging, bringing down masts and yards, destroying the outboard rope and beam steering gear. In return they received small shot and showers of arrows which damaged their own sails and rigging, but could not penetrate the timbers behind which most of the men lay hidden. Only the swivel gunners were exposed and they formed the bulk of the Portuguese casualties. Arrows quivered from the bulwarks and masts like porcupine quills.

By the time Sodre's squadron had worked right through the fleet, they had wrought such destruction on the flimsy craft that Kassim was beating a retreat towards the shore, leaving behind a trail of disabled hulls and shattered timbers, and drowning men clawing at the debris. The remnants of Cojambar's dhows were also moving away in whichever direction they could to escape the fire of da Gama's main body. The Portuguese tacked and steered after them; the caravels sailing close enough to get up with them, aimed at leisure with destruction, and sent several more to the bottom. The ships were not able to sail close enough to the wind, which in any case was beginning to drop; before long it died away altogether. The Muslims had their larger vessels towed towards the shore by rowing craft, and the caravels did the same in pursuit, while da Gama, 'seeing that the business was certain', had his ships' boats armed with falconets and swivels and twenty cross-bowmen in each and sent them to join the chase. So the battle ended in isolated boarding actions over a wide area in which the fire of the guns and cross-bows from the boats drove the enemy off the becalmed or towing vessels, which were then plundered and burned.

About midday a sea breeze sprang up and da Gama fired a gun and hoisted a flag signal of recall, meanwhile setting course for Cananore, 'giving to the Lord great praise for the great favour He had shown him'. Sodre, not content to let the victory pass without a secular demonstration, had the caravels take a number of enemy vessels in tow, and sailed with them to Calicut, where they were made fast to one another and set alight on the sea breeze so that they drove ashore; the caravels fired into the vessels and into a crowd which gathered on the shore to watch. So ended the first serious challenge to the Portuguese in the Indian Ocean. How many of Cojambar's vessels were destroyed is not known, but da Gama lost not a single ship, or even a boat, and Portuguese casualties were light. It was a massacre rather than a battle, but it should stand out in naval history as the first recorded sea battle fought to a pre-arranged pattern as a staff-off artillery action by squadrons sailing in close-hauled line ahead.

In the same year on the east African coast, a single Portuguese ship commanded by Ruy Marques, which had become separated from an outward-bound fleet, cruised off Zanzibar Island, and captured some twenty dhows laden with ivory, tortoiseshell, honey, rice, coir, silks, cottons and suchlike. The Sultan of Zanzibar sent 4,000 men in a fleet of canoes against him; Marques armed just two ships' boats with swivels and these killed thirty-four men in the leading canoes at the first discharge, and soon put the rest to flight. Marques followed, and landed in Zanzibar, forcing the Sultan to pay tribute and become a vassal of the King of Portugal. The Atlantic-gunned sailing ship was quite simply irresistible in the Indian Ocean.[11]

This 1503 battle was just a start. In 1505 Francisco da Almeida captured Mombasa in eastern Africa with a fleet of 22 ships and 1,500 fighting men. He also built a fort at Sofala to control a key route to inland gold mines, with marginal success. In 1506 he won another naval victory over the allies of Calcutta at Cannanore. In 1508 Affonso da Albuquerque took Ormuz, or Hormuz, on the Persian Gulf with 7 ships and 500 men, planting a fortress in order to cut off spice ships bound for Muslim ports. In 1509 Almeida led another squadron against an Egyptian fleet in Diu harbour in what proved to be the winning battle for sea supremacy in the Indian Ocean. Diffie and Winius describe this most decisive sea fight as follows:

> Once Almeida's navy was inside, one gathers that the Gujarati gunners ashore could not be sure whom they were hitting in the narrow harbour, while the Egyptian, Gujarati, and some Calicutian vessels had no room for manoeuvring and could be fired upon at point-blank range by Portuguese gunnery. In the bloody hand-to-hand mêlée of broadsides, grapplings, and boarding, the Portuguese demoralized and butchered the enemy. . . . One large Portuguese ship fired more than 6090 large cannonballs alone within a half day. . . . The Portuguese lost over a hundred men themselves, but they completely destroyed the enemy fleet and dyed the whole harbour crimson. . . .[12]

With sea superiority in hand, Albuquerque now took over the complementary job of hacking out by force of arms a series of fortified bases on the African *faetoria* model but on a much enlarged scale. He was a fifty-year-old Morocco war veteran out to cut off all possible Muslim trade, according to Diffie and Winius '. . . the most venerable and remarkable conquistador and empire builder of all'.[13] In a fight as big as the naval battle of Diu, he led two general assaults against Goa in 1510, captured the city and made it the capital of the Asian empire for the best part of the next five centuries. In an even more spectacular land assault in 1511 he attacked Malacca, or Malaka, controlling the rich traffic between the Indian Ocean and China Seas. As Diffie and Winius again describe this conquest, it was another tough fight against the odds. In their view Albuquerque's conquest of the biggest trading city in Asia with just 900 Portuguese and 200 Indian allies was equal to the Spanish conquest of the Aztecs by the conquistadors of Hernando Cortés. At one stage the defenders unleashed their secret weapon:

Affonso da Albuquerque (1453–1515),
principal creator of the Portuguese trading
empire in Asia.

Then, suddenly the sultan appeared in person with his full force of war elephants to crush the invaders. As the huge beasts bore down on the astonished Portuguese, a certain Fernao Gomes de Lemos frantically jabbed the lead animal in the eye with his pike, an instrument developed originally to halt cavalry charges in Europe. As the animal screamed and reared, he jabbed it in the tender parts; other Portuguese quickly emulated his tactics and wounded the other lead elephants. Trumpeting wildly, the animals wheeled and trampled the armies behind them. . . . Twenty-eight Portuguese had been killed outright and many were wounded, some fatally with poisoned arrows.[14]

But they attacked, the sultan fled, and Malacca became a key Portuguese base. It was Albuquerque's main contribution to the trade wars. In 1513 he failed in a major attempt to take Aden but in 1515 he recaptured Ormuz and then died. The Portuguese held Ormuz until 1623. By the time they captured Colombo in 1518, the main bases were all in place, except for Macao, which they reached in 1517 but took until 1557 to get extraterritorial rights from the Chinese emperor. In Japan they held trading posts and mission stations from 1542 to 1640.

By 1522 the Portuguese also sorted out their rivalries with Spain when they wiped out a Spanish trading post on Tidor in the Spice Islands of present-day

FERDINAND MAGELLANUS.

Portuguese captain Fernao da Maghelais (1480–1521), perhaps better known as Ferdinand Magellan, the first European to circumnavigate the planet.

Indonesia. Spain too had reached the far east but not yet in strength. In fact the major Spanish fleet to Asia was another disappointment. Portuguese captain Fernao da Maghelais, or Ferdinand Magellan, was commissioned by King Charles V of Spain in 1519 to find out the exact geographical relationship between America and Asia. As it happened, he left just as Cortés was launching his conquest of Mexico, which would convert an American barrier to Asia into an American treasure trove for Spain, with its own great worth. It took the Magellan expedition until 1522 to circumnavigate the globe and prove its correct size. Magellan himself died and the survivors came back under a junior captain named El Cano or Del Cano. So Spain now knew that Portugal had indeed received the best part of the Treaty of Tordesillas bargain of 1494, which did spoil somewhat the news and golden treasure from the capture of Tenochtitlan in 1521.

THE PORTUGUESE ASIAN EMPIRE AT ITS HEIGHT

By the middle of the sixteenth century Michael Pearson concludes that 'Portugal finished up with a string of some fifty forts and fortified areas, and a total fleet of up to 100 ships of various sizes in different areas'.[15] The total number of Portuguese in these bases was 10,000 but with a growing number of Portuguese Asian relatives attached very tightly to the native-born Lusitanian communities.

In India, for example, Sanjay Subrahmanyam estimates that three times the number of allied and related Gujaratis lived in Portuguese towns and that overall the Portuguese language became the language of trade, the lingua franca, from east Africa to China on the sea routes.[16] According to P.D. Curtin, the imperial organization was run from Lisbon and Goa. In Lisbon the *Casa da India* controlled the *carreira* or convoy system to and from Europe itself. These convoys were the king's monopoly but also the king's military and naval responsibility. In Goa local operations were under the authority of the *Estado da India*, with control over its own policy, armed forces and diplomatic relations. This semi-independent office forwarded the king's *carreira* to Europe but also raised its own tax revenues through a *carteza* or licensing system of all non-Portuguese deep-sea ships. To sail at all, foreign ships had to buy a Portuguese *carteza* or be subject to capture or sinking; it was, in effect, a maritime protection racket.[17]

How well did this system work? What were the benefits to Portugal, and what the costs? The prevailing argument is that the profit margins, especially for the king, were low, eaten up by administration and defence costs. Yet, the statistics cited by experts suggest positive gains throughout. For the crown the Asian import monopoly brought net profits of up to 90 per cent during the 1560s when the *Casa* was importing half of Europe's total spice supply and perhaps three-quarters of all the pepper. It was not the monopoly Albuquerque and Dom Manoel had planned but it was substantial. On average these imports between 1513 and 1603 consisted of 65 to 89 per cent pepper, 2.5 to 7.3 per cent ginger, 9 to 8.7 per cent cinnamon, 1.6 to 9.0 per cent 'spices' – that is nutmeg, cloves and mace from Indonesia – and 10.5 to 12.2 per cent textiles (after 1587). The *Estado* also did well. It only lost money twice between 1581 and 1687, in the years 1603 and 1684–7.[18] Nevertheless, the government part of all this imperial enterprise did not do as well as the private sector, or the so-called 'country traders'. Increasing numbers of Portuguese shipowners stayed in Asian waters carrying Asian goods for strictly Asian markets. They did have an edge over local shipping, the protection of the *Estado* combat vessels and other services. But they kept all the profits themselves. For Asians such as Bangladeshi cotton cloth manufacturers they provided cheaper transport to places like the Indonesian area and brought back less expensive rice more reliably. But for Portugal they were of no direct financial advantage. These private traders were in effect Asianized Europeans.

Subrahmanyam sums up shipping statistics. The total number of Portuguese ships departing for Asia was:

1497 to 1500	–	17 ships
1501 to 1510	–	151, the record years
1511 to 1520	–	96
1531 to 1540	–	80
1571 to 1580	–	50
1601 to 1610	–	71
1631 to 1640	–	33
1661 to 1670	–	21
1691 to 1700	–	24[19]

P.D. Curtin claims that of the sailings between 1500 and 1634, 28 per cent were lost, sunk or otherwise destroyed, and that of all the ships that sailed to Asia in 134 years, at about the average of 4 per year, only 470 came back to Portugal, a constant Asian drain on Portuguese ship supplies.[20] There was also a population drain, though this may have been beneficial in the long run by keeping population pressures back home within manageable bounds of natural and government resources. The total number of Portuguese emigrating to all overseas possessions were, according to Subrahmanyam:

1400 to 1500	–	50,000 (500 per annum)
1500 to 1580	–	280,000 (3,500 per annum)
1580 to 1640	–	330,000 (5,500 per annum)
1640 to 1700	–	150,000 (2,500 per annum)[21]

The period 1580 to 1640 was that of Spanish rule and included a large migration to Brazil in particular.

All this was very impressive for a small country that began in 1500 with under a million people comprising about 2 per cent landowning nobility and 80 per cent agricultural peasantry. The population density was among the lowest in Europe, at twelve people per square kilometre. This reflected a relatively poor set of agricultural resources. One person in thirty-six worked for the Catholic Church. By 1600 the Portuguese population was up to about 2 million. At the same time India alone had about 150 million people. But overall, Portuguese living standards were probably among the highest anywhere as a result of this thinly spread and very marginal economic and military ascendancy over great masses of Asian traders. The Portuguese achieved wonders by qualitative specialist intensity, and gained material rewards.

But their influence on either Asia, Africa or Europe in power terms remained insignificant. They were envied for their ships and profits but their old dreams about turning back and crushing Islam were now quite useless. In fact the Portuguese presence in the Indian Ocean did nothing but occasionally irritate the Muslim land powers. To the Ottomans, according to Pearson, '. . . the Indian Ocean was a sideshow . . .'[22] and instead of the Portuguese 'expanding' Europe by significant territorial gains in the East it was the Ottoman Turks who were quite spectacularly contracting Europe from Asia and Africa.

The Turkish push into Europe had begun at about the same time as the Portuguese expansion down the western coast of Africa. In 1448 Murad II beat the Hungarians at the second battle of Kosovo and in 1453 Muhammed II captured Constantinople. In 1499 Ottoman galleys beat the Venetian fleet and established sea power ascendancy for the first time in the eastern Mediterranean. In 1515 the Ottomans beat the Persians and in 1516 and 1517 they annexed Syria and Egypt. During his reign between 1520 and 1566 Suleiman the Magnificent drove the armies and navies of Islam steadily westward. In 1522 he captured Belgrade and in 1526 he beat the Hungarians at Mohacs and took much of their country. In 1529 he came close to taking Vienna, and in 1538 his admiral Barbarossa decisively defeated the Christian sea powers of the Mediterranean at

Prevesa. He was stopped only at Malta between 1563 and 1565 and his sea power was severely pegged back at the great battle of Lepanto in 1571. But the Turks could still besiege Vienna a century later in 1683. Compared with these power achievements the Portuguese made no real difference except to themselves, and as objects of imitation or envy for other Europeans. It was, in fact, the sea power of their much larger neighbour Spain that led the decisive Christian defence fleets at Lepanto.

In the 1580s Portugal itself disappeared as an independent country with its own king. Philip II of Spain, now running a country whose American empire greatly surpassed the Portuguese Asian empire in both wealth and power, and with an increasingly united and dominating home base in Europe, seized the Portuguese crown. In the decisive sea battle of Terceira in the Azores in 1582, Philip's fleet beat the Portuguese fleet, completing both dynastic takeover and sea power ascendancy. It took Portugal until 1640 to regain independence. During their captivity the Portuguese sustained losses in the East. In 1600 the English East India Company, based on the Portuguese model, began to set up rival trading stations in India, followed by the Dutch Vereenigte Ostindische Compangnie (VOC for short) in 1602. In 1605 the Dutch captured Portuguese Ambon and Tidor in the valuable Spice Islands of Indonesia; in 1622 the Persians drove the Portuguese permanently from the Gulf of Persia; in 1640 the Japanese expelled them; in 1641 the Dutch took Malacca from them; and in 1658 the Dutch captured Ceylon as well. At the end of the seventeenth century the English had set up and fortified competing bases at Madras, Calcutta and Bombay.

So it has been traditional to see the Portuguese in decline from around 1580 onwards, as Spain, the Dutch and the English all took over the initiative. But the Portuguese imperial shrinkage was not great after all. They still hold Macao and will outlast the British in Hong Kong. The profits to the Portuguese people levelled off but stayed healthy. It was just that European rivals now began to pass their plateau of gains, significantly using the methods the Portuguese themselves pioneered as starting points in their own empire building processes. A thin scattering of Lusitanian maritime and combat specialists thus did well for themselves and did a great deal to open up a global communications network that has continued to grow ever since.

BRAZIL

Meanwhile, Portugal also colonized a significant part of the New World, with consequences arguably even greater. Brazil was acquired by pure blind luck, entirely unexpectedly and it was initially neglected. The basic details are succinctly related by H.B. Johnson.[23] While news of the Cabral discovery of 1500 was still on the way, the only other Portuguese Atlantic interest was far to the north where, between 1499 and 1502, the Corte Real brothers reached the rich cod fishing grounds of the Grand Banks and set up a small fishing base in Newfoundland. In 1501 a second expedition to Brazil brought back a cargo of brazil wood, a plant important in the manufacture of woollen cloth dye back in Europe, which was cut and traded by the Brazilian Tupi Indians. Even with

Amerigo Vespucci on board – after whom the Americas were later named, largely because his public relations network at home was much better than that of Columbus – Brazil turned up nothing of interest to Portugal and Europe except brazil wood. The government of Dom Manoel therefore leased Brazil to a group of private traders between 1501 and 1505.

But by 1505 foreign ships, especially from France, were beginning to appear in the region and threaten Portugal's slender interests and authority more and more. They were looking for brazil wood and thinking of settlements. Therefore, in 1530, the crown appointed its first Brazilian governor, Alfonso da Souza, and sent him with 400 dubious Portuguese settlers – including convicts – to at least keep out the French. The settlers tried to recruit Tupi labour but the Amerindians were not enthusiastic, so in 1532 the first African slaves came in from the other side of the Atlantic, especially to provide labour for sugar production, which, by 1533, was developing into a major enterprise, much to home authority surprise. In 1534 King Joao III tried to speed up some of this promising but expensive colonization by granting most of Brazil to nobles in a series of hereditary captaincies or huge private estates in return for bringing out more settlers. The captains and their followers in the 1530s and '40s in turn demanded both more Tupi labour and Tupi land, which generated armed Tupi resistance. This drove the colonizers to concentrate in a series of fortified towns and to launch expanding punitive raids against the Amerindians in a fashion that had already been previewed by Spanish settlers on Hispaniola and other West Indian islands and which would be repeated again – without the demands for Amerindian labour – in Virginia and other European colonies in the Americas later. As in New Spain and New France, the Catholic missionary orders were brought in to convert the Tupis to subservience, with doubtful short-term results. Portuguese communities were growing, but slowly and with difficulty.

In 1555 a renewed foreign threat began to generate better progress. Some 600 French Huguenots under Villegagnon arrived, looking for a new Protestant home. In response, an energetic new governor, Mem de Sà, was appointed in 1558 to deal with them and by 1559 he was driving them out. In addition, he also wiped out 60 hostile Tupi villages by 1560 and brought in 34,000 pacified Tupi labourers for his fellow colonists by 1562. Unfortunately, half of these died during a huge epidemic in 1562 and 1563 but the remainder were enslaved. In 1565 Mem de Sà supervised the founding of Rio de Janeiro and by 1567 all foreign interlopers were driven out. By 1570 sugar planting began to expand rapidly to the point where, within a few years, Brazil had become Europe's largest single sugar producer. Most of the labour came increasingly from Africa. In 1570 there were already as many as 3,000 African slaves in Brazil. When Mem de Sà finished his term in 1572, Brazil had 8 towns, 207,600 Portuguese settlers and 6,000 other people working for them. Sugar output was growing towards new records, a culmination of sugar planting starting back in Madeira in the 1450s and gradually built up in Portuguese and Spanish islands until it found its best geographic and labour supply home in Brazil.

Although the government revenues from Brazil remained at only about 10 per cent of the revenue from the Asian empire, by 1600 – even under a Spanish king –

Brazil was a growing success and a source of much national pride, probably more so than all the African and Asian outposts. Dutch attempts to conquer it between 1624 and 1654 were repelled, huge gold deposits were discovered at Minas Gerais in the 1690s and later, and diamonds were found in the 1730s. These mineral riches compensated for the loss of sugar production leadership to English and French West Indian planters during the 1640s (who at least got their early African slave supplies from the Portuguese). From 1808 to 1821 the Portuguese monarchy itself took up temporary residence in Brazil. Again the Lusitanians took control over a vast area populated by very few people. This time they created a lasting new American culture, a significant expansion of Europeanized territory. And again, both settlers and government, especially the former, profited well. Those who copied their sugar plantation system with its African labour force in the seventeenth century also began to exert a more than marginal economic influence on European development itself, which some experts are arguing helped bring on industrialization. But of this indirect Portuguese impact there is more detail later under Anglo-French headings.

CHAPTER 4
Hispanic Frontiers in America

While Portugal expanded gradually, Spain did so suddenly in 1492 and 1493. While the Portuguese built new transport links with known parts of the world, Spain found new lands and millions of new people. In half a century Spanish colonizers overran the richest parts of two new continents with the most productive societies and the warmest climates, forced the Amerindians in their conquest areas to work for Spanish masters, become Catholics and speak the Spanish language, and found the largest deposits of silver at that time which they used to buy wealth and power in Europe and push along economic growth by materially expanding the money supply in global circulation. Other Europeans believed that during the second half of the sixteenth century Charles V and especially Philip II owed their dominant position among European nations to these American conquests. They were mostly wrong but the Spanish colonization of the New World was nevertheless a spectacular phenomenon, at least the largest geographic multiplication of European style human communities at that time.

It was all the more spectacular because it was so unplanned and so unexpected, by the colonizers as well as their envious neighbours. It was startling that the only country in Europe with the means and the attitudes essential for such huge conquests was Spain, or its two modern foundation parts of Castile and Aragon. Only this country had sufficient numbers of conquistador types to do the job; only this early Spain had a strong enough monarchy under Isabella and Ferdinand to fund, control and defend such colonial conquests; only it had the wealth, expertise and shipping capability – of a quality equal to that of the pioneering Portuguese mariners but of far more potential quantity – to carry out large-scale transatlantic colony building. And only Castilians had serious experience in colonizing lands populated by new and unfamiliar people, the Canarians and Guanches of the Canary Islands. They also had the Portuguese to copy and to envy for their larger expansion achievements along the east coast of Africa and to help them in this task, Castile and Aragon together were already several times larger than the small Portuguese nation.

Yet, unlike the Portuguese with their deliberately contrived expansionist strategy stretching over the best part of a century, the Spanish colonizers reacted suddenly to unexpected new opportunities. While still in the process of subjugating and Hispanicizing the native people of the Canaries – a process they only concluded in 1496 – the Spanish received new islands with unknown natives to conquer from Columbus: these new natives had gold as well. A generation later they found the Aztecs and then the Incas, and in the 1540s the world's greatest silver mines. Spain exploited each windfall to the full bringing about the Hispanicization and mostly effective cultural integration of surviving Amerindians but also exterminating millions of others. Charles V and Philip II seemed to profit much in power but were also encouraged to reach beyond their capabilities and so, in fact, weaken the Spanish hegemony and invite rivals to surpass them. Most of the wealth of the Americas probably stayed there, in the hands of the Spanish migrants who were best at seizing and controlling lands, mines and workers. The area and population of Spanish culture and European culture was expanded as never before but Spain itself probably spent as much energy and resources on this great effort as she gained. Nevertheless, her empire clearly surpassed that of Portugal and was unrivalled until the start of the seventeenth century.

ISABELLA AND FERDINAND

Traditionally Ferdinand is cited first but from 1479 Isabella, queen of Castile in her own right, was the dominant personality and intellect in her marriage partnership with Ferdinand of Aragon, which began in 1469. Castile was the biggest of the Spanish kingdoms. Even though custom dictated that the husband ruled the marriage, the 1479 contract between Isabella and Ferdinand as king of Aragon stated that they ruled their kingdoms separately. Isabella's kingdom was much bigger – she was also more able.[1] She also had the support of her nobles, who were the most numerous and qualitatively the most formidable fighters on the Iberian Peninsula and beyond. This nobility and their men at arms were conquistadors, still leading the long Spanish reconquest campaign against the Moors who were now driven back to Granada. From 1478 some of them were also beating up Canarians and Guanches – and fighting off rival Portuguese and other European colonists – in the Canaries. The contest for the Canaries had begun in the preceding century but, by the 1480s, Castilian conquistadors were winning. They were sending out armed and armoured migrants and missionary priests; they were seizing the land and more or less enslaving, or at least enserfing, the natives under a series of labour duty requirements sometimes called *encomienda*, derived from the word for command. The Canarians and Guanches were allocated to landowner conquerors to supply a labour service as an alternative to tax in goods or money, though such a tax was also imposed. Thus the Canaries were a school in which to learn how to conquer land and workers, as had been the reconquered parts of Moorish Spain back in Iberia.[2]

Isabella had especially close ties with the 2 per cent or so of her leading expansionist landowners who paid no taxes. In exchange, they surrendered their old medieval taxation rights over the 80 per cent plus of the agrarian peasantry and most of this went to the queen. The excuse was war emergency and this gave Isabella one of the most reliable and extensive tax bases of any monarch in Europe, with the possible exception of the kings of France. Only the Portuguese kings had as good a tax system but on a much smaller scale. Other strenghts came from power over money: by 1492 Castile was the most centralized and efficient monarchy in Europe next to Portugal, and Aragon was going the same way by example and pressure. Among many other things, centralized power could be translated into more formidable armed forces and larger overseas colonization ventures. But by the 1490s the main focus was on the expansion and unification of a Spanish nation under a single monarchy. The main method was the conquest of Granada, the last Moorish outpost in Western Europe. Two consequences of the Granada campaign were the expulsion of the Jews – part of an overall cultural homogenization policy aimed at stamping out long tolerated alternative religions and customs among 'Moriscos' (Muslims recently converted to Christianity) and 'Conversos' (Jews recently converted to Christianity) and others by means of the Inquisition – and the funding of an Atlantic voyage to find a quick route to India, promised by an Italian named Columbus.

The joint monarchy, or the Catholic Kings, as they were called, was the essential prerequisite to Spanish expansion at home and abroad. The armed migrants were already there by 1479 and Spanish merchants, mariners and shipbuilders shared with the Portuguese the best methods of long-range oceanic transportation so far devised. But it took an accident of birth, Isabella, and a fortunate marriage to a congenial Ferdinand to put together the concentrated resources and skills that, among other things, brought the long-awaited final victory over the Moors. Isabella's Castilian conquerors invaded Granada in April 1491. Sultan Muhammed XI surrendered the city on 2 January 1492, the day after the Castilian knights broke through into the Alhambra palace. The joint monarchs entered the city on 6 January.

COLUMBUS

In April 1492 Isabella officially authorized the first Columbus voyage. But who was this Columbus? And how did he convince a very hard-headed queen that he could find a short route to Asia across the Atlantic when all the leading university geographers agreed he was being quite ridiculous? There is relatively little reliable information about Columbus in 1492, instead there are great piles of contradictory assertions. Most historians accept that he came from a family of weavers in Genoa. He went to sea as a merchant and became a navigator and pilot along the Portuguese and Spanish African and Atlantic island trade routes; in other words, he was an Italian product of essentially Portuguese seafaring initiatives. His real or original name was probably Cristoforo Colombo but for some experts he was other people as well. Some argue he was a Spanish navigator named Cristobal Colon. Some say he was Jewish. Mascarenhas Barreto asserts that he was really a Portuguese secret agent named Salvador Fernandez Zarco, sent to take Spain off on a westward wild goose chase while the Portuguese got ready to open the real route to Asia without Spanish interference. In the short run, it seems Zarco succeeded in this mission brilliantly.[3] But there are also other Columbuses, claimed to exist by other national writers.

There is a bit less controversy about how Columbus came up with his misleading project but still no consensus. Some say he already knew America was out there. He appears to have visited Iceland and may have known about

Christopher Columbus (1451–1506). Three portraits from a variety of interpretations by contemporaries. The real Columbus is an obscure individual.

Greenland and Vinland. The Scandinavian route to Greenland was going out of use by the 1470s or '80s but was probably known by living northern mariners. Then again, Columbus may not have known about any of this. Another theory goes that in either 1482 or 1483 he actually met a group of Amerindian women adrift on the Atlantic. John Larner tells the story as follows: these Carib women in canoes from Guadalupe or Martinique, having been for a time left alone by their men, at a certain point

> . . . armed with bows and arrows, and with fishing implements, have put to sea. Perhaps they have been terrified by a volcanic eruption . . . perhaps they were hoping, in womenly solidarity, to establish their own community. As it is they were borne away into the Atlantic by strong currents. . . . They have survived on rainwater . . . on raw crayfish, or perhaps cannibalism, and the weed of the Sargasso. On their meeting with Europeans, they are taken and sold into slavery.[4]

Columbus met them, learned to talk to them and decided they were Amazons and subjects of the Great Khan. Some Amerindian feminists told him they came from Asia, which was only about ten days' sailing to the west. Most of the recognized experts, like Felipe Fernàndez-Armesto, think this is a silly story, though such opinions do not disprove anything either.

In any case, in 1492, after trying to sell his project to the crowns of Portugal, France and England, Columbus presumably convinced a victorious Isabella that some money was at least worth investing in an attempt to find an exclusively Spanish back door route to Asian spices and silks. It may be, on the other hand, that the project was much more practical and realistic, with a route to Asia as just an outside chance. Castile was still colonizing the Canaries. Portugal had Atlantic islands. Did Columbus believe he could find more islands for colonization? Isabella did in fact order colonization in 1493 without any hard evidence of the existence of Asia at all. In any case, Felipe Fernàndez-Armesto argues strongly that Columbus was mostly after such islands.[5] For Isabella, financing Columbus and then colonization from her own funds and by organizing private money as well, all appears to be a logical push for more power and territory. She was following the momentum of the Granada victory, the Canaries colonization and competition with Portugal. And only she had the resources and the will to undertake the most distant large-scale colonization project as yet attempted by Europeans, or anybody.

For Columbus himself, his public career began with his discovery, and it was not all success and glory.[6] He made the momentous crossing with two caravels and one quite small carrack between 3 August and 12 October, arriving somewhere in the Bahamas. By Christmas he had discovered Cuba and Hispaniola, lost his carrack by running her aground, and founded a fort called Navidad on Hispaniola, where he left behind a few men to cement amicable ties with the initially friendly Taino, or Arawak, Amerindians. It took him from 16 January to 17 February 1493 to get to the Portuguese Azores and then to Lisbon, where the local authorities heard his stories about having found an offshore Asian archipelago and let him go. On 4 March his fame began to grow. He brought some Taino natives, Taino gold nose plugs and other bits with him to Barcelona in April and there convinced Isabella and Ferdinand that he was indeed a hero and that they must follow up on his Asian outpost at once. They appointed him governor of Hispaniola, gave him other titles of his own devising, and on 12 September sent him back with a colonization fleet of 17 ships, 1,500 colonists, horses, cows, sheep, pigs, chickens and various European grains. He was instructed to round up the numerous poorly armed Tainos and make them work at food production and gold mining. On 3 November the expedition was back at Navidad, to find the advance guard gone, presumed wiped out by Tainos, and the fort destroyed. While the colonists picked fights with the original landowners and generally made themselves miserable and rebellious, Columbus sailed off to find the rest of Asia. Late in 1494 he discovered Puerto Rico. The next year he found Jamaica. As the colony dissolved further into disorder, however, he came back to take control, with little success. Between 19 September 1494 and March 1496, he governed badly. The Tainos refused to supply enough food and the settlers failed to grow any. The Tainos also refused to produce enough gold. The result was sporadic undeclared but ferocious war. The colonists set up fortified settlements and Columbus led repeated raids against Taino towns, which were unfortified.

The European animals multiplied all over the place but the colonists were dropping dead or running off – preferably home to Spain – at a growing rate.

Back in Spain in 1497 the queen supplied reinforcements but also expressed her strong desire for greater colonization efficiency. Again Columbus preferred to explore. In 1498 he sailed along the coast of Central America for the first time, wondering if he had actually found a new continent. In 1499 the colony dissolved into rebellious disorder that was worse than before. When Columbus tried to assert authority he was arrested as an incompetent and sent home to jail. The queen let him go, organized yet more reinforcements in 1502, and saw him off on a fourth discovery tour. He cruised the Panama area but then wrecked his ship and became marooned on Jamaica. Messages for help got through to Hispaniola but the colonists hated him and refused to rescue him. Finally, they relented with reluctance in 1504. Columbus got home just before his dear patron Isabella died. He died soon after, in 1506, not poor but more infamous than famous. Amerigo Vespucci, who had sailed with Columbus and also the Portuguese, was appointed the chief navigator of Spain in 1508 and then convinced Europe's map-makers to name the Columbus discoveries after himself rather than Columbus.

By Columbus's death all that Spain had gained from his efforts was one exceedingly expensive and disappointing colony and some claims to other pieces of land of similar type in the same region. These Antilles were recognized by the pope and Portugal as clearly Spanish. They had a little gold, some pearls and a few other minor export goods. But they were otherwise no better as settlement prospects than the Canaries and were a lot further away. Portugal was already bringing back boat loads of pepper and spices from the real India. Columbus had not done well.

HISPANIOLA AND EARLY CARIBBEAN COLONIES

Aside from the disappointments about Asia and gold and the inadequacies of leadership, why did Hispaniola degenerate into such a shambles? The funding was on an unprecedented scale of generosity and the colonists had experience from the reconquest and Canaries colonization to draw on. The two main reasons were probably ill health and the collapse of harmony between the incoming and the indigenous ethnic groups.

The prevailing expert view at the moment is that Eurasian and African diseases brought in by Spanish and other colonizers were so devastating to the Amerindians that over the next century or so 90 per cent of them were killed by such pathogens. Disease wiped out resistance to invasion. But on Hispaniola in the foundation years it was the Spanish settlers who had the devastating death rates. The first major epidemic, smallpox, struck the Taino people in 1518, by which time the majority were already dead from other causes. The only earlier epidemic was the syphilis outbreak of 1494, which affected the invaders after presumed contact with the Tainos.[7] Meanwhile, between 1493 and 1502, the colonists lost some 1,200 people out of 1,500, mostly due to death from illness.[8] Initially, disease may well have aided Taino resistance more than European invasion. Almost as popular among historians is the belief that, along with these diseases, superior European firepower was the other key factor in overcoming Taino resistance. Columbus did bring out 100 'hacabuche' hand cannon in 1493 and 100 'espingarde', smaller hand cannon, in 1495, well in advance of the general military adoption of gunpowder infantry arms in Europe itself; Spanish forces were using these weapons from about 1500. He also had ship's cannon and a few land cannon. But the Spanish invaders relied mostly on swords, helmets and chest armour. Swords were better than Taino hand weapons: in 1502, 300 invaders allegedly killed 700 Tainos with swords in just one fight. They also had horses and savage war dogs. All these armaments and advantages made Spanish colonists more effective man-to-man combatants. But, depending on whose Taino population figures we accept, there were between 666 and 200 Tainos to every invader in 1493. Swords, armour, horses and dogs could help even such odds but had the Tainos been concentrated at any time against the colonists it is more than doubtful that the invasion would have succeeded. In fact, the Tainos never managed to concentrate substantial portions of their warriors against the armoured swordsmen from Spain.[9]

There was no intention on either side to engage in full-scale war at the beginning. The sources here are thin and there is need for an up-to-date detailed reassessment but the outline of main events is clear enough. From their initial confrontation the two sides could not quite overcome cultural differences and widely divergent objectives. The 1,500 or so Columbus colonists were out for quick wealth from gold and then sought estates and workers to develop mines and agriculture, just as Spanish and Portuguese reconquest adventurers had sought estates with Moorish peasants from Moorish landowners for half a millennium and just as armed Spanish settlers were still doing in the Canaries. But back in Iberia peasants were used to changing lordly masters occasionally, and whether Moorish or Christian peasants, worked much the same to produce food or other primary products for their masters. In the Canaries and Hispaniola, and generally in the Caribbean, the native inhabitants were emphatically unaccustomed to European style peasant work and resisted being coerced into an existence seriously inferior to their pre-contact ways. So the invaders, who were mostly desperate to make sufficient wealth to cover their expenses and provide recompense for their huge personal risks, were much inclined to coercion. In Spanish law, heathen lands and labour could be seized by Christian men at arms. In certain cases where these heathen resisted the progress of Christian expansion particularly stubbornly, they could be declared slaves. In any case, the rights of the Tainos to their lands and liberties were not recognized. They could only gain such rights after accepting Christianity. So, for the armed Columbus conquerors of 1493, Hispaniola was already Spanish territory and the Tainos were already the third-class citizens of Spain with at least the same duties of work and obedience.

Needless to say the Tainos had very different views. They recognized from the start that they could not control the coming and going of these magically mobile intruders, and that some Spanish goods were extremely desirable or potent. But Tainos basically saw the colonists in Amerindian political terms. On the one hand they saw them as another group of tribespersons impinging on their particular territory and living area (which was bad) but on the other hand as potentially extra-powerful allied neighbours, or even adopted tribespersons, to make them much stronger and more secure in their ongoing rivalries with other Taino groups. These groups, or nations, were all more or less independent, living in open towns on just enough light labour agriculture and food gathering to be reasonably comfortable. Their staple food was manioc, or cassava; they produced only small surpluses. They picked up the odd gold nugget to make into jewellery; they had canoes for fishing; they had their wars but fighting was mostly ritualized and, in any case, seldom lasted very long. It would appear that they neither had the food surpluses nor the food transport technology to permit long campaigns. And so, while the invaders were mobile, had logistical capabilities for prolonged combat, had unity of objectives and of command, and were bent on making Tainos into Hispanic peasants, the Tainos stood divided and immobile and sought to absorb the newcomers into their cultural structure instead. At least some such attitudinal preconditions are suggested both by the limited sources and by the subsequent pattern of events.

On both sides initial instincts were benign. There was an urge to be accommodating. Early trade was fruitful: the Tainos appreciated the new manufactured items they got for their gold ornaments and their spare food. There was even the occasional inter-ethnic romance. The most prominent local Taino

Columbus meets the Carib people on his second voyage, in 1493.

leader in the first region of Spanish settlement was Caonabo, with an alluring and politically influential wife called Anacoana. Columbus and these Taino leaders launched forth on mutually beneficial negotiations. Their followers, however, soon began to fall out over the terms of trade. There were growing disputes over romantic issues. The gold ornaments were soon gone and so was surplus Taino food. But Spanish demands for gold, food and sex just increased. The Tainos began to realize these interlopers were going to stay. Individual fights broke out more and more frequently until they became group actions. Colonists were picked off in the open countryside, so they concentrated more and more punitive expeditions against unfortified – and as often as not unexpecting because innocent – Taino towns. These towns were now occasionally robbed of their cassava bread and burnt.

Within months of arrival Columbus declared all Tainos to be subjects of Queen Isabella and levied a tribute, or tax, of a small amount of gold or raw cotton per month on all adult males. Meanwhile, he demanded enough food from local tribes to feed his own people, at consumption rates both greater than Taino rates and exceeding Taino supplies. Most of the towns within reach refused to pay up. In 1494 Columbus declared Caonabo's people to be in rebellion against lawful authority. Four fortified Spanish towns – later to be followed by others – were set up close to Taino towns in the interior in that year. From these armoured swordsmen raided the Tainos and took their food. Some Tainos were enslaved. Columbus sent 500 such slaves back to Spain. Most of them died on the trip or soon after. In 1495 and 1496 Columbus organized a series of pacification campaigns. The people who agreed to cooperate had to spend more and more time digging for gold, to such an extent that their ability to feed themselves declined. Increased deaths from malnutrition and unaccustomed physical labour caused the death rates to shoot up. The colonists thus grew shorter and shorter of workers, and more and more violent. Some began to raid other islands for slaves. The Caribs were erroneously held to be cannibals and so could legally be enslaved. There were lots of Amerindian collaborators too, many fighting their own culture as Spanish auxiliaries. But most resisted as best they could. Of these, Canoabo put up the strongest fight. At Vega Real on 27 March 1495 he made his biggest effort, some say he had up to 100,000 warriors. But he got caught in his camp by 200 Spanish armoured infantry, 20 armoured cavalry, 20 armoured war dogs and some hundreds of Taino auxiliaries, and he lost. After some additional mass efforts of lesser note, his warriors relied mostly on small-scale raiding and ambushes, lacking the food supplies for long campaigns. Even so, the only way the invaders got rid of Caonabo was to trick him into believing they were making peace when they actually took him prisoner. He died on the voyage to Spain. His wife Anacoana worked towards a peaceful reconciliation but the governor Ovando, reinforced by the settlers who arrived in 1502, contrived to use her to assemble and then massacre many of the remaining Taino resistance leaders. Anacoana was arrested and publicly strangled. Ovando expanded Spanish settlements by increasing their fortified towns to fourteen. Juan Ponce de Léon led the last punitive campaigns against the hostile Tainos in the so-called War of Higüay in 1504, which broke all remaining resistance of any organized and large-scale type.

The Spanish ascendancy proved to be seriously counterproductive. Their objective was the acquisition of numerous Taino workers but these were now in serious demographic decline. Not that the settlers had prospered either up to 1502, by which time only 300 were left in the colony. Of the 2,500 reinforcements with Ovando, including the first European women, 1,000 died in short order. After this, however, European numbers began to rise. By 1510 Hispaniola had 10,000 European migrants. While their numbers rose, the Tainos died away. From a possible million in 1493 – more likely 300,000 or so but still a lot of people – they were down to no more than 60,000 by 1508. By the official census of 1514 only 22,726 Tainos were still listed as fit to work for Spanish masters. By 1540 there were hardly any at all. On the other hand, from 1505, European cows, horses and pigs first introduced in 1493 were swarming all over the island, in effect replacing the original human owners. By this time too most of the gold was gone and some of the colonists were settling for agriculture of limited profitability, while others were looking to new Amerindian lands to conquer.[10] Bartolome de las Casas, one of the early settlers, and a group of Dominican fathers from about 1510 began to denounce what they saw as the excess cruelty and ruthlessness which, in their view, had slaughtered the Tainos counterproductively and barbarically. The Spanish government passed the Laws of Burgos in 1513 to stop such abuse. But on Hispaniola it was far too late. And, in any case, a system called *encomienda* made surviving Amerindians everywhere liable for lifetime labour service to leading Spanish colonizers. The first Amerindian nations were overrun and almost exterminated. Whatever the main reasons, the strength of the invaders, especially their power to concentrate their resources more quickly and densely against dispersed defenders, was greater.

But the new American Europeans and their backers at home were discontented at the meagreness of the material pickings. They looked for better things almost from when Hispaniola was first discovered. The main focus was on the shores of Central America, the Pearl Coast, the region that became Panama and Venezuela. From 1504 to 1509 some of the more energetic Hispaniola settlers pooled their resources to fund a series of expeditions to collect pearls, some more gold and, increasingly, slaves in this area. Caribs were fair game for slavery. They lived in the Pearl Coast region as well as in the Lesser Antilles, the smaller West Indian islands to the east of Hispaniola and the bigger islands. But they resisted so strongly that no settlements succeeded in their area in this early period; they were militarily tougher than the Tainos. But the remaining big islands also had some gold and workers. In 1508 Governor Ovando helped to finance a group of conquerors led by Juan Ponce de Léon for the successful invasion of Puerto Rico. Ponce de Léon collected gold and built a productive estate, the proceeds from which he used to mount other invasion enterprises, especially later to Florida. But on Puerto Rico the successful European takeover soon used up all the gold as well as all the native Amerindians. In 1509 Juan de Esquivel and Panfilo de Narváez – later a leading Aztec conquistador – overran Jamaica with their privately organized armed settlers. All the Jamaica Amerindians were gone by 1519. In

1510 the Central American invaders finally settled at Darien but not before Juan de la Cosa and 70 men were killed in one battle with the Caribs, and another group of 300 under Hojeda lost 60 men, mostly to illness, but also in battle. In 1511 these conqueror types also overran Cuba, the last of the big West Indian islands with militarily unorganized native inhabitants. Most of this Hispanic imperialism – or in nineteenth-century British imperial history terms 'sub-imperialism' – was driven by private conquest urges, steady if unspectacular migration from Spain and private Spanish money, or money already gained from American gold (most of which was now used up). The hope was for bigger sources further west. Meanwhile the conquerors applied to royal governors for legal recognition of their estates, replaced Taino labour with Indian slaves from unconquered areas and would soon begin to import African slaves from Portuguese trading posts. By 1513, when Vasco Nunez de Balboa crossed the Isthmus of Panama for the first time and the word began to filter back that there was another great ocean out there, the first wave of this colonization process was finished.

In 1513 Ponce de Léon bought three ships and invaded Florida with a well-armed force of gold-hunters. The Timucua and Calusa Indians fought back so well that they drove the Spanish back to their ships. When he tried again in 1521 he was driven off once more and died of his wounds. Indian resistance was equally strong south of Panama and in the Carib islands east of Hispaniola. That left only the coasts north of Panama and Mexico itself. In 1517 and 1518 exploration parties were driven off by native people who seemed better equipped for war than any other native Americans.

At this point the result was that the crown of Spain had four large islands and a group of Panama mainland colonies which now sold some exotic natural products but mostly cowhides – from the growing herds of feral European domestic animals displacing the Amerindians everywhere in these colonies – back to Spain, for only modest profits. There was some cotton production too, and sugar looked promising, but this American empire was just a more distant and so more expensive version of the Canary Islands on the other side of the Atlantic. Back in 1493 the hope had been for a short route to Asian trade as well as lots of native gold. These blessings would make the crown of Spain richer than all others, and individual conquerors into great lords with vast estates. Some of the conquerors even made enough money to retire in modest comfort back home but for the most part these expectations were severely disappointed all around. For the human cost of the loss of an entire Taino culture – even though this was in fact deeply regretted by the authorities – Spain had some more territory, some thousands of citizens overseas, and also a working and slowly expanding transportation and commercial network across the Atlantic beginning to rival the maritime infrastructure of Portugal. But the power and glory dividend was minimal.[11]

THE AZTEC CONQUEST

It was at this point of diminished expectations that news of a great Amerindian empire in Mexico began to circulate among the leading Caribbean colonists. In February 1517 Governor Velàsquez of Cuba sent Francisco Hernàndez de Córdoba

CORTEZ.

Hernan Cortés (1485–1547),
conqueror of the Aztecs.

with 110 men to check up on the Mayas of Yucatan, reported to be city dwellers. There was immediate combat. Córdoba's men pushed inland to the city of Champoton under mounting Mayan attacks. Fifty were soon killed and the rest fled back to Cuba, where Córdoba himself died from his wounds. Governor Velàsquez then sent Juan de Grijalva, with 200 men this time, to try again in 1518. Their object was to break through Mayan defences. Despite deploying firepower superiority, especially cannon fire, Grijalva too was driven off and forced to return to Cuba. So the Governor prepared a third expedition in 1519, under Hernan Cortés. This arrived in Yucatan in February. Cortés had 450 armed and armoured volunteer fighters with 13 arquebus shoulder guns, 32 crossbows, 14 small cannon, and a cavalry wing of 16 horsemen. They were ready to fight it out with opponents now clearly recognized as tough and dangerous troops. In a major battle at Vera Cruz, later the site of San Juan de Ullua, the Spaniards beat the Mayas decisively for the first time. Cortés now convinced some of the local city states to negotiate, and began to build alliances. He was given Malinche, a lady slave, and from her and others learned of the mighty Mexican empire of the Aztecs in the interior. What he found out specifically was that it had masses of gold, great stone cities and hordes of food-producing workers and that it was ruled by what seemed to be a European style king or emperor not particularly well liked by his subjects. Cortés set out to try and seize control of this Aztec emperor. He ordered his men to start marching west.[12]

But who were these radically different new Amerindians, the Maya and the Aztecs? They seemed to be complex cultures parallel to but totally separate from the civilizations of the Old World. Together they were related Mesoamerican city-state cultures of which the Aztecs were the most prominent and final evolution by 1519. The Aztec empire began in 1428, evolving out of its Mesoamerican antecedents which began in about 1500 BC. The Olmecs, Toltecs, Mayas and others all built their societies on maize – corn – agriculture and city-state politics, and had governments that collected tax and gathered tribute of mostly food, labour service and sacrificial victims. The Aztecs themselves had a variety of names including Pipiltin, Mexica and Nahua or Nahuatl-speakers, but basically they were the citizens, both nobles and common workers, of Tenochtitlan on the site of present-day Mexico City. They ruled an expanding network of culturally similar city-states covering the central plateau of Mexico. With a population of 200,000 in Tenochtitlan in 1519, they kept a standing army of 8,000 warriors expandable in emergencies to a force several times greater. This army had characteristics unique to Mesoamerica and was not directly equivalent to European armies. The 8,000 Aztec warriors could travel 8 to 32 kilometres a day for a maximum of 8 days, or 256 kilometres in total, at the cost of 60,000 kilograms of maize made up into its portable form of tortillas.[13] By this means and by diplomacy they dominated a central Mexican population variously calculated at between 4 and 100 million people, usually accepted as around 25 million. This was a great feat by one city. But Tenochtitlan's control was limited. There was much conceded local autonomy but it was also necessary for the Aztecs to send punitive expeditions to repeatedly put down rebels in every direction. The empire stuck together more because of mutual convenience than effective central government. It was a loose confederation of tributaries rather than a united state and it had limited capabilities against serious external challenges. But it was prosperous in food and the basics of life and impressive in arts and cultural developments, with the prospect of greater things to come.

There was also a dark side. The Aztecs took Mesoamerican human sacrifice and ritual cannibalism practices to their furthest extremes. Half of the twenty months of the Aztec year had a holy day celebrated with some form of ghastly human sacrifice usually accompanied with at least ritual cannibalism. On special occasions there may well have been the kind of mass butchery of sacrificial victims described, perhaps a bit excessively, by R.C. Padden, who details '. . . lines of victims . . . strung out for miles . . .' being driven up temple pyramid steps to the sacrificial altars at the top hour after hour where they were '. . . slaughtered with machine-like precision . . .' by relays of priests wielding obsidian knives until they fell exhausted and the blood poured down the temple in streams:

> The holocaust went on unabated for four days and nights, with tens of thousands perishing on the slabs. . . . The stench grew so overpowering, the revulsion so general, that there was an exodus from the city. . . . According to some of the sources, Tlacaellel and his sturdier partisans stuck by their knives, and by the end of the ceremonial month it was estimated that they had butchered over 100,000 people in Huitzilopochtlis' honour.[14]

Even if this is an exaggeration, especially of the numbers, Aztec religion does appear to have had characteristics perhaps as revolting as those of Nazi and other Second World War civilian killing regimes. The whole religious rationale of the empire was to capture sacrificial victims for brutally demanding gods and the strategy and tactics of Mesoamerican warfare overall were geared towards capture rather than killing in ritualized fighting called 'flower wars'. Thus combat casualties were mercifully low but the fate of prisoners of war was horrible. In any case, this mass killing by Aztecs was later used by conquistadors and Catholic clergy as justification for the cultural annihilation of the Mesoamericans and for their Hispanicization.

Perhaps the most amazing thing about the Aztec story is their defeat. The discrepancy between conquistadors and Aztecs in the per person disposition of physical force was not nearly as great as between Hispaniola colonists and Tainos, while the discrepancy in numbers was immensely greater. The followers of Cortés did emphatically style themselves as the soldiers of King Carlos, as the representatives of the Spanish nation, even though they were self-funded and independent of royal command or even knowledge. Under Carlos I Spain was emerging as Europe's greatest power. Isabella had built the solid foundations by her death in 1504. In 1516 Charles of the Austrian house of Habsburg had not only taken over as Carlos I of Spain but also as Charles V, Holy Roman Emperor,

Montezuma, Aztec emperor, 1502 to 1520, captured by the Spanish conquistadors and killed by his subjects.

ruler of most of Spain, Austria, the Netherlands, parts of Italy, and other places. In 1517 this greatest European empire since the Romans actually began to break up. Martin Luther launched forth on a religious revolution. But in 1519 Luther's fragmenting ideology was still dormant, and Carlos was truly great. Thus the conquistadors defined themselves as the frontier shock troops of the world's most energetic state, leading the world's most aggressive religion (with the possible exception of Islam). Yet by European standards they were a small band of provincial desperados and Carlos was entirely unaware of their conceits about being his, and the pope's, agents. Nor were they exceptionally formidable in other ways. Cortés himself and a few others had some European military experience but the rest were men of ordinary attainments and lowly status. But to have Carlos behind them would at least be retrospectively important should they in fact conquer peoples with great riches and gold. Then they might be adopted as the agents of Europe's greatest king indeed. And they had another initial advantage over the Aztecs as well – they had the power to go to Tenochtitlan. The Aztecs did not have the power to go to Hispaniola, or any place outside central Mexico.

Beyond the access initiative, however, how and why these few hundred Spaniards managed to take over perhaps 25 million civilized city dwellers in a mere 31 months remain matters both for wonder and of controversy. There were, according to Bernard Grunberg, a grand total of 2,100 conquistadors of Mexico City altogether, but never at any one time. Over half died in the conquest effort. There is, in fact, specific information about only 1,212 individuals.[15] How did they overcome the greatest odds on any conquest in European annals at that time, against a foe which, uniquely among Amerindians opposing European invasion, met them with large-scale organized military resistance and launched forces against them equivalent in mass to big European armies? The two popular answers have been, as in the case of Tainos, pathogens and firepower. For example, in the middle of their war for survival in 1520, the Aztecs were struck by smallpox and seriously debilitated after massive mortalities. Disease made it easier for Cortés to conduct successful siege operations against Tenochtitlan. But there are experts who dispute the seriousness or even the existence of the 1520 epidemic. Francis Brooks has argued that the disease impact has been distorted by biased source material from the conquest time and that, in any case, there were never as many Aztecs alive in the first place as historians have believed.[16] Although serious disease assessments are now beginning by way of scientific analysis of human bone remains from key Amerindian burial sites, so far the Brooks argument is not widely accepted and most of the experts can only agree that it is not really possible to be sure either about the size of original populations or of the disease impact on them. But what, then, about the popular firepower superiority interpretation?

In his letters to Carlos I Cortés described his fights against Aztec forces at Cintla, Otumba and Xochimilco as full-scale European sized battles. The 75-day siege of Tenochtitlan he described in terms of major European sieges, in this case at least with considerable justification. He constantly stressed to the king the military superiority of the conquistadors, who '. . . had always been victorious, killing with crossbow, arquebus and field gun an infinite number of the enemy . . .'

Battle between conquistadors and Aztecs, 1520.

and doing great damage on horseback.[17] Conquistador Bernal Diaz recorded among other similar comments that, during the siege of Tenochtitlan, '. . . some three or four soldiers of our company who had served in Italy swore to God many times that they had never seen such fierce fighting, not even in Christian wars, or against the French king's artillery, or the Great Turk . . .'.[18] The Aztecs themselves were impressed by Spanish firepower. Fray Bernardo De Sahagun and his assistants collected Aztec narratives from surviving participants, such as the following view of Spanish weaponry:

> But the Spaniards shot iron bolts and guns. Many men were pierced by arrows and shot by guns. The crossbowman aimed the bolt well; well did he aim the bolt at the one whom he would shoot. And the iron bolt as it went, seemed to go humming, seemed to go hissing; it sped with a great rush. . . . And the guns were well trained upon the people; well did they aim at them. And when the shots fell, they went to the ground, there was a covering of the ground as if a mattress were stretched out.[19]

The conquistadors clearly had firepower as well as other military advantages.

But those historians who have assessed the conquest in the most detail and most recently do not now believe that superior arms and tactics by themselves were a very important reason for Spanish success.[20] The events and interactions were much more complex than merely a series of military encounters.[21] Ross Hassig's conclusions are as up to date and well-researched as any available, and he stresses the complexities of the role of politics in the invasion:

> Cortés and his men landed in Veracruz in 1519 and, despite clashes with various native groups on their trek toward the Aztec capital and an alliance with the powerful Tlaxcaltecs, the Spaniards and their allies were allowed to enter Tenochtitlan peacefully. A series of circumstances combined to make this possible. The Spaniards did not present themselves as a hostile force, they arrived prior to the harvest when Aztec soldiers were unavailable and unprepared for war, and they were largely oblivious to the perception of Aztec power that was so effective against other Mesoamerican groups. Once in the capital, the Spaniards seized the Aztec king, Moteuczomah Xocoyotl. The battle for Tenochtitlan did not truly begin until he was killed and the Spaniards were driven out, retreating to Tlaxcallan.
>
> The Spaniards brought new military technologies against the Aztecs, including sailing ships, cannons, guns, crossbows, and steel swords and lances, as well as horses and war dogs. However, the Spaniards were so few – numbering in the hundreds – and the Aztecs so adaptable in their responses that most of this technology was not decisive. For example, Spanish lancers were devastating against open formations, so the Aztecs quickly shifted tactics, avoiding open battlefields and shifting to broken terrain where horses could not be used with effect. The Aztecs also relied on passive defenses, such as camouflaged pits and sharpened stakes which effectively curtailed the use of horses.
>
> But the Aztec political disruption was devastating. Moteuczomah's successor, Cuitlahuah, died within eighty days of smallpox introduced by the Spaniards and was succeeded, in turn, by Cuauhtemoc. Customarily, each king began his reign with a show of force to ensure the continued allegiance of his tributaries, but Cuitlahuah had died too soon and Cuauhtemoc, hobbled by the presence of Spaniards, adopted a conciliatory approach. Safe in Tlaxcallan, the Spaniards also made overtures to Aztec tributaries in the east. Disgruntlement at the Aztecs and the Spaniards' military ability drew many former tributaries into the Spanish camp, especially because the Aztecs could not send enough troops to every town to ward off incursions. As defections continued, Aztec forces shrank until they could no longer send an adequate force against the Spaniards without leaving Tenochtitlan vulnerable to attack in the increasingly unstable political situation. The Aztecs adopted a defensive stance, withdrawing to Tenochtitlan to await the erosion of Spanish logistical and political support.
>
> Cortés began a series of campaigns against Aztec allies around the lake shore, most of which the Aztecs countered by using canoe-borne troops. With the disruption of planting and its food supplies dwindling, the Spanish blockaded

Conquistadors in combat with Aztecs during the battles for Tenochtitlan.

the city with thirteen sailing ships until famine and pestilence brought Tenochtitlan to its knees. Although Spanish weapons technology did play a role, Cortés's victory was more political than military, disrupting Aztec allegiances through the death of two kings and augmenting his own meager forces with tens of thousands of native troops while undercutting the Aztecs. With the ultimate fall of Tenochtitlan, the rest of Mesoamerica fell to Spanish domination with little or no struggle.

Resistance to Spanish domination continued for decades and even centuries among peripheral groups in the deserts to the north of Mesoamerica and hidden in the jungles to the south. Nevertheless, the Spanish conquest effectively brought large-scale indigenous warfare to an end.[22]

What did the conquistadors and Carlos gain from this amazing imperial coup? In brief, they won loot, mines, estates, taxes, patronage, territories, citizens, Christian converts, glory and international envy – just about everything any of them had dreamed about. Yet none of this was really enough, and none of it changed either Spain or Europe nearly as much as it changed Mexico and the Amerindians themselves. The loot was, and is, the most famous of these gains. It consisted of tons of gold ornaments and utensils, accumulated by the Mexica ruling class over generations, much of it of great intrinsic artistic and historical worth and merit. The conquistadors seized it as fast as they could but the bulk of it was probably lost within just weeks and months of acquisition. It was perhaps not easy come, easy go, but whatever the 'come–go' process was, it was quick. By the end of 1522 most of the Mexica treasure was thinly dispersed between Tenochtitlan and select points all over Europe. A great proportion of it sank into the muddy bottom of the lake on which Tenochtitlan was built, along with the bodies of conquistadors caught escaping the city along its causeways in the dark on 30 June 1520, during the big defeat and retreat of the campaign called 'The Night of Sorrows'. After the rest was split up among conquistador survivors according to their rank, with Cortés getting most, a full 20 per cent had to be collected for King Carlos as his legitimate tax. The conquistadors were keen to pay. Without the king's retrospective recognition of their deeds as legal Spanish conquests of non-Christian and thus outlaw people they could neither hope to spend their shares in public nor get allocations of landed estates as their territorial shares, another primary objective of theirs second only to the gold itself. But not all of the king's 20 per cent, or royal fifth, nor all the privately consigned gold as well, got all the way across the Atlantic. News of the Aztec treasure had reached western Europe already in 1520, while the Mexica still fought on. Some of the gold had also arrived in Spain. Thus, in 1522, French sea raiders, mostly from the Dieppe area, were already lurking in thoroughly armed ships off the main Spanish ports, and they appear to have intercepted substantial amounts of the loot. Finally, the biggest remaining concentration of the gold went straight into the coffers of the Habsburg empire, to be disbursed for mostly military purposes all over the king's European possessions. The gold was most welcome and much appreciated but it was only a small temporary addition to the general tax revenues of Charles V. Furthermore, there was now a new civil and religious administration needed in Mexico and a new and clearly vulnerable sea route to protect. All this cost the king a lot of money, probably at least as much as he got in Aztec treasure. The crown had already supplied two armed caravels to specially protect West Indian convoys at the European end as early as 1512. Now, in 1521, Carlos had to reorganize all his America transport fleets again and supply five armed escort vessels. In 1524 he created a colonial administrative headquarters called the Council of the Indies to run the new empire, and in 1528 had to increase the size of the fleet escorts again. So perhaps the greatest gains the king received were not the loot bonanza at all but rather the glory of expanded territory and the considerable patronage which came in the form of numerous new appointments for colonial government posts, jobs for his key nobility and people of the Catholic Church. If the envy of other leading

Europeans was an advantage, then Carlos I got that too. Meanwhile, Martin Luther at the Diet of Worms in 1521 officially declared the opening of the Protestant Reformation, and neither loot, patronage, glory nor envy helped the emperor very much in coping with this potential disaster.

The conquistadors spent their gold even more quickly. There was more in Mexico but it was in the ground and hard to get. Cortés had barely finished fighting before sending out reconnaissances in search of gold mines. He grabbed the best ones for himself. The gold slowed to a trickle, especially as Spanish masters took command of Aztec miners and each group had to adjust to the other's practices before production could resume, let alone expand. The bulk of the conquistadors, and the early settlers with enough money to follow them to Mexico, resorted mainly to agricultural estates, already in operation under Amerindian landlords and bosses, and worked by a diligent and skilled food-producing Amerindian farming class. The conquering migrants simply removed some of the Mexica nobles and put themselves in their places. Other Mexica landlords retained their lands and workers and carried on much as before. Descendants of some of these are still members of the modern Mexican elite but they were a minority. Most of the lands, along with the villages of workers on them, were allocated to new Spanish masters under various legal structures, pretexts or customary conventions under the three general evolving headings of *encomienda*, *repartimento* and *hacienda*. The Catholic Church sent missionaries and took estates also, especially on the outer reaches of Mexico where the Amerindians were less cooperative. The Spanish built towns and cities and lived in these. The Amerindians stayed in their rural villages. There were serious adjustment difficulties in this change of regime. The Amerindian population declined steadily for the next eighty years or so, partly because of European disease, partly because of more work in mines than before, and partly because of European livestock, to note only main reasons. Mexican corn and bean-based agriculture was very efficient but not set up for coexistence with the domesticated cows, horses, pigs, sheep and donkeys eagerly introduced by the invaders. In the long run the Mexicans benefited from this livestock. In the short run these animals from Europe found a fence-free and predator-free feeding bonanza in Mexican corn fields and as they multiplied, caused serious Amerindian starvation until the necessary trade-offs could be set up. It took two generations or so to adjust livestock and Amerindians comfortably to each other. By the end of the sixteenth century the native Mexican population began to recover and then grow. It had never been in the kind of terminally rapid decline as was the case in Hispaniola and the islands of the Greater Antilles. In fact, the conquered Mexicans had remained rather uniquely prosperous throughout their great adjustment. John C. Super argues that at least the majority of them had continued to eat better than just about any workers anywhere else:

> Sixteenth-century Spanish America may have been unique. While much of the world fought against shortages and famines, Spanish America produced surplus quantities of grains and meats. It is both sad and ironic that one of the greatest population losses in history occurred during this period of good

food supplies. Yet food surpluses helped Indians withstand disease and social upheaval. The surpluses also hastened conquest and colonization, aiding Spaniards to explore and build new societies. As the new societies confronted the tensions of the late sixteenth century, they could still rely on adequate food supplies.[23]

By finding a farming peasantry that they could take over much like their Spanish ancestors of the Iberian reconquest had taken over Moorish peasants from conquered Islamic estates, the conquerors of Mexico succeeded in creating a stable and eventually prosperous new society. Earlier historians have seen this conquest as either a case of straight physical coercion or of the displacement of an Amerindian with a European culture, or the cultural survival of Amerindian ways in isolated regions. In all these interpretations the emphasis has been on cultural incompatibility. James Lockhart, however, has recently reasserted the conclusions of Charles Gibson that Amerindians and Spanish invaders had so many institutions and practices in common or of similar type that there was cultural accommodation and convergence rather than confrontation and annihilation:

> The presence of Europeans among Indians unleased a long series of vast epidemics that had nothing to do with the intentions of either party, but resulted from the combination of the historical attributes of both sides. Likewise, in the cultural sphere, the degree of contact between the two populations helped shape centuries-long processes combining gradual transformation with deep continuities, depending on the relative attributes of the two. Wherever human beings come into touch, there will be both conflict and cooperation, both congregation and avoidance; some things on both sides will be strongly affected, others less so. In the central areas, contact was relatively close from the beginning, and with a quickly and steadily expanding Hispanic sector, it grew ever closer in a cumulative trend covering centuries.
>
> Another important defining characteristic of the Spanish American central areas as opposed to the periphery is the widespread interaction of indigenous and intrusive cultures on the basis of coincidences that allowed the quick, large-scale implantation among the indigenous people of European forms, or what appeared on the face of it to be such. Only in areas resembling central Mexico were large and lucrative *encomiendas* possible, only there could hundreds of rural parishes be set up and independent Indian municipalities on the Spanish model be made to function. In many ways, the Europeans and indigenous peoples of the central areas had more in common than either did with the other peoples of the hemisphere.
>
> The coincidences, however, though real, were inevitably and invariably imperfect, leading to mixed forms. Absolutely unaltered survival and total displacement are equally rare in the history of cultural contact in central Mexico. In the early stages, what one typically finds is the preliminary identification of intrusive and indigenous elements, allowing an indigenous concept or practice to operate in a familiar manner under a Spanish-Christian overlay. Over the centuries, stable composite forms and patterns took shape,

owing some traits to one donor, some to the other, and some to both. By the late eighteenth century, almost nothing in the entire indigenous cultural ensemble was left untouched, yet at the same time almost everything went back in some form or other to a preconquest antecedent.[24]

All these positive developments were under way by the end of the 1520s. They were vital to the future of both Spanish and Amerindian Mexicans. To a degree they were still being played out politically in 1994, in Chiapas State, under the national presidency of another Ponce de Léon. But at the time they were marginal to Spain and irrelevant to Europe. Once the loot was gone, Mexico lost its influence.

INCAS, SILVER AND MANILA

But just as a disappointing Hispaniola led to Mexico, so Mexico now led to other and greater treasures, of global significance this time. Other conquistadors followed the Cortés model. Expeditions, including those of Ponce de Léon, struck out into the lands north of the Gulf of Mexico and south of Panama, all after new golden cities. Only one of these succeeded, that of Francisco Pizarro. In 1532 Pizarro found the only other Amerindian empire of great lords, cities, golden ornaments and productive agricultural peasants, the Incas of present-day

Francisco Pizarro, conqueror of the Incas.

Inca warriors as they would have been armed at the time of Pizarro's arrival in 1532.

Columbia, Bolivia, Peru and Chile. There were fewer Incas in this high altitude Andes mountain region in 1532 than there had been Amerindians in Mexico in 1519, and it is probable that they had suffered severe demographic decline during the 1520s due to disease epidemics that may have been smallpox from European sources. In any case, in May 1532, Pizarro entered the territory of an Inca empire of perhaps 8 million well-ordered and efficiently governed Amerindians with 106 armoured swordsmen on foot and 62 armoured lancers on horseback.[25] The Inca emperors were more powerful than the Aztec leaders had been and their military forces were probably more formidable than Aztec equivalents. But Pizarro's desperados were very lucky. First, the empire was temporarily disorganized because of a civil war between two brothers claiming the throne. Second, the brother who was just in the process of winning, Atahualpa, was campaigning near the coast at Cajamarca, or Caxamarca, right on the road taken by Pizarro's band. If the Spaniards had any plan at all, it was to imitate Cortés by seizing the Inca emperor and then getting him to transfer all wealth and power to themselves. As it happened, the first large group of Incas Pizarro's men encountered included the very person they were after. Peaceful negotiations were organized at a formal parley in the small enclosed town square of Cajamarca. The Inca elite, with thousands of victorious troops in the area, came to look at these strange new folk from the west – the Pacific coast – unarmed. Pizarro saw his chance, opened fire on several hundred of these nobles in a confined space, and unleashed his armoured swordsmen and lancers in a general massacre lasting about two hours during which each Spaniard is supposed to have hacked and slashed to death as many as fifteen unarmed Incas. Atahualpa was seized intact. It appears that by this one dastardly, treacherous deed the majority of his top civil, military and religious administrators were wiped out on that day.

Atahualpa, the last Inca emperor,
captured by Pizarro in 1532 and
subsequently killed.

Pizarro proceeded to rule through Atahualpa as Cortés had tried to do through Montezuma, or Moteuczoma Xocoyotl, but with relatively brilliant success. There were some tense armed confrontations as bands of conquistadors fanned out over the empire to check their winnings, but by July 1533, after collecting some tons of gold and silver booty at Cajamarca on Atahualpa's orders, Pizarro felt sufficiently in control to dispense with the Inca emperor himself and had him executed. A string of new puppet emperors was appointed and there was some more fighting and tension of a minor sort but by 1534 and 1535 the invaders were setting up Spanish municipal corporations at Cuzco, Quito and Lima, and the Inca workers were now producing food, gold and silver for European rather than indigenous masters. So the conquest itself was quicker, much less military and much more complete than Mexico had been. But the long-term adjustment to Europeanization proved much harder. There were still thousands of the old Inca nobility at large, and they were discontented. In 1536 Manco Inca, originally a collaborator, led a rebel army against the new regime, starting a series of savage Inca insurrections that lasted until 1572 when the Vilcabamba-based insurgents under Tupac Amaru were put down and Tupac was executed. After that there were wars against other Amerindians, especially in the south where the Araucanians made much trouble in the 1590s. There were other violent problems in the new Spanish viceroyalty of Peru as well, made by the conquistadors themselves as they now began to fight over mines, estates and high offices. In 1537 civil war broke out between the followers of Pizarro and his brother Hernando and the men led by Diego de Almagro and old Mexico conquistador Pedro de Alvardo. In 1538 the Pizarro troops defeated and killed Almagro but in 1541 Francisco Pizarro was in turn killed by Almagro's people. This civil violence continued on and off until the battle of Pucarà in 1554 and the political situation remained unstable and dramatic afterward. At this stage, all territorial expansion in Spanish America was at an end. An easy conquest thus brought a difficult new regime. Spanish masters and Inca workers did merge politically, economically and culturally, despite the much longer armed resistance of the Inca nobility. There was also a clear population decline, as there was in Mexico. By one estimate, in Mexico in 1580 there were 1.9 million Amerindians remaining and by 1605 there were just 1 million; in Peru in 1572 there were 1.3 million and by 1620 these were down to 0.6 million.[26] After this, numbers in both places began to rise again, but it is clear that this adjustment to a new amalgamated culture was a costly process for the first three generations or so. Total Spanish migration to the Americas between 1506 and 1600, in some form of compensation, came to about 400,000 persons.

In the short run, a great heap of gold and silver loot once more flowed into Spain. Pizarro's treasure may have been smaller but a larger proportion got through to the king and the financiers and merchants who sustained the new conquest. This loot, too, was quickly dissipated. But again there were gold mines, and also silver mines, and together with those of Mexico they began to make the flow of precious metals across the Atlantic rather important. By the 1530s gold and silver was the biggest Spanish American export, followed by cowhides and sugar. But these new colonies still remained economically and therefore politically marginal, essential only to their own people's long-term prospects. Again, the conquistadors had been lucky beyond belief but settled down shortly to merely provincial prosperity.

But there was one more stroke of Spanish colonial luck, the biggest of all, the great silver discoveries of the 1540s. The first finds were at Potosi in present-day Bolivia in April 1545. Potosi turned out to be a very large mountain of silver ore, the biggest single concentration of this precious metal discovered up to that time. As more and more Inca workers were taken off their potato and llama farms and conscripted to dig as fast as possible, there appeared to be a corresponding population decline among them. Not to be outdone, the mine owners of Mexico found huge silver deposits at Zacatecas in 1547 and at Guanajuato in 1550, not quite up to the haul at Potosi, but with similar effects on Amerindian workers. Finally, in 1559, the Spanish mine owners found mercury at Huancavalica in the viceroyalty of Peru. When mixed with silver ore, this metal greatly increased silver production and made the lower ore grades profitable. So, from 1545 onwards, the flow of silver out of Spanish America became huge for the first time, and everybody agreed that it began to shape the known European, and Asian, world in important ways.

The quantities involved have been recently assessed and summarized. In the early 1530s Mexico and the Inca lands produced up to 23,000 kg of gold per year. In the 1540s this sank to 10,500 kg per year and declined to 1,000 kg for the rest of the century. The total amount of gold Spain gathered from Hispaniola in the New World until 1660 was 164,000 kg. By contrast the figures for silver were 85,000 kg per year by the late 1530s, rising to 153,000 kg per year in the 1540s, and peaking at 280,000 kg per year in the late 1580s. The total value of this from 1555 to 1600 was about 24,000 million *maravedis* collected by the crown alone as its tax share. The private sector imported another 79,000 million *maravedis'* worth. The value of a *maravedi* was approximately the same as an English pound, worth a lot more then than it is now.[27]

All this silver and gold had its economic and political impact. It was fashionable to argue that this American bullion drove up European prices, causing inflationary pressures that stimulated general economic growth and so laid down the material preconditions for the rise of capitalism and industrialization. Recent analysts are not so sure. In the sixteenth century, as Carla Phillips concludes, there were a number of fundamental growth factors that coincided in western Europe including population growth, an increase in per capita food production, a large increase in internal European as well as external world trade, and also a big increase in money supply. Clearly, the silver from America did not shape population growth, in fact, it probably reduced the Amerindian population. But no doubt it did also help to stimulate trade and manufacturing to some degree.[28]

What is clearer, however, is that this mineral bounty made Spanish colonists, merchants and administrators more wealthy than just about any other European elite. Even more important, it brought unprecedented wealth and power to the Spanish government and the Habsburg monarchy.[29] Carlos was already the envy of all other monarchs. He abdicated in 1556 in favour of his son Felipe, or Philip II of Spain, Austria, the Netherlands, Naples and other places, including Mexico and Peru. All rivals agreed that Spain and Philip owed their prosperity and power to American bullion, and many in France, the Netherlands and England planned to divest him of this bonanza by fair means or foul.

But there were two more additions to be made to this Spanish money machine. From a base of outposts begun in 1564, Spanish colonizers moved to occupy key points in the Philippines on the other side of the Pacific. In 1571 they founded Manila as a transit point between America and China. In 1580 Philip seized the crown of Portugal by right of inheritance, and subsequently by right of might. Manila was vital to East Asian trade. The Chinese demanded gold and silver cash money for the silks and porcelains the European traders wanted so badly. The Portuguese were always looking for such cash to meet the Chinese demands. Japan supplied some silver to China but from the 1570s it was Spanish galleons from Lima and Acapulco that began to dominate the Chinese cash market, and so diverted increasing shares of Chinese trade away from the Portuguese. Chinese silks now began to go to Europe across the Pacific and then the Atlantic, as Columbus had envisaged originally. But this great gain in taking over the Portuguese empire was not enough for the Spanish. Philip took the lot, and he and his successors held it until 1640. Most of the wealth of this empire remained in private Portuguese hands and under Portuguese administration but Philip gained more rich tax revenues from the Portuguese domination of the Asian luxury trades. By the 1580s Philip controlled the world's largest long-range transport fleet in the Atlantic, his American shipping, to which the Portuguese Asian fleet was now added. There were galley fleets in the Mediterranean, junk fleets in Chinese and Japanese waters, and the French, Dutch and English all had growing Atlantic transport fleets. But none of these were predominantly long range; most were for coastal transport. Spanish American shipping alone grew from about 100 ships carrying 9,000 tons of goods in the 1520s to about 200 ships carrying up to 40,000 tons in the 1580s, or about twice the size of the Portuguese Asian fleet. While this was only about a tenth of all Mediterranean shipping and a twentieth of total European shipping of all kinds, Spain now had not only the world's largest precious metal reserves but also a near monopoly of oceanic transportation. Over 90 per cent of all European wealth was still generated back home in internal production and trade but Spain had the bullion and luxury sectors, the very high value glamour items. With these economic advantages it was a wonder that Philip II did not exert greater power and domination over European politics than he did.

THE WORLD EMPIRE OF PHILIP II

Philip retained dominant European power throughout his reign from 1556 to 1598 but from the 1580s, as Spain reached the peak of its world power, the growth of his authority and the economic primacy of his empire began to slow and in relative terms to decline. Spain's range of power now stayed constant. Perhaps the psychology of being at the top generates a degree of complacency. In any case, others began to make wealth at greater rates, to build rival fleets and to challenge Spain's military and naval power. It took other counties until the 1640s to take all the main initiatives from Spain but this rising rivalry was well under way in the 1580s, at least in its formative stages.

Philip had his greatest triumphs between 1571 and 1582 against the Ottoman Turks and the Portuguese and their French allies. He also had his biggest setbacks between 1568 and 1588 at the hands of Dutch rebels and the navy and mariners of Elizabeth I of England. In one sense these victories and defeats suggest that he attempted to exercise power beyond even his unprecedented means. Spanish defences were pushed too far in too many directions for the American silver and Asian luxuries to sustain. Most authorities seem to agree that the American bullion tempted Philip into political overexpansion. He was trying simultaneously to stop the Muslim invasion of Europe from the Middle East, North Africa and the Balkans, to convert Amerindians and Asians to Christianity, and to stamp out the spread of Protestantism north and east of his own Spanish borders. At the same time he was also trying to rule five main European kingdoms with elite interests that were often in serious conflict and to fend off hostile French and English governments. In this sense it may well be that the riches of the Americas and Asia were eaten up by Spanish self-defence expenses. Battles won Mexico, Peru and Portugal and beat the Turks but they used up more tax money than Philip raised.

But the victories were spectacular. In 1571 the Ottoman Turks were probably the greatest political and cultural threat to Europe. Until 1566 they had advanced north-westward under Suleiman the Magnificent at an accelerating rate, especially threatening Mediterranean sea transportation with growing war fleets. They had beaten Venetian galley fleets under the Genoese admiral Andrea Doria at Preveza in 1538 and again at Djerba in 1560. In 1571, having captured Cyprus, the Turks were ready for more victories, with 273 war galleys under the command of Ali Pasha. The Christians, with 200 galleys under Don John of Austria, were officially the fleet of Pope Pius V, with soldiers and nobles from all over Europe on board. But the Spanish contingent was the main core and with that contingent the Christians decisively beat the Muslims on 7 October. The immediate effects of this triumph were rather small but the winners agreed that Philip II had finally stopped the Turkish advance by sea, and as time went on it became clear that Turkish power in Europe had indeed peaked. It was Philip's greatest victory.

Philip's second triumph was due as much to good luck as to good management, his seizure of the Portuguese crown by asserting right of inheritance. He was in fact one of the stronger claimants to the vacant throne but to consolidate his rule he also had to fight. This time he again resorted to sea power but now in the Atlantic, thus demonstrating Spain's maritime and oceanic supremacy. In 1582 the pretender to the Portuguese throne, Dom Antonio, raised a mainly French fleet, including some English ships, under Philip Strozzi in the Azores to stage an armed overthrow of Philip. The latter responded by sending twenty-eight ships under Lepanto veteran the Marquis of Santa Cruz. In July the two fleets met in the first great sailing ship battle at the island of Terceira. Santa Cruz drove off Strozzi and landed naval infantry to occupy the rebel bases. Only two French ships were actually sunk by Spanish gunfire but it was a decisive victory and confirmed Philip as ruler of all the oceans.[30]

He had, by this time, also ended all serious threats to his Atlantic and Pacific communications by French and English seaborne raiders. French pirates operating from ports in Normandy began to attack Spanish vessels from America along the Iberian coast from the early 1520s, capturing some of the Aztec gold sent by Cortés in 1522. In 1537 Jean Ango of Dieppe and his brothers captured a small Spanish treasure fleet. Others started to sail as smugglers to Africa and the Spanish Indies looking for cargoes of hides, dyewoods, other colonial products, and bringing slaves who could be sold for big prices to Spanish American colonists. In the 1550s these French raiders began to operate in small fleets under Francois le Clerc and Jacques de Sores, looting towns in Cuba. They were joined by English raiders and smugglers, and superseded by them in the 1560s. In 1562, 1564 and 1566 John and William Hawkins and John Lovell took small fleets of contraband goods, especially African slaves, to the West Indies and made hefty profits in their trade with the colonists, conducted under the threat of English gunfire. In many ways this armed commercial insinuation was similar to earlier Portuguese practices in the Indian Ocean and China Seas. The difference was that Asians could not or would not meet Portuguese armed intimidation with effective military and naval retaliation. But Spain did. After each wave of raids, Spanish authorities upgraded their Indies convoy systems. By the 1550s and 1560s these were so effective that no bullion fleet was captured again until 1628, when it was taken by the equivalent of a full-scale Dutch battle fleet. Thus, from the 1550s, the raiders were turning to the less well-defended colonial towns themselves. By the 1560s, however, Spanish authorities began to fortify and garrison their main colonial ports. The new defences proved their worth in 1568 at San Juan de Ullua, the main eastern port of Mexico. John Hawkins had a successful smuggling trip but then got caught with his fleet in San Juan by one of the two main annual Spanish convoys consisting of eleven transports and two heavily armed escorts commanded by the officer in charge of all Indies defences, Pedro Menendez de Aviles. The English tried to talk their way out of the situation but got shot to pieces by the Spanish ships and shore installations. Only 200 of them got away in one big ship, commanded by Francis Drake, and one small ship. In 1572 Drake was back for revenge and more plunder, this time operating as a straight pirate with no more than one crew. But he had to attack in a different way because of the improved Spanish defences. He tried to ambush a silver-carrying mule train crossing the isthmus of Panama and after considerable difficulty captured part of it, winning considerable wealth and much fame for himself back in England but doing the Spanish empire little harm. In 1577 Drake tried again. Queen Elizabeth I herself was unofficially interested in smuggling and plunder and invested in the earlier Hawkins ventures. She now invested in a Drake expedition of five ships, four of them small vessels, aimed at striking the only main undefended Spanish colonial region left, the Pacific coast of Peru and Mexico. Drake captured one ship there with enough silver to bring himself, the Queen and the other investors a very large profit when he returned to England in 1580, having, rather incidentally, become the first English captain to circumnavigate the entire globe. Elizabeth knighted him: England loved him: Philip demanded his arrest. But Spain continued to become more powerful and England remained exceedingly weak.[31] Drake and Hawkins would sail against the Spanish empire again but as admirals of war fleets during formal hostilities. Meanwhile, back in 1565, Menendez de Aviles turned to deal with the only serious European attempt to capture a North American settlement which was carried out by French Huguenot Protestants under René de Laudonniere and Jean Ribault in Florida. Menendez had sufficient ships and professional government troops to round up several hundred of these armed interlopers, to put them all to the sword, and to rebuild the fortress of St Augustine so strong that such a foreign challenge would not happen again.

The serious challenge to Spanish power came from within Europe rather than on the colonial peripheries. This was the Dutch Revolt, or 80-Year Revolt, traditionally considered to have begun in 1568.[32] Charles V had politically attached the old dutchy of Burgundy to Spain with the other Habsburg lands he inherited. This was the region of present-day Belgium and the Dutch republic, or the southern and northern Netherlands, which sits on Europe's main river systems where they empty into the North Sea. This region had the best inland waterway system in Europe, especially in the north with the Meuse, Scheldt and Rhine rivers linking the Atlantic coast. It had a position that was central to the main European population concentrations and it was already beginning to specialize in both inland transport services and services between the Baltic and Mediterranean seas. As part of the emerging Spanish empire it began to carry more and more Spanish colonial trade and Portugal relied on Dutch supplies and distribution of its Asian goods even before 1580 when it became part of Spain too. So by the 1560s the Netherlands was the fastest growing transport and trade centre in the world, urbanizing at Antwerp faster than anybody else. The increasingly mercantile ruling elite was fast catching up with Spain's town-dwelling rural landowners as the richest in Europe. The trouble was that from the 1550s Philip II tried increasingly to Hispanicize this influential group of people. He appointed outsiders from Castile and elsewhere to run the administration, thus cutting out important local leaders like the mercantile aristocrats of the house of Orange and the princes of Nassau. He tightened tax impositions in order to raise military and naval defence funds. He stationed more and more troops – often not promptly paid and so dangerous to the local people – for his anti-Protestant wars. There were other problems as well. By 1568, however, more and more Dutch towns and elites protested and some refused to obey Philip's administrators and orders. There were riots, and violence began. In 1576 the revolt got serious. Unpaid Spanish troops at Antwerp decided to pay themselves and went on a rampage, devastating the powerful merchant community. In 1585 the Duke of Parma's troops besieged and captured Antwerp in an effort to end further resistance and the rebellious merchants lost what was left of their economic power. The leading families fled north to Amsterdam with their remaining money and took their commercial infrastructures with them. They also became increasingly inclined to Protestantism, organized their own armies under the princes of Nassau and declared themselves a separate and independent republic. Philip had the finest army in the world (when it was paid) but the invincible Spanish *tercios* became bogged down at the endless river lines which crisscrossed the northern Netherlands. The battle against the Dutch rebels became a long siege operation. Dutch commercial funds gave them the money for the latest fortifications and the princes of Nassau adopted improved firepower tactics against the *tercios*. Neither side backed down yet neither side could beat the other decisively. The ongoing Netherlands war now began to drain more and more wealth out of Philip's empire, because of military and naval costs and also from the loss of Netherlands trade services and the rise of Dutch trading competition.

The Dutch disaster brought trouble in the shape of the English as well. Hawkins and Drake were serious pests but imperial defence measures had dealt with their kind of threat. In 1582, however, English ships had joined in against the Spanish fleet at Terceira which defeated the Portuguese counterattack against Spanish takeover. The Dutch and English began to form a Protestant alliance against Philip. In 1585 Elizabeth I, seeking to weaken Philip's power which she probably saw as a long-standing threat to her own political survival, began to send soldiers to help the Dutch rebel forces. This was in effect an English declaration of war. The Duke of Parma therefore got new troops together and launched a strong reconquest campaign. The Spanish grip on the southern Netherlands was much tightened; Antwerp was cleared of all lingering rebels. But the hold of the rebels over Amsterdam and the north was not weakened, especially now that they had English support. Philip decided to mount the greatest sea and land offensive in history to wipe out both the Dutch rebels and the English Protestant queen in one great move. Thus what became the Spanish Armada campaign of 1588 was launched.

In both English and American historiography the defeat of the mighty Spanish Armada by Elizabeth's Seadogs[33] is one of the great naval victories of all time. It has been held up as proof that the England of Hawkins and Drake was both smarter and braver than the empire of Philip. Spain was rich but backward. Spanish ships and fighting men were inferior. Hawkins invented the superior English 'race-built' galleon, while the Spanish admiral Medina Sidonia, actually not a sailor at all, commanded old-fashioned carracks without gun carriages and the English could reload their cannon many times faster with these. In any case, the English had the initiative at sea since Drake's circumnavigation of the globe between 1577 and 1580, and clearly since Drake and Hawkins again raided the Spanish Caribbean with over twenty ships, sacking Santo Domingo and Cartagena. They followed this up in 1587 with a raid on Cadiz, which materially delayed Philip's Armada preparations. When the Armada finally did sail with supposedly 130 ships – against a much smaller English fleet – it went first to pick up Parma's *tercios* in the Netherlands for an amphibious assault on the London area. The Spanish fleet was thoroughly outgunned by the better equipped Seadogs, forced to put in to Calais harbour, broken up by clever English fire ships, and then driven up the Channel and north-west around Scotland and home. Only 67 out of the 130 Armada ships survived this brilliant English defence.[34] With all this display of English superiority, the big question was why it was the Spanish who had a maritime empire and not the English.

This nationalist interpretation is now thoroughly altered. Research carried out on Spanish sources is now coming out in English as a result of pioneering work by historians like Felipe Fernàndez-Armesto, M.J. Rodrigues-Salgado, J.L. Casado Soto and others. In fact, the Armada had better ships than the English. The galleon type was far more likely a Spanish invention than a Hawkins invention. As Casado Soto points out:

> New research on the 1588 Armada campaign and the results of intensive investigation into Spanish naval construction during Philip II's reign clearly discountenance the deeply-rooted, traditional and wholly negative views of Spanish shipping in that period. Spanish naval architecture was probably at the forefront of the most sophisticated technological movement of the time.[35]

In fact, the Armada entering the Channel in 1588 consisted of only 117 ships (the English had the larger fleet with 226 ships), the English only sank one Spanish ship by gunfire – or any other means – and the damage to the Spanish side was entirely due to adverse weather conditions in the Atlantic west of Ireland on the return voyage, causing a loss of not more than 35 ships rather than the previously assumed 67. Of the ships lost, almost none were Spanish built; they were either Mediterranean or Baltic auxiliary ships and of an inferior type.[36] This force was defeated but not by the English or their less numerous Dutch allies. It was defeated mostly by weather conditions and also by a strategic plan that was overambitious for the technology of the age. Medina Sedonia had to first pick up Parma's *tercios* from a Channel port but neither force had any means of communication with which to coordinate the complex logistics of such an army–navy link-up. It was tough enough to do this kind of thing in 1944 at the D-day landings. In any case, when the link-up failed, the operation was over.

But Philip and his commanders were not demoralized. They had created the mightiest ocean fleet at that time, which consisted of 66,000 tons of shipping, 18,539 soldiers, 7,666 sailors and 2,088 rowers, 2,431 guns carrying 13,000 lb of cannon balls and costing 256,588 ducats a month.[37] Philip in fact raised and sent two more such Armadas against England in 1596 and 1597. Under his successor, a fourth Armada in 1601 landed troops in Ireland. The weather again defeated the second and third Armadas, and the invasion of Ireland was quickly repelled. In retaliation, Drake and Hawkins took a fleet to the Spanish Indies again in 1595. They were stopped in their tracks by much improved Spanish defences and both died during the voyage. In short, despite the failures of the otherwise unbeaten Armadas, Spain continued to rule the waves and to control the bulk of the American, African and Asian trade. Spain left only the relatively undesirable coast of North America north of Florida open to rival European colonization. The French and English made weak colonization attempts but before 1607 achieved nothing. All the important oceanic frontiers remained firmly Spanish.

But 1588 was nevertheless a turning point. The initiative slipped from Spain towards the Dutch, the English and the French. The main reason for this was probably the mounting cost of imperial defence, as most dramatically shown by the Armadas themselves. The problem was in part Spain's lack of the raw materials and skills needed to create all the armaments. The metals, chemicals, timber and many experts came from other parts of Europe, especially the Netherlands. Spain had to import bronze cannon from Flanders in the Netherlands and from Germany, copper from Hungary, gunpowder from Italy, masts from the Baltic and hemp from the Netherlands and Germany. Thus, by yet another calculation, the Spanish colonial gold and silver imports between 1555 and 1600 came to 23,827 million *maravedis* but at his death in 1598 Philip II owed his creditors 31,875 *maravedis*. In fact, Philip declared himself temporarily bankrupt in 1557, 1560, 1576 and 1596.[38] Perhaps this was the price that had to be paid for a century of enlarging Europe's overseas territories in the most spectacular and profoundly influential of all the imperial expansions of Europe. In 1600 Spain had slowed down to just about a full stop. But its modest population of under 8 million people in that year – and especially the far less numerous Castilians who had been at the cutting edge of the frontiers of conquest – had achieved the all-time greatest colonization record. Spain laid the foundations for the European take-over of the western hemisphere. Spain set the model. Spain, through envy and fear, created much of the motivation. Her successor imperialists often became wealthier than her Castilians but on a per person basis they achieved less with more.

CHAPTER 5

The Maritime Ascendancy of the Dutch

Between 1585 and 1609 the two main Dutch provinces of the northern Netherlands, Holland and Zeeland, with less than a million people and few natural resources except plenty of water, simultaneously fended off the full military and naval power of Spain and built Europe's wealthiest trading empire. Up to the 1580s Spain led Europe in empire, wealth and power. By 1609 the Dutch were succeeding in their rebellion against Spanish rule and power and on a per capita basis were surpassing Spain – and all the rest of Europe and most of the rest of the world as well – in the creation and accumulation of wealth. The revolt against Spain officially lasted eighty years, from 1568 to 1648, but the critical period was from 1585, the Spanish sack of Antwerp, to 1609, the start of a twelve-year truce with Spain. By 1609 Dutch fighting power was good enough to make independence irreversible, though twenty-seven years of war still remained to be fought out. This same critical period of the first Spanish truce was also the time that the Dutch gained their lead in shipping and trade. From 1621 to 1648 they consolidated and expanded this lead by creating an overseas empire, modelled on the Portuguese and Spanish examples but with their own innovations, which then became examples for the English and the French. From the 1620s to the 1660s the Netherlands was the world's leading maritime power and Europe's wealthiest country. But by the 1680s it was totally eclipsed by the power of France and the maritime ascendancy of England, and the Dutch leadership – though not their accumulated individual wealth – was finished.

To some historians the rise of the Dutch has seemed miraculous. For Jonathan I. Israel, how could the smallest and newest of Europe's nations, low on population, soil quality, minerals, timber and other essentials, manage to command by the 1640s about

> . . . half of the world's total stock of seagoing ships. . . . Dutch supremacy in world trade and shipping revolutionized the world economic order and transformed the pattern of Europe's colonial expansion. . . . Never before – or perhaps since – has the world witnessed such prodigious concentration of economic power at a single point.[1]

Even if this is a considerable overstatement and the gap in economic energy between the Dutch and their neighbours was not in fact so huge, how and why they managed to get even a marginal lead while conducting a desperate revolutionary campaign against Europe's strongest armed force is still a big question. Many simple answers have been proposed, covering either the survival against Spain or the great wealth processes more or less separately. An early view focused on Protestantism. Protestants were the forces of good and Protestantism generated hard work and a simple lifestyle. Protestants could therefore defeat Catholics in battle because they were theologically and therefore morally right, and they were more industrious and saved more money. Unfortunately, not all the Dutch rebels were Protestants and Protestants outside Holland and Zeeland did not become as economically strong as the Dutch. Another theory, by Pieter Geyl,[2] stressed Dutch geography. The dense river network of Holland and Zeeland provided natural defences as well as superior interior transport facilities. Other experts stress other aspects. Richard Unger focuses on superior ship technology and Jonathan I. Israel argues that it was the unique combination of business and political elites in a system where Dutch governments supported Dutch merchants and entrepreneurs better than anywhere else that gave the Dutch the lead. In the end Richard Unger concludes that the reasons were so complex and intertwined that there is no simple explanation for either the Dutch rise or the subsequent Dutch stagnation, because '. . . there is no single explanation for pre-industrial or industrial growth'.[3] But some causes do stand out, and some features of the Dutch ascendancy were at least very unique to their unusual success if not the main or the total reasons for it.

THE DUTCH LOCATION

As Pieter Geyl pointed out a generation ago, the geographic position of the northern Netherlands provided their residents with a wide range of advantages over their neighbours, although there were the limitations of poor natural resources and very little living space as well. By the sixteenth century the superficial appearance of Holland and Zeeland was not very physically appealing. The weather was marginal with constant cold winds coming off the North Sea, the land was flat and the soil, cleared of trees, was best suited to pasture. Much of it was wetland and much of it cut up by more natural waterways than any other country in Europe. The people spent more time than anybody else on boats just to do their daily duties and amusements. But the longest and most navigable west European rivers flowed through these provinces, including the Meuse and the Rhine, and it was unique to this area to be able to travel by boat all the way down to the Mediterranean through southern France – after a few crossings from one set of riverine headwaters to another, made easier by man–made canals and locks of various types. Thus the Dutch had the best water access to the interior of western Europe, which they shared only partly with the Flemings immediately to their south. In the 1580s water transport was by far the cheapest and quickest way for moving bulk products. In addition, Holland and Zeeland were on a key transition point for Atlantic ships sailing back and forth between the

Mediterranean and Iberia in the south and the Baltic, Scandinavia, North Germany and eastern Europe in the north. Since Dutch ports in winter froze up much later and for a shorter period of time than Baltic or north German ports, they were important transfer and concentration points for the Baltic trade. That trade was rapidly expanding during the sixteenth century as Polish and Ukrainian landlords opened up new wheat-producing regions, manned with serf labour, which grew grains for the European market rather than for local consumption as in earlier times. This serf-grown grain was beginning to feed the west European town and city dwellers, accelerating the rate of urbanization. There were also vital timber products from Scandinavia and other parts of the Baltic shoreline, which were used for general building construction and shipbuilding. To the south, Iberia produced salt supplies essential to the Baltic area and other places produced wine and cloth for the Baltic market. The Dutch sat right in the middle of this bulk trade route, the most important commercial network in Europe, and their rivers distributed these and other goods into the European interior. Finally, there was the North Sea herring fishery, which had migrated from previous Baltic concentrations to the coastal waters of Holland and Zeeland in the fifteenth century. By the 1580s herring, salted with Iberian salt, was the most important protein source in the diet of ordinary Europeans, and the Dutch were the closest fishermen to this natural bounty, which they supplied to the Europeans right up to the 1990s.

So the Dutch had the best water communications in Europe, on the most prosperous bulk trade routes, closest to the best fishery. But the Flemings, the French and the English were also nearby, if not quite as central, and there were a lot more of them, living in larger and thus stronger political structures. And the official overlord was Spain, with its empire including the Portuguese dominions, which had the most wealth, war strength and overall power of anybody. The Dutch, therefore, could not become important just by sitting on their good location. They also had to make the best possible use of it. They applied extra effort and built up extra skills in a number of ways. But the most obvious of these were their achievements with ships: they became ship specialists.

SHIP TECHNOLOGY

By the 1590s the Dutch were the best shipbuilders in the world. With the launching of their *fluyt* oceanic transport design in about 1595 they created the most economical and efficient bulk cargo-carrier in history. It was not especially original, being derived from the best European models as they evolved from the late Middle Ages, including the trendsetting caravel and carrack types of the Iberians. It was also derived from their own herring *buss* type, the North Sea fishing ship that, in its turn, came from earlier European and Dutch models. The herring *buss* by the mid-sixteenth century was bigger than other fishing vessels, could stay out in rough weather for longer, could marinate the catch of herring in salt-water solution on board, thus improving freshness, and could be both built and manned more cheaply than previous models. It was fleets of herring *busses* that enabled the Dutch to extract the full benefits from their geographic proximity both to the herring fishery and also to sources of Iberian salt. Thus they created the technology that enabled them to dominate completely the west European salt herring market. This was not a market of spectacular profits. Salt herring were food for the relatively poor but they were also a staple and it was a large mass market, if a humble one.

The *fluyt* of 1595 was the final version of several experimental types. It became the standard design for ocean transports throughout Europe until the end of the eighteenth century. It had, among other features, a wider hull with a flatter bottom for better cargo capacity and small harbour access, more economical use of timber in the structure, a more flexible sail plan – including a removable top mast system – more pulleys, block and tackles and other mechanical aids for sail manipulation, and it required a smaller crew per ton of cargo. All these things were refinements and improvements rather than radical changes. Just as important were the shipbuilding techniques involved. *Fluyts* were constructed by mass production methods. These had been used in Venetian shipyards earlier but again the Dutch extended and improved them. Wind- and water-powered sawmills cut up the imported Baltic timber in standard sizes; multiple hulls and masts were assembled in standard ways. Thus by 1600 Dutch shipyards produced more ships from a given timber supply faster and considerably more cheaply than the leading Spanish yards were doing. Richard Unger quantifies the resulting Dutch shipping ascendancy. While some have estimated that the northern Netherlands built up to 1,000 ships per annum and ran a fleet of 20,000 sails, the reality in the 1630s was more modest but still impressive. Unger estimates 3,000 ships at any one time, of which 500 were herring *busses*:

> The total tonnage would have been between 450,000 and 550,000. That was probably as large as the Dutch merchant marine ever got in the Republican period. If the total of seagoing vessels in seventeenth century Holland and Zeeland was between 3,000 and 4,000, and assuming a life expectancy of a cargo vessel of ten years and of a fishing vessel of 20 years, then for the Dutch merchant marine alone shipyards had to produce an average of between 300 and 400 vessels per year of which more than half were over 100 tons. Though exports probably never equalled domestic consumption, production for foreign buyers may have been as much as 50% of total output.[4]

There were probably 100,000 people or 2 per cent of the Dutch population building these ships.[5] Nobody else in Europe could match this fleet size and ship output. The Iberian leaders of the sixteenth century were decisively surpassed by the Dutch.

But this was not the case in warship production and operation. Portuguese, Spanish, English and other merchant ships were strongly influenced by their combat requirements. These other European countries all had strong government naval departments or admiralties that dictated design and construction rules of long-range full-rigged ships such as the Spanish and English galleons. These oceanic carriers were in many ways fighting vessels first and cargo transports second. They all carried cargo and most were privately owned; up to about 1630 no purely fighting ship existed. But these vessels were designed to be conscripted into state service as combat units in emergencies, as in the case of the Armada campaigns. But not among the Dutch. After their revolt, especially after their loss of Antwerp, the Dutch had no strong admiralties capable of dictating combat requirements. Instead, they designed transports first and then put guns on them and fought with them second, in reverse order to common practice. This did two things. Dutch transports were better designed in all ways and therefore superior to all others. But in the long run the Dutch lacked naval strength. They did produce a modified *fluyt* called a *pennance* out of which the European combat frigate evolved in other countries. The *pennance* was at least in part for war use but compared to their bigger neighbours, the Dutch did not create a specialist and professional navy, continuing to rely on civilian equipment in temporary war roles throughout. This saved them defence costs and increased trade profits. It even brought important naval victories at times. But by the 1660s it made them into a relatively minor sea power as well.[6] According to Jaap Bruijn, it took the Dutch until 1653 to build their first specialist navy and that was too late to match England and France.[7]

In the shorter run, however, the Netherlands had their shipping ascendancy firmly in control soon after 1600. In part this was also a reflection of Dutch urbanization, which was the highest in Europe. Along with shipbuilding, the Dutch led Europe in a whole range of manufacturing and food-processing industries. They were prominent not just in salt herring export but also in cheese and butter production and in barrel manufacture; barrels were vital for food transportation. Perhaps their lead in sauerkraut export was no big blessing to world cuisine but it kept ship's crews healthy on long voyages by providing vitamin C. The Dutch also led in things like clock, instrument and advanced machinery and tool output, and Amsterdam became a major centre for the printing industry, turning out books of importance, especially science and Protestant theology, at an unprecedented rate. These expanding Dutch towns and cities were all linked internally and to interior Europe by the densest river and canal network anywhere, making transport and storage the cheapest available. For all these reasons, plus the fact that after 1585 the Dutch rebels deliberately choked Antwerp's competition by maintaining a near-permanent armed blockade of the Scheldt river estuary on which Antwerp's trade relied, the Dutch created the biggest commercial warehousing, storage and transshipment facilities of their time. Quality advantages brought quantitative superiorities at least in shipping and commerce.

INFANTRY FIREPOWER

The Dutch achieved all this while under intense military pressure from the elite fighting *tercios* of Spain, against whom they maintained continuous operations from 1585 to 1609 and from 1621 to 1648. The *tercios* were regarded as the best troops in Europe right until their defeat at the hands of the French at Rocroi in 1643. The Spanish kings had them in large numbers as well. The Dutch rebels never developed a professional infantry of equal reputation but they held their own against the best nevertheless, this time by creating superior infantry tactics. They substantially increased the volume of effective musket fire generated by infantry formations in battle. The adoption of infantry firepower arms had been pioneered by Spain in the late 1490s and the first part of the sixteenth century. By the advent of the Spanish *tercio* system in the 1530s, about one third of all Spanish infantry were equipped with matchlock arquebuses and muskets, while the remaining two thirds protected the slow shooting musketeers with their medieval-style pikes and their swords. These Spanish troops were the first to rely substantially on what were called shot, or gun shooters, and the massed application of these matchlock guns – with their long reloading time and low accuracy beyond a 50 to 80 m range – gave them superiority over troops with fewer firearms. The proportion of shot to pikes and swords had increased slowly during the century. From the 1580s the Dutch greatly accelerated this trend, making infantry guns majority instead of supplementary weapons. They did this without any large technological innovations, simply by applying existing European weaponry to battle situations in better ways. The leaders in this tactical initiative were the three princes of Nassau.

These three men were the landed aristocrats William Louis, Count of Nassau, and Stadtholder in Friesland, his brother Prince John, and Maurice, the son of William of Orange. William invented volley fire. In 1594 he proposed six ranks of musketeers, each rank firing in unison in turn so that the opposition was subjected to waves of bullets at short intervals. As volley fire spread as the preferred tactic in the next century, the ranks were reduced to three. William and Maurice then added linear instead of compact block formations. Thus the width of the ranks of musketeers was increased, bringing more guns to bear on the enemy. In 1597 John brought in the third change, the control of troops in battle by standardized drill methods and words of command, so that formations could be manoeuvred reliably under the stresses of combat. The idea of drilling soldiers first came from the writings of classical authors such as Vegetius and Aelian, whose works were being revived by Dutch printing houses from the 1580s.[8] These drills, missing from European warfare since Roman times, made volley fire and linear tactics work on the battlefield. By 1600 the proportion of musketeers and arquebusiers to pikemen in Dutch infantry units was the highest in Europe, seventy-four to forty-five, putting the shooters in the majority for the first time.[9] Infantry now dominated cavalry on the battlefield. So the Dutch had an advantage that may have been one of the critical differences between survival and defeat by much larger forces under excellent commanders like the Duke of Parma. Again these advanced tactics came from refinements and more intensive specialization.

The Dutch defenders also relied very heavily on their water defences, supplemented by the new and expensive cannon-proof fortifications first created in Italy in the last part of the fifteenth century. On land the 80-Year Revolt was fought mostly as a series of sieges, with the Dutch compensating for numerical inferiority by better fortifications and larger volumes of defensive artillery. These things took enormous amounts of money and the commercial success of the Dutch merchant elite provided enough of this to counter the Spanish attackers funded by American silver. But success in defensive siege warfare, as in infantry combat or in sea fighting, was never certain despite these advantages. And Dutch combat efficiency was very much interlinked with commercial efficiency.

POLITICAL ADVANTAGES

Aside from exceptional military and naval efficiency the Dutch also held out because their enemies were busy fighting elsewhere. Spain, with a largely hostile and more populous France between her own and the Dutch lands, and with opponents everywhere, could never bring its full power to bear against the northern Netherlands. The Armada campaign, in which more resources went to the English side of the operation than the Dutch, was a case in point. Philip II also had his Muslim enemies in the Mediterranean and the Balkans and his overseas imperial bases and communications to protect. These defence burdens got no easier for his successors, who from 1618 onwards became embroiled in the Thirty Years War as the principal Catholic protagonists. Despite the continuing weakness of the French monarchy France too became a growing menace under Cardinals Richelieu and Mazarin, until Louis XIV ascended to power in 1661. The Dutch also fought in the Thirty Years War and worried about French designs on their borders. But their proportional commitment was smaller than that of their enemies. Instead, they used the opposition's wartime preoccupations as opportunities for overseas raiding and the taking over of the seaborne trade of the combatant powers. The English began as Dutch friends and allies but became rivals by the 1620s. Their internal political instability, culminating in the English Civil War until 1649, also kept them from effectively challenging Dutch oceanic enterprises, even when these were damaging to English interests. So the Dutch maritime star rose while the European powers were busy fighting each other.

The Dutch were also successful because they already knew exactly where and how to attack their busy Spanish and other enemies overseas, and because it had been their earlier participation in Spanish and Portuguese trade as the subjects of Charles V and Philip II that had helped to build the foundations of their economic successes. The rich trades, Portuguese Asian goods and Spanish bullion, had, until 1576, and no later than 1585, flowed to the rest of Europe through Antwerp, the great distribution point for these high-value goods as well as the bulk trades between the Baltic and Mediterranean. Many of the Amsterdam merchants had begun their careers as middlemen and distributors for Portuguese and Spanish imperial trade by virtue of their political affiliation to the Spanish crown, which was also the Portuguese crown from 1580. They had been excluded from the respective imperial shipping services and from direct access, as were also all other non-Spanish or non-Portuguese Europeans, but they had made money from these empires and they knew more about them than any other Europeans. Those who rebelled took the money and knowledge with them and by the 1590s set out to try and capture at least some of the Iberian overseas trade directly for themselves. The weakness and discontent of a conquered Portugal after 1582 was their first target. Spanish America itself was too strong, as well they knew. As the Dutch offensive gained momentum after 1602, the international political preoccupations of their existing and potential rivals with their own expanding wars much facilitated Dutch overseas expansion.

They had an internal political advantage as well. Jonathan I. Israel argues that, while they had their landed aristocrats like the princes of Nassau, it was the urban merchants who controlled the Dutch republican government. This was the reverse of the normal hierarchy in the bigger countries like Spain, Portugal, France and England. The confederated governments of Holland and Zeeland were a commercial oligarchy. They used political power to support and expand trade and industry, instead of using trade and industry to sustain political power as their opposing and rival aristocratic monarchies did. As Israel puts it, 'Dutch merchants . . . could rely on their government to adhere to its undertakings, to pay its debts on schedule, and not to tamper disreputably with savings or with the currency. Elsewhere, including in pre-1688 England, businessmen could have no such confidence.'[10] State intervention was decisive in building Dutch wealth and the Dutch empire. 'The federal state and its extensions, the East and West India Companies, were ever on the alert for challenges to Dutch trade supremacy and prompt to suppress them.'[11] But this same oligarchy neglected to build a specialist navy and could not make the northern Netherlands into a first-rate European power no matter how much money they made. It may be that Israel overstates his case because it is based on a very tight correlation between government and business. Surely the Portuguese and Spanish monarchies, who, in fact, created their trade and colonial empires in the first place with the taxpayers' money, had close ties with their merchants also? The *Estado da India* was a state enterprise throughout and the Council of the Indies in Seville was fully immersed in the workings of the Spanish colonial economy. Spanish warships carried cargo and were rented to merchants, while Dutch trading ships were armed and occasionally used for combat. If there was a difference, it was again a difference of degrees and perhaps of psychology. When the French turned to overseas empire building, they followed the monarchy controlled Spanish and Portuguese models. The English did, however, follow the Dutch more closely. The main point is that the Dutch elite was highly united both in business and politics, in trade and war. It had to be to prosper among its bigger and better resourced neighbours, even though these were preoccupied much of the time with problems of war and revolution.

OVERSEAS TRADE AND COLONIES IN THE EAST

The Dutch began their quest for Asian trade at about the same time as the English. In fact the English were a bit ahead of them. Captain James Lancaster sailed to Asia in 1591 to exploit Portuguese weaknesses and returned in 1594 with huge profits that impressed the Dutch as much as the English. In 1601 the English were the first to create a large and well-funded East India Company in London which, by the end of the eighteenth century, was poised to conquer the entire Indian subcontinent. English trading fleets and the early Dutch fleets, fourteen of them with about sixty-three ships by 1601, sailed into Portuguese dominated waters together and until 1623 sometimes fought Portuguese war fleets sent to wipe them out together as well. They protected each other's ships in Asian waters. But up to 1602 this cooperation did not bring much profit to the small independent Dutch companies involved so far. The risks and overheads ate up what profits they could get from cargoes they had to sneak past Portuguese naval patrols. So in 1602 the little companies, following the model of the confederated Dutch local governments, joined together into the VOC, or the United East India Company. The VOC government charter gave it a complete monopoly on Asian trade, the authority to wage war in self-defence, build fortifications, operate combat fleets and conduct its own diplomacy with Asian states and authorities. It was both an instrument of Dutch trade and foreign policy, of commerce and war, and was controlled by a tight oligarchy of elite merchants who also ran Dutch affairs generally. In practice the VOC was both a capitalist and a state authority, though in theory it was entirely private and merely commercial with self-defence capabilities.[12]

It took time for the VOC to get going in the face of its opponents and competitors. The 'First Fleet' got to India in 1604 but made only modest gains and arrangements. The biggest achievement was the capture of a Portuguese fort on the Indonesian island of Amboina in 1605, kept as the first small Asian territory of the VOC. In 1606 the 'Second Fleet' was driven off from Malacca and in the same year the 'Third Fleet' was driven out of Indonesian waters by a Spanish battle fleet from the island of Tidore. In 1609 two VOC ships got to Hirado in Japan and in the next year they set up a factory there with Japanese permission. This was an important start, because Japan was the only other major silver producer supplying the huge Chinese market besides Spain. The Dutch soon began to carry Japanese silver very profitably to China, thus in effect gaining an alternative silver source – more expensive than Spanish silver but still better than none – of their own. This was the first of two main gains in the East by the company, on which its commercial prosperity was subsequently based. But in 1610 these profits were still a long way off and the VOC was not succeeding in its efforts to break significantly into the Portuguese monopolies.

At this point Jan Pieterszoon Coen began to advocate a new approach, the conquest of more Asian land. This would be a similar venture to Amboina but on a bigger scale with its settlement of Dutch colonists growing their own Asian spices, especially the vital Indonesian trio of nutmeg, cloves and mace. The settlers could use Asians as slave labour. In 1611 the Company was allowed to build a factory at Jakarta in Java, and Coen urged that this place should be further colonized, but the 'Heeren XVII', the seventeen directors of the VOC, thought this would cost too much. It took Coen until 1619 to rise high enough in the company hierarchy to begin to shape policy. He was, in effect, governor in the Indonesia region until 1623 and again from 1627 to 1629. He did not manage to get many Dutch settlers out but he did build the first small European territorial and political empire on Java which was the second main and most important reason for Dutch economic success in the East.

Coen conquered Jakarta and renamed it Batavia. He then conquered the surrounding lands, in particular the Molucca island group to the east and north of Java, which was the original source of all the cloves, nutmeg and mace that the

VOC wanted to remove from Portuguese control and then totally monopolize for itself. The Portuguese held out only on Timor and the Spanish continued to operate out of Manila and from Tidor and Ternate, but from the Coen assault and destruction of Jakarta in 1619, the western tip of Java was the core of Dutch power in the East and Batavia was the governor's capital until it was finally recaptured by the Asians. (These were the Japanese samurai warriors who came as paratroops and naval assault units between 3 February and 4 March 1942, just over three centuries later. From Coen's contacts with their ancestors in Harado and Deshima, the Dutch had recruited Japanese samurai as combat troops in their original Indonesian conquests.)

These conquests were vital to the success of the VOC, illustrating both its specialization characteristics and the fact that just trade alone with Asians was not sufficient to generate a big enough level of profit to cover the huge transport and defence costs involved. Both Coen and Heeren XVII had to supplement their qualitative advantages in transport, commercial methods and combat with opportunism, because neither their European rivals in the East, the Portuguese and the Spanish – shortly to be joined by the English – nor the Asian rulers were easy to overcome or even influence. So from 1619 the VOC looked for a weak point to exploit. That weakness was on Java and its neighbouring islands, where, among other things, the spread of Islam had fragmented local authority and especially weakened the empire of Mataram. C.R. Boxer explained the decision to go for territorial conquest:

> One reason why the directors were prepared to use force in the Moluccas when they hesitated to do so elsewhere was that the local rulers possessed no warships of any strength, and the spice-growing districts were mostly on the island coasts and exposed to the reach of Dutch sea-power. Dependent as they were on the importation of rice, cotton textiles and other necessities of life from Java, Malaya and India, the inhabitants of the Spice Islands were in no position to take reprisals against the Dutch for real or fancied wrongs, as were, for example, powerful kingdoms on the Asian mainland. Moreover, the spice trade was for long regarded as the principal objective of the Company's activity in the East Indies, and as the actual or potential source of its greatest profits. Hence the Heeren XVIII enthusiastically supported, when they did not actually initiate, aggressive action in the Moluccas, at times when they deprecated or forbade the waging of offensive warfare elsewhere.[13]

The methods Coen used here and on Java, methods subsequently imitated by governors such as Anthony van Diemen, of later Australasian fame, were as ruthless and violent as those of Albuquerque, Cortés and Pizarro, though on a much smaller scale. The popular scholarly impression has been that the Indonesian conquests were copies of the Portuguese seizures of Diu, Goa, Malacca and other bases, which included both Asian cities and their hinterlands. In this view, held for example by Geoffrey Scammell and C.R. Boxer,[14] western Java and the Moluccas were armed trading post colonies similar in type but not as extensive as those of Portugal, or even of Spain in the

Philippines. They were even somewhat similar to Mexico and Peru. In fact, they were most similar to much later English examples in Bengal from the 1750s onwards. They were very innovative.

Quite unlike the Portuguese, Coen and his successors conquered not just a trading post hinterland for purposes supplementary to trading, such as extra security and fresh food supplies, but they also conquered an agricultural community and a private source of trade goods production. They conquered the spice farms, their primary objective. Coen's efforts to drive the Asian owners and farmers into slavery under Dutch migrants did not succeed well. The VOC could not attract enough such settlers. Coen's soldiers first destroyed all farms producing basics such as rice in spice-growing regions and spice farms in inaccessible areas or areas open to European rivals. Thousands of Indonesian farmers were forceably relocated or driven off their lands. Dutch bosses with gangs of slaves or native farmers obedient to them took over in large areas within the Batavia control zone. This produced a combination of a European-owned plantation system with a taxation system imposed on Asian workers. Thus the VOC created a near monopoly control over the supply of nutmeg, cloves and mace and also gained an independent source of revenue, profiting from the taxation of Asian productivity. None of the other Europeans at this stage actually became large-scale Asian landowners and tax gatherers.

Setting up this monopoly and taxation system had its costs. Military operations continued decade after decade. In 1623 one of Coen's colleagues, a man named Van Speult, ordered the beheading of ten Englishmen, ten samurai and one Portuguese, at what had so far been a relatively friendly rival English outpost on Amboina. The 'Amboina massacre' wrecked the old Anglo–Dutch harmony permanently. The two Protestant interlopers into the Portuguese Asian empire had a tradition of alliance going back to 1585 and the Dutch Revolt. They had shared the Armada 'victories'. They had fought the Portuguese in the East together and had escorted each other's ships. But Amboina was one of the spice-producing islands that the VOC wanted total control over and the English had to go. But they did not have to have their heads chopped off. One act of gratuitous terrorism ended a mutually beneficial alliance and started a long enmity that flared into full-scale war in the 1650s, much to the disadvantage of the Dutch. There were other reasons of course. But excesses in monopolizing spice supplies were not without their costs.

By 1623 the VOC in Asia was already permanently ensconced. It operated 90 ships, had 2,000 European soldiers (exclusive of mariners and Asian auxiliaries), 20 forts and 4 big fortresses at Batavia, Banda, Amboina and Ternate, valued at 6 million guilders.[15] This was the core. The war with the Portuguese continued elsewhere but the Dutch made gains against them in the East in only three other areas. In 1641, after many tries, they finally captured Malacca. In 1656 they took Colombo after a long effort, thus driving Portuguese influence largely out of the important cinnamon island of Ceylon. Also, in 1638, the Japanese government banned all further trade with the Portuguese; by 1641 the only European traders allowed became the Dutch at Deshima, where they remained Japan's sole contact with the rest of the world for the next 212 years. There were complex reasons for this Japanese isolationism and also for only continuing the Dutch contact.

Portuguese Catholic missionary initiatives were a big part of this Japanese decision. But the VOC now had exclusive access to the only other important silver source aside from Spanish America with which to buy high demand Chinese textiles and luxuries, and later the even more profitable Chinese tea. Japanese silver was the key and the VOC had a near monopoly of this also.

OVERSEAS TRADE AND COLONIES IN THE WEST

For the Dutch people at home, however, VOC profits were still not enough. The northern Netherlands had imitated the Portuguese Asian empire on a smaller scale and by spice monopoly and taxation seemed to outdo the model substantially. But the Portuguese empire also lived on, especially in its Indian bases, at Macao, and, despite the best Dutch efforts, in Timor, too close to the Moluccas spice monopoly for comfort. Between 1609 and 1621 the VOC consolidated its Asian foundations successfully because hostilities with Spain were suspended, mostly through mutual exhaustion. The war resumed in 1621. The VOC effort had not been enough to save the new Dutch state from the Spanish menace. The oligarchs therefore turned to a new company, the West Indies Company – *West Indische Compagnie*, or WIC – to strike against the Iberian enemy by war, trade and colonization across the Atlantic as well.

The WIC was set up along the lines of the VOC but the military and naval components were larger still.[16] The main objects were, first, to capture Brazil from the Portuguese and take over the Brazilian sugar industry as a Dutch monopoly. By the 1620s this was becoming Europe's largest source of sugar, and demand for sugar was becoming limitless. The alternative temperate climate source of sugar, the sugar beet that could be grown in Europe itself, was not discovered until the nineteenth century. So, again, the Portuguese were targeted as the weak link in the Spanish empire. To grow plantation sugar took African slaves, so the next objective was control of Portuguese African trading posts. A small colony in New Netherlands, later to become New York, and another one at the Cape of Good Hope were minor but supplementary territorial objectives. Aside from these, the other main aim was the defeat of Spanish power, especially on the seas. The only territorial and commercial ambition that worked out was the capture of a part of the African slave trade and a weak colony at the Cape. As a money-spinner the WIC failed to compare to the VOC. As an engine of sea power, however, it brought naval victories against the Spanish oppressor and full independence by 1648.

The greatest colonial impact of the Dutch in the Atlantic world was their indirect contribution to the development of English and French North American colonies from the 1620s. Their slaves and shipping services were probably essential for the growth of the Lesser Antilles sugar plantations of the English and French, as well as for the growth of the Virginia tobacco industry, which would be so important to the foundation of settlements on the Atlantic coast of North America. Dutch trade with the Iroquois Amerindians also shaped the development of New France in important ways. These contributions are dealt with in detail in subsequent chapters. For present purposes the WIC story can be summed up chronologically without pursuing the complexities of unsuccessful initiatives.

Henry Hudson's ship Half Moon *on the discovery of the Hudson River for the Dutch, 1609.*

A general Dutch interest in profiting from Atlantic empires predated the WIC. Dutch fur traders joined English and French counterparts as early as 1607 in the area that became New York and New England. By 1619 Dutch slave-traders sold the first twenty Africans to the struggling English colonists of Virginia for their newly discovered tobacco culture. But it took the WIC until 1624 to capture Bahia in Brazil and until 1630 to capture nearby Pernambuco. The aim was to seize prosperous Portuguese slave-worked sugar plantations in much the same way as the VOC was seizing Indonesian spice farms. But the Portuguese resisted, and while some African slaves could be collected by smuggling, it took the WIC forces until 1638 to capture a main slave source, Elmina itself. Again the Portuguese held on to their other slave ports more or less solidly. Back in 1624 the Dutch also launched their first colony of settlements at New Amsterdam, actually purchasing Long Island – the present site of New York City – from the Mahicans after some earlier casualties inflicted by these original owners on a small group of unhappy and unwell Dutch colonists. In the 1640s the local Amerindians were largely driven off or wiped out and the colony developed strong commercial links with the Iroquois in the interior, but even while sitting on the best North American east coast harbour and on a river network second only to the St Lawrence for control of the continent's vast network of internal navigable waterways, the WIC failed to attract enough Dutch settlers to hold its ground. By contrast, the English settlements to the south in Virginia and especially to the north in New England grew in European population at the fastest recorded rate for overseas settlements so far. In 1664, during hostilities largely proceeding in the English Channel, the English easily conquered New Amsterdam and made it into New York.

The WIC's efforts were greater in Pernambuco than in the north. After all, North America north of Florida was the part Spain had decided was not worth settling, which made it available to others but not highly valued. Brazil was better but harder to get. In 1628 the WIC did make a great gain in the south. Admiral Piet Heyn captured an entire Spanish silver fleet, carrying 3.3 million pesos worth of the precious metal, at Matanzas on the coast of Cuba. This was the largest single influx of profits in the WIC's history. Spanish authorities had

The capture of the Spanish silver fleet by Dutch admiral Piet Heyn, off Havana, Cuba, in 1628.

their silver fleet commander publicly executed by having his throat cut. But in terms of territory gained, the pickings were meagre. In 1634 the company captured the small Lesser Antilles islands of Curaçao, Aruba and Bonaire, and these it kept. But, compared to the plantation islands the English and French were now developing as engines of sugar profits, especially St Kitts, Martinique, Guadalupe and Barbados, these small colonies remained minor enterprises. Despite helping the Portuguese free themselves from Spanish rule in 1640, the Dutch faced rebellion in Pernambuco in 1644. By this point they were spending about twice as much on defence as they were making out of their Brazilian sugar. The revolt rolled on until 1654, when the Dutch, now under their most serious naval competition from the English at home, gave up the Brazilian effort. It had been a drain rather than a gain and the great booty of Matanzas had been only temporary compensation.

But the WIC fleets did further the material cause of Dutch independence. The wealth and the practice of empire east and west paid off on 21 October 1639, at the Downs in the English Channel. Martin Van Tromp, with 100 small Dutch transports converted for temporary combat, sailed against 70 bigger and more specialized Spanish warships. Clever use of fire ships and tactics produced a resounding Dutch victory. The Spanish fleet was just about annihilated, with 7,000 casualties and 1,800 prisoners taken, for a Dutch loss of 1 ship and 500 dead. The following year a WIC fleet smashed up another Spanish war fleet at Itamarca off the Brazilian coast in a smaller action but one of great assistance to Portugal's fight for independence. Thus, between 1639 and 1640, the Dutch permanently crippled Spanish sea power worldwide and helped reduce the Spanish empire considerably by freeing the Portuguese empire. In 1643, while the Thirty Years War and the English Civil War were also raging, the French ended Spain's infantry leadership at Rocroi. Thus, in 1648, when the main wars in Europe ground to a halt, the Dutch had done enough to win full independence from a generally reduced Spanish power. They had done a lot of the reducing.

In 1652 the WIC made its last small initiative at the Cape of Good Hope. The objective was simply to build a resupply base for VOC fleets, where they could stop for rest, recreation, fresh water and fresh food. Jan Van Riebeeck took a few dozen settlers out to Table Bay, landing there on 6 April. With difficulty he built a small permanent colony, lasting under Dutch rule until taken by the British in 1806. It was the foundation of the Afrikaner culture of present-day South Africa but it was a very small gain in the context of the 1650s.

THE LOSS OF DUTCH MARITIME LEADERSHIP

Independence coincided with predominant influence in trade, colonies and European power politics. There was no loss of wealth, merchant fleets or commercial scale. In fact, by the 1650s the Dutch nation was greatly increased in population and much improved in most of the other qualities and attributes which had given it a slender lead in international competition so far. The problem now was that England and France, with much bigger populations and natural resources, had caught up with the specialist skills of the Dutch. In some areas these big neighbours were now more specialist than the Dutch. As noted earlier, the Dutch did not finally get around to building an up-to-date specialist navy with ships for combat until 1653. By this time the English had been building a navy for war alone since the 1630s and France was about to begin a major navy building effort under Louis XIV and Jean Colbert in the 1660s. Jonathan I. Israel argues that, in fact, the Dutch remained at the leading edge of trade and shipping well into the eighteenth century. 'By 1651 England was resorting to the deliberate use of force to disrupt Dutch commerce; only the efforts of the Dutch state prevented Dutch shipping from being swept from the seas, until, in the end, this is precisely what happened in the 1780s and 1790s.'[17] But at the same time the English state grew much stronger than the Dutch and so did the French. In the first Anglo-Dutch War, 1652 to 1654, the English navy won four sea battles, the Dutch two. In the second war from 1665 to 1667 the Dutch regained the lead, and Dutch ships even sailed up the Thames and bombarded London. In the third conflict, 1672 to 1674, they won against the English navy again but Louis XIV invaded them by land. Meanwhile the English navy, English commerce and English colonies all grew rapidly nevertheless. So did the French equivalents. The Dutch did not grow. By the 1680s, when Louis XIV rose to preponderant power and authority in western Europe, the Dutch, along with Spain and Portugal, were no longer recognized as leading European powers. The leaders were France, with the largest national population, and England, with the largest navy and a merchant marine now equal to the Dutch.

It seems clear enough that the Dutch developed a qualitative lead in oceanic shipping and global commerce in both bulk and rich trades. For half a century they excelled at creating and operating marginally superior technologies and techniques ranging from catching and preserving herring in brine to infantry volley fire. From about 1600 to 1650 they also managed to build and operate the world's largest single merchant fleet, thus adding quantitative superiority to their qualitative edge. From these initiatives they became per capita the richest Europeans for the entire seventeenth century and beyond. Theirs was a commercial *tour de force* as Portugal's was an imperial one.

But superior proficiency and wealth did not translate into international power except in terms of a successful independence fight against an otherwise overcommitted imperial Spain. And while high capability is an undeniable part of this successful fight, so is the fact that the enemy was far more embroiled in the expensive wars of the first half century of the 1600s than the less-committed Dutch were. At least until 1648, and until the ascent of Louis XIV in France in 1661, their enemies and rivals were distracted by expensive wars with each other. Thus the Dutch impact on Europe's overseas frontiers was less powerful than contemporaries thought. In Asia they tried to replace a thoroughly crippled Portuguese hegemony but they only got the Spice Islands and Ceylon. The former they conquered only because local rulers were fortuitously very weak at the time. They exploited a lucky break. Beyond this, it is doubtful if they made as much money out of the VOC trade as they did out of less glamorous European trades. In Africa they gained slave-trading posts and proceeded to supply rivals with much needed labour for very profitable rival enterprises. But even this was a small proportion of the total slave trade. On the other side of the Atlantic they got some small and not very profitable Caribbean islands. Elsewhere they got nothing permanent at all in terms of territory.

The Netherlands did have the strongest fighting fleets for half a century, even if these were civilian transports first and combat vessels occasionally and second. Between 1588 and 1652 the only fleets as strong were Spanish and English. By 1639 the Dutch were the top European sea power, and recognized as so. Portugal built its empire in part because it had the best fighting ships. Spain built its empire first because it had Europe's best land soldiers and then the best sea forces as well. It is in this sense a wonder that the Dutch colonial empire was so limited. But the full explanation for the rise and fall of wealth, power and colonies is the sum total of many complexities. So far most experts agree only that the Dutch took the lead because of outstanding sea power achievements and lost it because they were outnumbered by their opponents.

CHAPTER 6
English Colonists, 1607–92

Until the 1980s English colonization in America was interpreted as part of England's superiority and leadership in Europe. A brilliant and efficient Queen Elizabeth led her fighting and trading Seadogs, with their superior ships, against backward and incompetent Spanish imperialists towards the foundation of a new and better type of colonial empire. From 1603 the Stuarts were a disappointment but Parliament and the English gentry retained their superiority and continued to build American colonies into the most populous, wealthy and economically important of them all. The Civil War between 1642 and 1649 was a minor setback but basically England led colonization throughout because of the special quality of her maritime and political excellence. The wealth of the old empire then brought about world industrialization, the world's greatest territorial empire for Britain up to 1914, and global leadership for the USA from 1945 onwards.

The experts now argue that this Anglocentric view is wrong. The Elizabethans were a failure at colonization. At the foundation of Virginia, England was both weak and backward. Until the mid-seventeenth century her colonies were largely financial failures and, in any case, generated no wealth to speak of and certainly no power. When the colonies did begin to prosper from the 1650s they did so gradually and separately. England only reached the rank of leading European power, after France, between 1692 and 1713, partly by virtue of home economic growth but mostly because of state specialization in naval sea power development. The Royal Navy brought European power to England (and Britain after 1707), although only because the defensive importance of the Channel exempted the English government from the greater costs of a large standing army and land warfare. The American colonies did grow in number, size and population but only because nobody else really wanted them. Even the Dutch had more power than the English and went after the established riches of the Portuguese empire; at the least, in New Amsterdam, they picked off the second-best waterway system along the mainland North American coastline, next to the French on the St Lawrence. Unlike all the other oceanic empires, until the 1690s the English colonized without major state participation. Their government was largely disinterested in what their colonists were up to and unconscious of the concept of 'empire' itself. When awareness coupled with the necessary power finally came, the colonists were already Americans and the French were in an excellent position to dominate all of North America. The Atlantic empire became the scene of a growing political conflict with the Americans and a rolling war with the French, and both in the end combined to beat the British state in 1782.

This critical reassessment is itself under scrutiny and there are many complexities that qualify the broad outlines. Was the first British empire really the inferior product of an inferior state, which finally failed altogether and benefited only the colonists themselves? The wealth generated by the English colonists and the Americans to 1776 was the greatest overseas economic achievement to that time, but was the overall impact on the European economy and power structure minimal? Was the periphery indeed peripheral, as Patrick O'Brien argues?[1] Was most of the profit used up in the expansion of colonial territory, population and development and of little external usefulness anyway? The resulting United States was big but did not become a world leader in either economics or power politics until the Second World War. All these and many other complexities, traditionally obscured if not obliterated by nationalist egocentricities, still need untangling. What follows here is only an introductory effort, with a few of the larger current issues posited as examples of the interpretive complexities involved.

ENGLAND AT THE START OF AMERICAN SETTLEMENT

It is neither very easy to quantify English colonial wealth and power nor English wealth and power generally. As Patrick O'Brien and Stanley Engerman say, '. . . the seventeenth century is a statistical dark age . . .'.[2] The figures that can be reconstructed, however, indicate that England was not particularly populous in 1600. The country had about 4.1 million people, packed in at a density of 47 per square kilometre. This was 7 per cent of the overall population of western Europe's six main countries. Holland had 1.5 million people and a density of 63, France had 19 million and a density of 46, and Spain had 6.8 million and a low density of 17.[3] France had the most people, the Dutch had the most wealth and the highest volume of trade per capita, Spain was probably the second wealthiest per person but internationally the most powerful, and France was rapidly catching up with Spain. In people, wealth and power, England was a third-rate competitor. The English economy was growing, but slowly. Most activity was still rural and the ruling elite was a landowning country gentry, only differing from European counterparts because they were somewhat less dominated by a very few aristocrats and somewhat more involved in commerce, especially through interaction with the London merchant community. This elite most closely resembled that in Portugal in about 1500, though the Portuguese had been much more aristocratic. Most of the English elite's, or gentry's, wealth still came from agriculture and most exports still consisted of raw wool which went to the European mills of Flanders and northern France, along with rival wool supplies from the aristocrats of Spain. A promising iron industry and shipbuilding industry were also beginning to grow and the English exported fish in competition with the Dutch. An English merchant marine was also growing. The London-centred gentry funded English East India Company predated its powerful Dutch equivalent by two years, and until 1623 English Asian fleets competed and cooperated actively with the Dutch all the way out to the Spice Islands in Indonesia. The raiding, trading and preliminary colonization attempts of the Seadogs, along with early West Country fishing expeditions to Newfoundland's Grand Banks cod fishery in competition with the fishing fleets of Portugal, France and the Dutch, all held the promise of successful future oceanic enterprise, but none of these efforts were very impressive yet. What was missing was the kind of intensive political support for oceanic pursuits that had been so prominent in Portugal and Spain and was now dominant in Holland and Zeeland.

The English government did relatively little to encourage English trade or oceanic expansion, either under Elizabeth I, despite her Seadog leader reputation, or under the very much less popular Stuarts. There were many reasons for this weakness but the main one was lack of money. Elizabeth, James and Charles collected proportionately less taxes than continental rulers. In Portugal, Spain and France, the late medieval monarchies had all made bargains with their aristocracy that gave them increasing control of national tax revenues in return for certain privileges. The crowns got the money while the landed elites got rights to offices, tax exemptions and other benefits. In this way the kings and queens all got gradually more dominant and became centralizing monarchy governments. For a variety of reasons, this tendency in England was countered by the rise of parliament in Tudor times. The English crown had some revenues of its own but the gentry in Parliament retained control of the bulk of the taxes. Elizabeth had to bargain with parliament for most of her money in a rather outdated medieval way. The gentry voted funds for national security purposes but for little else. Thus the Queen maintained her father Henry VIII's specialist navy – more specialist than anybody else's warships – but had little money left over. James I did marginally worse in bargaining with Parliament, and Charles ended up at war with his MPs. Therefore, Elizabeth did not follow up the American initiatives of her grandfather Henry VII who had provided the funding to send John Cabot, or Giovanni Gaboto, to claim part of the New World north of the Caribbean for England in 1497. The Cabot voyages produced nothing but English participation in the Grand Banks cod fishery and minor fur-trading ventures. Henry VIII was too busy dissolving the monasteries for overseas ventures. By nationalizing the Catholic Church, Henry did make a lot of money but it was a once-only income and he spent it all on his war with France. So Elizabeth could afford no more than the occasional loan of one of her naval ships to Hawkins or Drake on their Spanish empire trading and raiding voyages from 1568 onward. Beyond that, all she could do was issue licences to gentrified private colonization individuals or groups such as those headed by Sir Humphrey Gilbert between 1578 and 1583 and then Sir Walter Raleigh between 1584 and 1602. The Raleigh group actually tried to settle Virginia when, in 1585, a few dozen colonists landed at Roanoke Island: then they disappeared. New expeditions went out in search of them but without success, and it was all a complete failure. The reason was underfunding. Raleigh did no better under James I. In fact, James had him executed in 1618 for mismanagement of raiding expeditions in Spanish colonies.

But, jointly, the English government, monarch and parliament did have a unique navy. Potentially this could be used like the Portuguese had used their sea power in Asia and elsewhere. It might even counterbalance a Dutch sea power that was based on armed transports rather than on purpose-built naval ships such

Sir Walter Raleigh, early English promoter of colonies in North America.

as those Elizabeth used to fend off the mighty Spanish Armada. In 1588 she had between seventeen and thirty-three royal warships,[4] built specially for combat rather than commerce. However, they were still not combat ships only. Elizabeth rented some out to people like Hawkins to use as commerce carriers. They could, like Spanish galleons, carry cargo as well as fight but their main purpose was still more naval than that of other European ships with combat capabilities. Their job was to provide national security primarily in the English Channel in a European context of mounting international hostility. In 1600 there were only enough vessels for coastal defence. There were no spare navy units for the overseas empire in 1600, indeed not until 1655 when Cromwell finally used part of a much-expanded navy, now up to 109 ships,[5] to conquer the Spanish island of Jamaica in the Caribbean. By this time the English had pioneered the adoption of the first true battleships, based on the 100-gun *Sovereign of the Seas* launched at the government dockyard of Woolwich Arsenal in 1637. But even in 1655 the bulk of this navy was still needed in home waters to fight the mighty fleets of the Dutch. The English navy did not gain European coastal superiority until the great naval battle against the French at La Hogue-Barfleur in 1692. Up to the 1660s there was no full-scale English land army except during the English Civil War: the crown could not afford one. There was only a poorly armed and ill-trained militia. The navy was the only viable defence force. In 1607 when Virginia was founded, this navy was too small to build overseas empires with. Those empires had to be started by the private sector with considerably less government support than had been the case with the Portuguese, the Spanish and the Dutch.

So the English East India Company, chartered by Elizabeth in 1600 but otherwise on its own, made only slow progress in its effort to get a modest share of Asian trade. Between 1619 and 1623 it had an accord with the Dutch VOC under which it cooperated with the Dutch against the Portuguese and Spanish but in the latter year the Dutch massacred the company's people on Amboina and so drove the English out of the Spice Islands more or less for the next century. In India itself the East India Company had a modest outpost at Surat from the 1630s to the 1660s but it was only a minor player here until a major windfall gain in 1662, when Charles II's Portuguese queen brought the dowry of Bombay. When the company added Calcutta to its gains in the 1690s, it was finally on the way to eventual commercial and then political domination of the subcontinent. But total domination only came to the East India Company after the Battle of Plassy in 1757, under a much more powerful national government than that of 1600.

THE FOUNDATION OF VIRGINIA

The 1607 Virginia effort succeeded more quickly but began as a rolling disaster and financial tragedy dragging on until well into the 1620s. Again there were many reasons for this but once again underfunding was central to the problem. A group of gentlemen investors set up yet another Virginia Company, got aristocratic sponsors and a licence to settle and take possession of American land roughly in the middle of the temperate east coast of the continent. The location was both political and second best. Spain was fortified at St Augustine down in Florida and threatened to exterminate all interlopers in the north as well as the south, as had been done to Huguenot colonists in Florida itself in 1566. Like other Europeans, the English wanted the most southerly American lands possible. They hoped to find more Mexican treasures, or at least gold and silver mines, and tropical exotica, dyes, herbs, spices and similar high-value goods bringing high scarcity value prices in Europe. They knew about Amerindian furs and fish to the north but these did not produce enough profit to merit colonization. They also knew that to the north of Virginia it got a lot colder in winter than they were used to. So Virginia was not a preferred location but the best they could manage. Their second main problem was that they needed quick profits because too little money was invested for too short a time. The third problem was the illness of the colonists, combined with Amerindian hostility. All the main European foundation colonies in the Americas sustained massive settler death rates in the first few years. On Hispaniola, in Brazil, later at Quebec in 1609, New England in 1620 and New Netherlands in 1624, at least half of the first colonists succumbed to the maladies of acclimatization and the various shocks of environmental unfamiliarity. Virginia was about as bad as it got. There are many versions of the early death toll numbers. J.J. McCosker and R.R. Menard may not have the last word but their summation is based on recent research:

Captain Argall of the Virginia Company meets Powhatan, 1614. Argall is reinforcing the colony with people and supplies.

The death rate at Jamestown was appalling: about 60 per cent in 1607, 45 per cent in 1608 and 1609, and over 50 per cent in 1610. The colony was severely mismanaged, both at home and on the scene; relations with the Indians were strained, to say the least; food supplies were inadequate; and no profitable staple exports were found. Investor interest quickly waned: roughly five ships and 300 colonists left England for Virginia each year from 1606 to 1611, but from 1612 to 1616 a total of only seven ships and a handful of souls made the voyage. In 1616, a decade following the initial landing and after an investment of well over £50,000 sterling and the migration of more than 1,700 settlers, Virginia counted only 351 European inhabitants. Its survival as an English colony in the Americas was far from certain.[6]

The colonists were incompetent. The first wave included a minority of gentlemen investors, who did not intend to do work, and their servants, who received no clear orders about what sort of work should be done. The object was to gain wealth quickly but just finding enough food proved too difficult. There were no precious metals lying about, no tropical delicacies or luxuries for the picking, and the only food around was Amerindian corn which the owners were not generous enough with, probably because their own surpluses were

Captain Smith takes the King of Pamaunkee prisoner, 1608.

Captain John Smith, the military commander of the Virginia settlers, fights an Indian chief.

Captain John Smith amuses Pocahontas with toys as part of his efforts to pacify the Amerindians.

small. The summers were hotter and the winters colder than at home. Virginia did not even have a lot of furs to collect for the European fashion accessories market. There was plenty of land, fish, game, trees and too many Powhatan, Pashpahegh and other Amerindians. But there were no quick riches and there was not enough food. Even the water at Jamestown was too salty because the James river was tidal. The settlers who did not succumb to illness and malnutrition got into increasingly violent disputes with the local Amerindians as they demanded more and more food supplies. From 1609 to 1614 they were at war with the Powhatans.

And the Amerindians almost drove them out.[7] The settlers fortified Jamestown but were so tightly besieged at times that it became too dangerous to leave their buildings even briefly. The Amerindians liked to ambush Englishmen who went into the woods just to answer nature's call, let alone take longer trips. The colonists retaliated by organizing raiding parties to attack Powhatan villages and especially their cornfields at harvest time. There were few big fights, however. The Amerindians had the numbers but they were scattered and had small food reserves, so they could seldom bring more than a small proportion of their warriors against the English for short periods of time. Their invading enemies, while sick and hungry, were nevertheless constantly reinforced from England and had better boats and armaments. The English colonists did not start out with European war skills of any importance but they did begin to import advanced snaphance flintlock muskets and the Virginia Company directors sent out some old helmets and body armour from the Tower of London and other home armories. So they organized themselves into militia units of bodies of armoured musketeers, learned their own drill, became their own security forces without any reliance on England, and so set the standards and practices for subsequent armoured musketeer militias in the later English and Dutch colonies as well. These units did not always do well against Amerindians but ultimately they always prevailed, particularly when the European populations exceeded those of the local Amerindians. But while the early Virginians pioneered these methods they themselves, while remaining relatively few, barely survived. After making a peace based more or less on mutual exhaustion in 1614, they coexisted with only occasional incidents of violence until 1622. In that year the Powhatan leader Opechancanough, increasingly worried about the continuing English reinforcements and their territorial expansion inland, was able to organize an all-out Amerindian assault against the invaders that killed 347, or a quarter of them. But by this time his people were already outnumbered and were driven westward in the resulting revenge campaigns, after failing to stay together under arms because of food supply limitations. He organized another mass attack in 1644, again killing many settlers, but to even less effect. By then the English were permanently based in Virginia.

The reason the early colonists survived was because the Company supplied just enough money, resources and people to keep the settlement going until they found something to begin to cover these large costs. That something was tobacco, already grown in the Spanish Caribbean, and already smoked by a small and

The Massacre of 1622; the Powhatan people kill 437 English colonists in Virginia.

wealthy minority of mostly upper-class Iberian addicts. Here was a high-value crop that grew well in Virginia on the virtually free land available. Poor English workers could be brought out as 'indentured servants' and contracted to work as temporary slaves for any master who could afford to buy their papers for a period of usually four years. They got their passage paid in exchange. By the 1620s some of the tobacco planters also began to import real slaves from Africa. Tobacco certainly worked as a moneymaker:

With the discovery of tobacco the Virginia boom was on. From 1617 to 1623, when the initially high prices for the crop began to falter, an average of fourteen ships left England for Virginia each year, bringing with them a total of roughly 5,000 new planters, while English investors pumped at least £100,000 sterling into the venture. Despite annual mortality rates nearing 50 per cent, the colony's population tripled, approaching 1,300 in 1623. Difficulties remained, but the English foothold along the Chesapeake Bay was at least secure.[8]

Migration and population growth became continuous as tobacco profits paid the costs of transport and all the goods needed to clear the land, build farms, build towns, fight Amerindians and administer economy, society and politics. But only a percentage of settlement and foundation debt was covered. By the time of the American Revolution in 1776 Virginia was still substantially in debt to British investors who kept funding its growth. So were the colonies founded later. Only a small elite of large plantation owners generated most of the tobacco profits; more than 90 per cent of the early settlers from the 1620s onward were indentured servants or other poor labourers who worked for the new American tobacco landlords, at least to start with. But this was not the situation for long. The tobacco plantations took up the tidewater lands on the navigable tidal parts of the many good Virginia rivers. Tobacco wore out the soil quickly, so by the 1630s the plantations began to migrate inland. Even so, there appeared to be endless tracts of other lands for the taking, even by humble workers with few resources. Amerindian resistance in defence of these lands was already seriously reduced by 1622 and, in any case, Amerindians lived in widely scattered and retreating communities. So, ambitious indentured servants, either at the end of their contracts or illegally breaking them earlier, could simply pick a hundred or so acres of their own as it pleased them, chop down some of the abundant trees for a cabin, fencing and fuel, and begin to grow their own patches of corn among the resulting stumps. Each year they could chop down more trees and so grow more corn, supplying plantation workers on the tobacco estates with food or selling corn in town. For protein they had abundant game and fish if on a river. In particular, they had an endless supply of pork for frying, curing and pickling. Michael Williams has detailed this amazing bonanza in *Americans and their Forests*.[9] Shortly after the foundation of Virginia and its offshoot Maryland, perhaps by the 1640s at the latest, wild pigs of the razorback hog variety began to appear in large numbers in the woods. They came from Florida, where De Soto's Spanish invaders had first introduced them between 1538 and 1541. Bacon, ham, pickled pork and spare ribs all became rich colonial staples. Thus if the poorer colonists had the nerve, energy and luck to overcome isolation, Amerindian hostility and a host of hardships and fears, they could become largely self-sufficient farmers in a few seasons. Colonial administrators were so eager to open new lands and start new food supplies that they mostly recognized squatters' claims and gave these pioneers full property rights. Many ex-indentured servants died and many failed in efforts such as these, perhaps the majority in the early days, but many also succeeded. They were the founding generation of the independent small farmers who, in turn, became the most typical Americans by the end of the century. Their surpluses did generate trade internally and in small ways externally too, and they helped the tobacco planters make profits and pay debts. The news of their successes filtered back to England and attracted other economic migrants looking for their own farms and bringing development capital with them. But they too, like the planters, were mostly in debt to English merchants for the provision of the necessities of European culture essential for their survival. They contributed more to colonial growth than to English wealth and, above all, they improved their own living standards to levels well above those of small farmers or urban workers in Europe. They were mostly a benefit to European America and themselves.

Virginia became the model for the colony of Maryland, which was established as a refuge for persecuted English Catholics in 1634 but soon became much like Virginia itself. In the 1650s Virginia settlers also began to colonize the lands to the south which became the plantation colonies of North and South Carolina by the end of the century. The only other notable development in this settlement region was the progressive increase in the importation of African slaves. Tobacco could be grown without slaves but with them profits could apparently be maximized. For the Virginia and Maryland area the total European population by 1630 was up to 2,400, and there were already 100 Africans present. By 1650 there were 12,000 Europeans and 300 Africans. By 1670 there were 29,600 Europeans and 2,500 Africans. Laws were now passed to make all Africans born in Virginia slaves also, a New World legal device called chattel slavery. By 1690 there were 68,200 Europeans and 7,300 Africans. By 1780 there would be 428,400 Europeans and 303,600 hereditary African slaves.[10] By the 1690s the Amerindians were down to a few scattered reservations of a few hundred persons each. In less than a century Virginia and Maryland, with the Carolinas following, were transformed into largely self-sufficient European majority cultures with minorities of influential slave-owner elites, both growing through migration but more and more by a natural increase in population rates, whose expansion was unmatched anywhere except in New England immediately to the north of them.

But how were these expanding communities ruled? In 1624 King James I revoked all previous relevant charters and grants giving political functions and power to the companies and other grantees who began the settlement of Virginia so badly. The king appointed a royal governor and in theory Virginia came under his direct rule. He thus gained appointive patronage powers with which to reward his political supporters and he was supposedly the only one who could give settlers clear legal title to the land. But James imposed no taxes on the colonists. At the time the situation was far too desperate for them to be able to pay any. As the royal administration developed, with governors dropping in and out on what were more or less temporary visitations, the leading residents set up a House of Burgesses on the model of parliament and taxed themselves to provide local services, at levels well under English ones. During the decades of turmoil throughout the English Civil War, Protectorate and Restoration, from time to time royal governors tried to assert greater control. In 1676 Nathaniel Bacon raised a small rebellion against Governor Berkeley. The main objective, however, was to clear Amerindians from some of their remaining lands. Bacon died unexpectedly and royal authority, such as it was, was restored. But the incident did show the weakness of control that the home government had in this region. Its control over New England, which began its rather different growth with somewhat similar results, was even weaker.

THE FOUNDATION OF NEW ENGLAND

With Virginia, New England set the strongest patterns for English colonization in North America. The founding settlers were very different from the early Virginians. They were political and religious rather than economic migrants and they came not as gentlemen adventurers with servants but as a complete social slice, a prosperous gentry and merchant upper class, a less wealthy rural and urban working class, their own accumulated capital rather than other people's investment, and all their wives and children. They were the politically alienated Pilgrim Fathers and Puritans. For religious reasons they felt England was too evil to stay in and, after some of them tried the northern Netherlands and found them almost equally hostile, they decided that the North American wilderness was their version of the biblical promised land, a new homeland for God's only true chosen people. They were not the first religion-based political refugees out there. The French Protestant Huguenots had tried unsuccessfully to find their promised lands in Portuguese Brazil and Spanish Florida in the 1560s. Maryland also began as a Catholic refuge for the New England dissident settlers in the same decade. Other such religious migrations came later, notably that of the Quakers into Pennsylvania in the 1680s. The Pilgrims were the first English variant of such groups and the Puritans by far the most influential and numerous. They too had adjustment problems but, since they came in fully articulated self-sufficient social groups with transport, supplies and capital goods, they created stable and lasting communities more quickly than the Virginians. And almost from the first there were so many of them that they outnumbered the local Amerindians. They achieved full self-sufficiency between 1620 and 1640.

The Pilgrims organized themselves as a colonization company roughly on the Virginia model in order to gain royal assent for their seizure of American lands. Between 22 July and 9 November 1620, the *Mayflower* carried 102 of their first settlers (not all Pilgrims, however) to Cape Cod in present-day Massachusetts. In December they settled at Plymouth, declaring themselves a self-governing nation. About half of them succumbed to sickness in the first winter, as was typical of all the European foundation colonies, but other Pilgrims arrived and their numbers grew slowly. They were very lucky in their choice of location. As Neal Salisbury has pointed out in detail, the local Amerindian nations had just been devastated by a severe wave of European diseases contracted from earlier arrivals and casual fur-traders. The surviving Pequots, Narragansett and Wampanoags were both weakened and dispersed well away from the Massachusetts coastline. They would resist the Puritan invaders later, in the 1630s and again in the 1670s. But in the 1620s the Plymouth area of the Pilgrim 'Fathers' – and mothers – was deserted. Amerindian cornfields cleared and ready for planting stood abandoned everywhere in the region, greatly facilitating the start of independent Pilgrim

One of the early Pilgrim Father vessels arriving in New England, 1620.

food production.[11] Since the area as a whole seemed decidedly unattractive to other Europeans, compared to warmer parts to the south and better fur-trading parts to the north, nobody disputed the Pilgrim occupations from the European side either. By 1626 they bought out the remaining London investors who had helped fund the migration and became economically self-sufficient, setting up local government institutions with a view to full political independence.

During the 1620s some non-political economic migrants also began to arrive in what became Maine and New Hampshire, organized by small chartered companies of the Virginia type. The Pilgrim settlement made it easier for them in terms of supplies and gave them some degree of security. But the main Pilgrim sequel came to Boston in 1630 with the arrival of a second and much larger wave of dissidents in eleven ships. These were the first of 20,000 Puritans, again an entire social section of all classes except nobility, with whole family units. By 1640 they were all settled, mainly in Massachusetts but expanding northward also. These 20,000 settlers in ten years were the largest transposition of Europeans across the Atlantic so far. Like the Pilgrims they too brought their capital goods with them and they too wanted to match economic independence with political independence, particularly seeking to exploit the English Civil War crisis and its aftermath.

As in Virginia and Maryland, the land was 'free' after the remaining Amerindians had been driven off it. The New England soil and climate were less productive, however. The fur trade was to the south in New Netherlands and to the north in New France. The fish were quite a distance north. High-value crops like tobacco did not grow well. Like Virginians, the Puritans became quickly self-sufficient in food, for the same sorts of reasons. They too had wild hogs and in any case European livestock thrived mightily. But, like Virginians, they remained dependent on European imports to sustain a European material culture[12] and had little in their region to trade with Europe. They began debt free but did not stay that way. By the 1640s they needed to start selling things to outsiders, and began

The treaty of the Pilgrims with Amerindian leader Massasoit at the founding of New England, 1620.

to find markets for food, livestock, horses especially, timber products, such as barrel staves, and dried fish in newly developing West Indian plantation colonies. This was promising. They were creating their own commercial hinterland, in competition with traders from Europe itself: they were starting to build a new economic empire. But it was a small start and they remained rich in basic self-sufficiencies but poor in money. The usual settling-in troubles reduced 20,000 migrants to 13,700 by 1640. By 1650 the numbers were up to 22,900, and by 1660 to 33,200. By 1710, as economic activity finally speeded up from the 1660s, the total number of New Englanders was up to 115,100 people.[13] The last part of this growth came not only from an expansion of agricultural settlements that filled up the remaining good land but also from a great expansion of their regional and Atlantic trade. The growth was slow but steady and their economic system was very broadly based on most of the essentials of continuing prosperity. They even created manufacturing industries based on abundant and cheap timber supplies. They made barrel staves that were essential for food transportation and storage but they especially built more and more ships. While the New Englanders did not have a vast inland trade like the Dutch back in Europe, they did parallel the Dutch patterns of shipbuilding, bulk food trading and long-range Atlantic commerce. All this, of course, was still minuscule by European standards and still required much European capital for it to develop. That capital came increasingly from the sugar plantation business.

These Puritans also struggled for political independence. The elders who led them to Boston in 1630 had Geneva as their model of a godly and genuinely Christian community. They were in fact religious fanatics bent on creating a tightly centralized theocracy. They privately renounced the authority of their Catholic-seeming Anglican King Charles and set up Harvard College in 1636 as a Puritan indoctrination and minister training institution. Almost from the start there were groups who objected to the Boston dictators. Some were not as puritanical as others and increasing numbers of new settlers were not Puritans at all. These tended to move into the more remote parts of the settlement and spread out of Massachusetts into Connecticut, Rhode Island, Maine and New Hampshire. This relatively free land thus ruined the hopes of the Boston theocracy for an American model of a fully Christian community that, by its example, would then also convert Europe and the world to the one true faith and proper lifestyle – theirs. These elders also had to fight the home authorities. Technically they were English subjects holding their land under crown licences and grants. They did better against the king than against their fellow non-Puritan migrants, largely because of the political breakdown at home. In 1641, before king and parliament went to war with each other, Massachusetts declared itself to be an independent 'commonwealth', that is, a republic. In 1643 there were enough Puritans in Connecticut to join Massachusetts in a political alliance called the New England Confederation. This first era of American independence lasted precariously until the restoration of the Stuart kings in 1660, when each of the New England colonies again had to submit to a royal governor. But even then the New Englanders paid almost no taxes to the mother country and continued to tax themselves modestly for their own internal needs.

The reception of Roger Williams by the Indians, as the New England colony expands during the 1620s.

Puritan control and centralization no doubt gave them the determination and unity to set up their foundation communities and institutions more effectively and permanently. By the 1660s that control was fading away but the essential economic and political structures of the most populous European American community so far were in place.

Like the Virginians, the New Englanders also wiped out any hostile Amerindians by their own devices. In the process they developed their own military forces. Even though the Pilgrims and the 1620s groups found the land mostly empty of Amerindians because of earlier epidemics, they too created a militia system like the Virginians. The Pilgrims and Puritans called up all adult males, gave them muskets and armour, and marched them around according to the volley fire drills that had been invented by the Dutch and were being perfected by the Swedes under Gustavus Adolphus on the European battlefields of the Thirty Years War. In 1637 they sent their armoured musketeers against the villages of the Pequots, scattering these original owners inland and clearing more lands for European settlers. In 1675 war broke out between the settlers and the increasingly pressured Narragansett and Wampanoag Amerindians, the militant core led by chief King Philip. At a cost of 600 English killed and 1,200 houses destroyed, the armoured musketeers, with considerable support from Amerindian allies of their own, smashed the last Amerindian strongholds in their region and ended all further hostilities in New England. The handfuls of surviving Amerindians sometimes assimilated, sometimes survived as cultural fragments on small and poor reservations, but mostly fled westward out of the way of the settlements. Their resistance nevertheless did leave a strong military legacy. In both the foundation colonies the settlers generated the militia system, a citizens' defence structure that was in fact far more elaborate than European equivalents. In Europe defence increasingly became the monopoly of the professional army. England lagged behind the continent but even here the first permanent army regiments, growing out of Cromwell's Civil War formations, were instituted by the 1660s. In Virginia and New England the colonists developed the most heavily armed and thoroughly trained citizen soldiers anywhere outside of Switzerland. William L. Shea argues that by European standards the Virginians came to tolerate a very high level of firearms ownership. In 1622, for example, in response to the Opechancanough assault, the colonists decided on the general armament of all male settlers more or less permanently. They also tended to adopt advanced models of guns such as snaphance flintlocks earlier than Europeans did.[14] Patrick Malone adds to this the development of superior marksmanship practices in New England. The Puritans, with their European-style volley fire, learned from much more skillful Amerindian practices of sharpshooting to rely on aimed fire and individual accuracy. Such shooting skills were more suited to American woodland warfare and were the basis of later American firearms proficiencies and enthusiasms.[15] These authors and others do not demonstrate that the colonists became militarily superior to either Amerindians – on a man-to-man basis – or to European professionals, though the latter superiority is implied. But the colonists did become self-reliant in war and they did begin to create mythologies of sharpshooting frontier heroes.

In 1664 four English navy frigates sent by King Charles II sailed into New York Harbour and accepted the Dutch surrender of their colony at New Amsterdam and New Netherlands, settled by them since 1624. Migration was slower than that of the English and the Dutch specialized more in the fur trade. They had the best river access to the continental interior next to the St Lawrence River to the north and so became linked with the Iroquois confederacy of Amerindians living south of the Great Lakes, principally as suppliers of guns. In 1664 the English conquerors took over this Dutch role. New York became integrated into the New England colonization and expansion patterns rather than the plantation-centred structures of Virginia. New Jersey, Pennsylvania and Delaware grew out of this conquest, thus rounding out the English settlements. Along with the Dutch and some Swedes, from 1682 Pennsylvania included considerable numbers of Germans but throughout these colonies the English ethnic component was in the majority and the socioeconomic and political patterns of Virginia and New England were dominant. By 1700 there were 228,000 Europeans altogether, 90,000 in New England, 33,000 in the middle colonies around New York and 105,000 in the southern colonies.[16] They were growing quickly in people, territory and self-sufficiency and England was getting very little benefit from them because the crown and government still had very little control or interest in them.

THE WEST INDIAN PLANTATIONS

There was much more English interest in Barbados, St Kitts, Bermuda, Jamaica and the other islands of the Lesser Antilles in the Caribbean. While the mainland colonies had gradually created their own mixed and self-contained economies, since the 1640s these small West Indian islands had much more suddenly become the Atlantic world's most prosperous sugar producers. The English shared this bonanza with the French, having obtained the techniques and concepts from the Portuguese with some inspiration from the Dutch. As noted earlier, the Portuguese began to produce sugar from cane on Madeira way back in the 1430s using African slave labour. Their small output found a ready market in Europe where demand expanded endlessly. The only other sweetener available was honey. In the 1570s the sugar plantations of Brazil, again worked by African slaves, greatly increased the supply of sugar and brought the best profits from any American product, except gold and silver. Therefore, in 1630, the Dutch West India Company began its long effort to conquer these Brazilian plantations. Meanwhile, from the 1620s, a variety of European settlers began to move into the Caribbean islands that had been left unoccupied by Spain. These were raiders, pirates, 'buccaneers' who settled as the hunters of the feral cows let loose by Spanish colonists earlier – and dried the beef for seaboard provisions into a form called 'boucan' – and some gentlemen with indentured servants (as in Virginia) seeking to grow things like tobacco. Spanish authorities at first sent armed patrols to drive them out but as Spain's military commitments expanded everywhere, the new interlopers were increasingly left alone. On the island of St Kitts, English and French planters settled together in the 1620s. On Barbados, planters began to make money from tobacco, using English indentured labour. In 1635 the French settled Martinique and Guadalupe but ran into trouble with the undefeated Carib Amerindians who had so far survived a century of Spanish contact without cultural annihilation because their islands had lacked attractions desirable to the invaders. Now the French planters wanted to grow tobacco. The Caribs fought in defence of their lands for twenty years before they too were overrun. But, in the meantime, from 1637 the English began to grow sugar cane on Barbados, which spread rapidly from there to the other new island settlements, including those owned by the French. They found they could outproduce the Brazilians and make limitless amounts of money.

On Barbados the English began to grow sugar cane with white wage labour. By the 1650s, however, they were switching to African slaves sold by Portuguese and Dutch traders, and increasingly by English and New England smugglers as well. African slaves may or may not have been cheaper than some forms of European workers but the point was that Europeans were not prepared to do the intensely physical work of cane cutting and sugar making that was involved, even when animal power, windmills, water wheels and other labour-saving methods were applied extensively. African slaves could be much more easily coerced into doing such work than Europeans. Enslavement tore Africans from their social and cultural context and isolated them in an alien environment where they had little option but to obey their masters as best they could. Their survival rate, averaging ten years only, indicated the rigours of plantation work, as well as the costs of continuous labour replacement.[17] In human terms it was unmitigated horror, economically it was a brilliant success. According to McCusker and Menard, by 1650 there were already 15,000 African slaves in the English West Indies plantations, though there were also 44,000 white migrants. In the mainland colonies together there were not many more Europeans, 55,000, and only 2,000 Africans in Virginia. By 1700, by this estimate, there were 234,000 Europeans and 31,000 Africans on the mainland but on the islands the Europeans were down to 32,000, while the Africans were up to 115,000.[18] The slave importation trend got much steeper into the eighteenth century, in the end African slaves numbering 8 million, or some eight times the size of European migration up to the end of the eighteenth century.[19] In the decade from 1650 to 1660 the African population in America grew at the rate of 112.8 per cent.[20] Ralph Davis sums it up:

> By 1667 the number of proprietors of land in Barbados had fallen from 11,200 to 745; between 1650 and 1680 thirty thousand white people left the island; the number of slaves rose from six thousand in 1643 to thirty-five thousand in 1680; and in 1673 Barbados exported some seven thousand tons of sugar, roughly a quarter of the output Brazil had reached after a century of operation.[21]

By 1700 the English islands together produced 22,000 tons of sugar.[22] As Barbara Solow adds, from 1660 England exported more sugar than all other colonial products. The same was true for France, and earlier for Brazil.[23]

Yet the economic impact of this phenomenal West Indian sugar expansion was greater on the English mainland colonists than it was on the home country itself. Led by the New Englanders, these colonists took over the plantation supply and transport systems. They became the middlemen of the sugar trade and collected the largest proportion of the profits, with only some home merchants noticing and complaining. They set up what an earlier generation of historians called the triangular trade of the Atlantic, in which sugar went to Europe – and mainland America – capital and goods went from England to the West Indies and the mainland, and food, fish and barrel staves, for molasses barrels especially, went from the mainland to the islands. In fact, there were other angles as well. Increasingly, New Englanders and other colonists sailed to Africa and brought back the slave labour as well, in competition with the Portuguese and the Dutch. As the mainland fleet of transport ships grew to pass all other shipping rivals in 1700, including the English and the Dutch, the colonists themselves took the sugar and molasses to Europe and brought back European goods. They did not exclude the English or Dutch carriers but they did begin to exceed them. After 1650, when the first rum was distilled on Barbados and became the preferred beverage of the Atlantic seafarers, the New Englanders also got deeply into the rum trade. They took molasses back to Boston and other mainland ports, made their own rum and then, among other things, sold it to Africans to purchase slaves. All these activities were only beginning by the 1660s. They reached their full extent a century later when the total value of all commodity exports from the English colonies came to £6,475 sterling per average year. In 1768 sugar amounted to 60 per cent of all colonial exports. Slave-grown tobacco from the southern mainland colonies added another 18 per cent. New England supplied 78 per cent of all its exports to the West Indies.[24] Before 1700 the foundations of a new American Atlantic trading network were firmly in place. Barbara Solow, with others, argues that this was one of the most powerful economic engines driving England toward eventual industrialization. It was the only real reason why the mainland colonies grew both rich and prosperous. African slaves were the basis of all this growth.

Older interpretations about the importance of free or cheap ex–Amerindian land and about the kinds of population flow that brought unprecedented levels of capital, labour and skills to New England and then other colonies are not necessarily displaced by the African slave argument. More quantification of surviving economic statistics is going on. There were other major factors speeding American development. The settlers paid little tax in the colonies and the barest of duties on some of their products to England. In 1733 the British government finally imposed a Molasses Act, with a duty on foreign sugar and molasses imports, to stop trade with the Dutch and French. The colonists complained but, compared to the taxes back in England and in other empires, this was a ridiculously low imposition. Until 1764 they were left to spend their money on themselves and they spent it on pushing their farms westward to the first natural barrier beyond the tidal reaches of their coastal rivers, the Appalachian mountain ranges. They also grew more tobacco, added rice and indigo, caught more fish and built more ships. So the new as yet loosely unified country they were creating in North America by 1700 or so was the product of a number of happy circumstances, not just of slaves. Unlike the West Indies islands, the mainland colonies also had a high and growing degree of independence. The Caribbean plantations, with shrinking European populations, remained highly dependent and politically fragile.

THE FOUNDATIONS OF ENGLISH SEA POWER

Instead of breaking free from English rule entirely, as some already wanted to do, these colonists from 1688 put up with increasing English intervention in their affairs. The reason for this was their external dependence on English protection, especially from the rising power and competition of an imperial France. In turn, as their naval power expanded for largely European reasons, the English authorities came more and more to see the Americans as subordinate subjects to be exploited in new ways for national purposes. At the least they could help to weaken the national enemy France in North America itself. This would be not much more than self-defence for them anyway. Thus, as for the first time in the 1690s England gained a degree of international power leadership on the oceans, on both sides of the Atlantic there was a mutual discovery of empire, a new recognition of mother country and colony relationships. While the French stayed in North America in strength, this new relationship prevailed – but not for much longer.

Despite its lead in naval organization and specialist warship building, England remained internationally weak even on the water until the 1650s. The inadequate rule of the first two Stuart kings, their inability to set up a centralized government integrating parliament and an adequate tax base, meant that England actually had very little means with which to control its North American colonists anyway. The navy was kept at home for coastal defence. There was not enough money to use it to carve out colonies as the Portuguese, Spanish and Dutch had done. From 1642 to 1649 the nation fought itself in a very expensive Civil War. In terms of expenditures on fighting, it could have been much worse still. Spain and France were hostile – so were other Europeans – but between 1618 and 1648 they too were busy fighting the Thirty Years War, a much bigger drain still. During the Civil War the navy also fought against itself. But at the end, the Lord Protector of the new English republic, Oliver Cromwell, did at least have organized and battle-hardened sea and land fighters. The army was mostly reduced but Cromwell expanded the navy. For the first time the English head of state had adequate tax resources. He now turned to imitate the earlier oceanic empires.

To expand his taxes further still Cromwell relied on tariffs and duties on English and foreign seaborne trade. To expand the English part, he and the gentry elite supporting him decided to use the navy to shoot down the competition, specifically the dominant Dutch with their numerically superior trading fleet. The excuse was that Dutch ships instead of English ones were, among other things, still carrying the bulk of England's colonial trade. In 1651 parliament passed the first Navigation Act excluding foreign ships from English colonial commerce. In 1652 the English navy sailed to do battle with the Dutch in home waters. The fighting lasted from July 1652 to April 1654. It was a stubbornly contested sea war, with more fleet battles than ever before. The English navy had bigger ships with bigger guns, throwing a heavier weight of shot per broadside than the Dutch. The English supplemented their men-of-war, or ships of the line, with armed transports also but most of the Dutch fleets were made up of such armed transports only. The English fleets were bigger. According to Modelski and Thompson, the English navy had as many as 124 ships in 1652, 134 in 1653 and 140 in 1654.[25] Furthermore, the Dutch admirals, led by Tromp and de Ruyter, had to protect their vast merchant convoys as their first duty and so could not manoeuvre as freely as the attacking English under Robert Blake and George Monck. The English had fewer merchant ships to defend. The result was four victories for the English, three victories for the Dutch and one draw, with the greater numbers of ships on the winning sides. In other words, it was stalemate and Cromwell's first resort to force against his commercial competition had largely failed. On the other hand, Dutch defence costs and ship losses cut deeply into their maritime primacy and weakened their campaigns in key places like Brazil, which they had to evacuate in 1654. They did not have a big enough resource base to succeed in a long contest of this kind against a larger nation with qualitative naval superiority as well. But in 1654 they still had the power to frustrate the English.[26]

Cromwell's navy, nevertheless, was now stronger than Spain's, which had been decisively defeated by the Dutch in 1639 and 1640: the French were still not in the race. So Cromwell went to war against Spain from 1654 to 1659, and in 1655 sent Sir William Penn with thirty-eight ships of the line to capture Hispaniola, or at least Santo Domingo, the original core of Spain's American empire. This was the first English government effort at serious conquest overseas. It was certainly the first overseas deployment of a professional English fighting force. Penn actually failed but he did capture the less well-defended Jamaica instead and so added another island to the sugar-producing plantation islands centred on Barbados. It was the first English imperial conquest.

In 1658 Cromwell died and in 1660 Charles II was restored as the third Stuart king but he was, in effect, under a watchful parliament. Under the Stuarts the developing English war machine declined. Most of the remaining army was demobilized. The navy was maintained, by parliament particularly, as a commercially useful but not politically dangerous force. Armies could be used to make tyrannies like Cromwell's or to support absolutist kings such as Charles I had tried to be[27] while navies were cheaper – and Parliament agreed with Cromwell's anti-Dutch policies.

So the Second Dutch War was fought out between 1665 and 1667 as a second round for control of Atlantic sea lanes. The Dutch fleets were now more professional and specialized and the English now had fewer ships than in the first war. In 1662 they had had up to ninety-four ships of the line while the Dutch had up to eighty-three.[28] On two occasions the Dutch achieved local numbers superiority in battle and won. The English won one battle and a fourth battle was a draw. English operations were crippled by the great plague of 1665 and the great fire of London in 1666. A Dutch fleet sailed up the Thames itself and caused widespread alarm. But it was another stalemate, and again the Dutch were weakened. The English navy sent four frigates to New Netherlands. They were enough to capture New York.

The third Anglo-Dutch War from 1672 to 1674 was more decisive but it was also more complex because the French navy joined in on the English side. From 1661 Louis XIV began to consolidate centralized power over Europe's largest country and the superior scale of his tax resources was rapidly translated into one of the most formidable European war machines. By 1665 he had Europe's largest single army and it was also the most modern and effective one. That year Louis had enough expensive soldiers to spare to send the first professional regiment ever to Canada to fight the Iroquois Amerindians. Spain and Portugal had occasionally sent professional units overseas but much smaller ones, mostly for garrison duty in coastal fortifications. For the first time France had enough money to send over what, in these terms, was a small European professional army, equipped for full offensive operations. Gradually from this point on America would become an extension of European battlefields. In the meantime, however, Louis also appointed the very talented Jean Colbert to build the world's best navy and to conquer for France a greater overseas empire than anybody else had. By 1672 Colbert's shipyards were turning out the best specialist warships ever produced, qualitatively superior to both the Dutch and English designs. There were already eighty-three of them, while the English were down to fifty and the Dutch had seventy-seven.[29] France was speeding on the way to naval superiority. With the English as allies, Louis set out to crush the Dutch and conquer the Netherlands, or at least some of the Netherlands. But the Dutch fought back brilliantly, exploiting the communication and cooperation troubles of the joint Anglo-French fleets. They won four big battles and drew one. The English made peace but the Dutch war with the French continued in the Mediterranean, the West Indies and on their own borders until 1679. They lost two battles on the sea but held their ground on land. The overall result was that the French had now finished Cromwell's job of reducing the Dutch to a second-rate sea power, as much by military as by naval pressure. The Dutch were worn down by sheer French superiority of land and sea resources. From here on they swung over to the English side, especially when William of Orange, their national leader, became King William III of England in November 1688. Now it was the English and Dutch fleets against the French as the general European War of the League of Augsburg got under way because of the ambitions of Louis XIV.

The Stuarts had let the English fleet run down. William III and parliament now hastened to build it up again. Parliament restructured the national finances and found new and ample funding, which was to make the English – and British – state the most financially sound nation in Europe in the next few decades. But in 1690 France still deployed 100 line of battle ships, of the highest quality in the world. England was down to seventy-one and the Dutch were down to sixty-one.[30] At the Battle of Beachy Head on 10 July the French admiral de Tourville, with seventy ships of the line, decisively defeated thirty-six English and twenty-one Dutch battleships, and won sea power superiority. It was a bad start for the Parliamentary rearmament campaign.

But that campaign produced results only two years later. At the Battle of La Hogue, or Barfleur, sixty-two English and twenty-six Dutch battleships decisively defeated the French fleet of forty-five ships. The French turned to commerce raiding with smaller combat units, capturing 4,000 English and Dutch trading vessels by 1694, but the English and Dutch fleets set up the first effective blockade of the French coasts, starved Louis of essential trade and customs duties, and by 1697 helped to drive him to peace.[31] From here on the English navy retained at least some margin of superiority over the French fleet for over two centuries. But the Dutch now could not afford to stay in the race. Their navy and transport fleet went into relative and absolute decline. Their tax base could not sustain the Anglo-French levels of armed competition. Around the turn of the century England for the first time had a preponderance of sea power, a working instrument of empire at last. The trouble was that the French had almost passed

The Battle of La Hogue–Barfleur in 1692. The English navy gains ascendancy over the navy of France.

her by in their sudden imperial drive of the 1660s and 1670s. England's new consciousness of empire in America was blighted by a rising French territorial, military and naval threat to the north, west and south of the now so promising English colonies. The naval margin of superiority over the French was slim. In the first instance, the colonists in America would have to do a lot of the fighting against the advancing French by themselves.

CHAPTER 7

The State Colonization of France in North America

As Europe's largest and strongest seventeenth-century monarchy, France was the last to build an overseas empire and produced the least impressive colonies. But in political and military terms the French effort was as heroic as the Portuguese, Spanish and Dutch achievements had been in their different ways. Relative to English colonization, the French version was positively exciting. In terms of the immense geographic range and control attempted by mere handfuls of French imperial operatives, no other empire was vaguely equivalent, not even the Portuguese in Asia at their fullest extent. By the 1680s a few hundred French officers and adventurers laid claim to all of North America except the narrow English strip east of the Appalachians between Florida and the St Lawrence basin. Neither England nor Spain credibly challenged this claim. Two forces made this possible: a network of Amerindian alliances massively greater than anybody else's and the determined resolution of the home government's minister, Jean Baptiste Colbert, to improve French colonization. The short term results were escalating wars among the Amerindians and between the French and English Amerindian supporters and European colonists, with no material dividends for the French state. Perhaps there was glory and prestige, and perhaps the English opponents were reduced in their wealth and power. But Colbert's scheme failed. In the long run a new French Canadian culture, with 'Cajun' offshoots on the lower Mississippi River, was firmly planted on the banks of the St Lawrence (its nearly 7 million people now stand on the brink of their own first national independence) but even they have lived for over two centuries within an English culture that swamped them and extinguished their direct links with France in 1760.

The main reasons for the rise of this French empire and the founding of the Canadians are still under discussion. The central role of the Amerindians in particular continues to be revised. Old conceits about the special benevolence of French people toward indigenous nations in America and elsewhere are now discarded, replaced by interpretations of mutual dependence and exploitation; the French and Amerindians also brought great harm to each other, with the greater harm going to the Amerindians. But interdependence was a necessity: earlier historians were not much concerned with such abrasive interactions of cultures.

Harold Innis and his lesser predecessors instead attempted to interpret the origins of Canada mostly in economic and geographic terms.[1] It was the fur trade that created New France, as later staple primary products like timber and wheat were to finish the job of building a transcontinental Canadian nation. Private French merchants and Amerindian hunters craving European manufactures together built and sustained a trading network radiating mostly northward and westward from the Great Lakes at the approximate centre of the continent. The trade flowed along rivers and was carried in Amerindian birchbark canoes – it was the basis of everything. William Eccles rejects this view.[2] The fur trade was never profitable enough to create a colony. The French government had to subsidize the trade, to send over state colonists, soldiers and diplomats, and to pay for most of the empire building with revenues extracted from the agricultural peasantry of France. Eccles has the support of the present consensus. But economic and political purposes do not always explain their own supposed consequences. Geography and culture competition, and the course of events themselves, all continue to complicate the story, and all that seems clear for now is that some interpretations seem to be more convincing than others.

THE FUR TRADE

French fishermen began to visit the Grand Banks cod fishery probably as early as Portuguese and English ones, perhaps in the 1490s. Some of them began to trade with Amerindians on the Canadian mainland and what became the Acadia region of present-day Nova Scotia and New Brunswick. There was a modest but high value fur market back in Europe. Fishermen from the other countries on the Grand Banks also traded for furs, but the French seem to have gone into this business on a somewhat bigger scale. Aside from the fish and furs, however, the future Canadian mainland had no particular attractions. Instead it had frighteningly cold and long winters. So King Francis I did not send explorers to claim this area until the Giovanni Verazzano expedition of 1524, long after the English monarchy of Henry VII had sent John Cabot. Verazzano, like Cabot, claimed much of the entire Atlantic coast for his king. Subsequently, Jacques Cartier sailed up the St Lawrence River in 1534, claimed what became the core of New France, and thoroughly annoyed the Iroquois people living at the future sites of Quebec and Montreal. He found more Amerindians with furs to trade, survived a Canadian winter but observed that the river below Quebec froze solid for the entire winter thus cutting off communications with Europe completely, and returned to France with no further achievements. The monarchy was not tempted to colonize on this basis. Furthermore, civil war between 1562 and 1598, followed by minority kings from the assassination of Henry IV in 1610 to the majority of Louis XIV in 1661, wiped out the possibilities of strong colonization support from the government. So the foundations were left to private merchants with royal licences, much as was the case for the English colonies. Early efforts to set up a fur trade centre of some sort began on this basis in the 1580s but with no success. In 1598 the Marquis de la Roche took fifty convict colonists to Sable Island. Only eleven survived the ensuing settlement effort. In 1604 another group

Jacques Cartier (1491–1557),
discoverer of New France in 1534.

of merchants finally planted a settlement in Nova Scotia, located at Port Royal from 1605. This became the main community of a most precarious French Acadia, with no more than 500 settlers half a century later, which was so weak that it was actually conquered by the English and given back a total of nine times by 1710. Acadia did not even have a lot of furs and the colonists had to survive on marginal agriculture. So the real beginning of the French empire in America was Samuel de Champlain's reoccupation of a now deserted Iroquois town site at Quebec in 1608, the year after Jamestown was founded far to the south. By doing this, Champlain and his few dozen ailing companions occupied the entry to the most extensive natural water communication on the continent, the main northern link into the Great Lakes system. Only New York's Hudson River gave similar communications opportunities, but on a markedly less advantageous scale and in part tied into the St Lawrence system as well. Therefore Quebec on the St Lawrence gave Champlain's traders the best contact with the largest number of Amerindian nations north of Mexico, and thus the best access to the furs that the northern groups of these native people were eager to supply. In terms of cornering the fur trade, Champlain's little colony was a brilliant success.

By itself this trade was not enough to build a strong colony, despite the arguments of H.A. Innis. Generations of Canadian students have been persuaded that the fur trade was a great and rich commerce, spinning enough profits to sustain a continent-spanning French empire. Some experts who agree with the importance do not always have a clear understanding of the details. For Eric R. Wolf the 30-lb beaver itself has become '. . . a small fur-bearing animal weighing about 1½ pounds'.[3] Even by comparison with Virginia tobacco it was a marginal enterprise throughout, more economically important to Amerindians than to Europeans. By the time Champlain died at Quebec in 1635, there were still fewer than 200 French colonists in residence, with little prospect of growth and no incentives greater than those from the fur trade alone.

What was this fur trade and how did it operate? There was a long-standing eastern European and Scandinavian fur trade in Europe by the time the early fishing fleets began to sail to the Grand Banks. It was a small-volume luxury trade in mink, marten, fox and other decorative skins from animals becoming extinct in the populated parts of western Europe. But by the turn of the seventeenth century, beaver furs were added to the old list because of their felting qualities. The hair was shaved and made into felt hats for the rich. As hat brims expanded during the seventeenth century, the beaver fur market grew with them. Even though it took several beavers to make one hat, the hat market was an elite market and it did not need more than a few hundred French traders and agents to collect all that was needed. But for the Amerindians the beaver furs became their most important commodity, which they could exchange for European tools and weapons, on which they became thoroughly dependent. Initially it was easy for them to collect these skins. Beavers lived in timber pile lodges in the water. When things froze over in winter they were quite helpless against men with sharp steel axes – they were also easily trapped. Thus the animals were hunted out of all the areas closest to the French traders within a few seasons, and so Amerindians in the south and east had to get them from Amerindians ever further inland to the west and north. The economic, political and cultural consequences of the ensuing expanding competition for beaver skins were far reaching. The Amerindians turned against each other in a growing series of wars. They allied themselves increasingly to rival Europeans according to location and whether they could supply them with the new necessities from Europe. They became tied up in the rivalries of different European expansionists as allies, dependents or enemies. The French proved the best suppliers for the bulk of the peoples of the Great Lakes and Mississippi region but some sided with the Dutch and English. The southern tribes relied more on other products such as deer skins. Beaver, however, influenced these changes and interrelationships the most dramatically.

There were two other fundamentals shaping this transforming and mostly destructive cycle of trade, food and transportation, and both were mainly Amerindian contributions. The food was corn, grown best in regions with the least beaver, and traded to sustain the fur trade with its essential human fuel. The transport was the great Amerindian contribution to inland waterway transport, the birchbark canoe. Birch grew best in beaver country and was not prolific in corn country. This too had its complicating influences. The canoes were the creation of the Amerindians of the St Lawrence and Great Lakes regions of the northern river networks, which interconnected with waterways that flowed down into the Hudson-Mohawk, Ohio and Mississippi systems and much further into northern rivers going all the way to Hudson Bay and the Rocky Mountains. The canoes themselves were light but strong. They could be made to carry a dozen or more paddlers and some tons of cargo, including bulky items such as barrels of gunpowder, brandy or flour. They could even carry small cannon, although these could not be discharged on board. They could be rapidly 'portaged' around rapids and waterfalls and from one river system to another. They gave the Algonquan people who used them the highest degree of inland mobility in the Americas, excepting only the Great Plains Amerindians who domesticated feral Spanish horses in the eighteenth century. Neither Virginia nor New England Amerindians had birch for canoes, and even the Iroquois (or Five Nations people) and the Ohio Valley people had only limited access to this vital tree and its bark.

Because of the canoe the fur trade was the quickest and most articulated long-range transportation network on the continent, with strong strategic effects. Those who had both birches and beavers, plus the skills and urges, could dominate the continent in a great arc from Quebec in the north to the mouth of the Mississippi in the south, surrounding the coastal colonies of the English. The centre of this canoe net was the St Lawrence and lower Great Lakes region. From here France was able to send its agents paddling to the Arctic, the Rocky Mountains, and to the Gulf of Mexico. But while the range was massive, few people were needed to work this system. It provided maximum geographic spread with minimum personnel. As long as the few were not challenged by denser blocks of population they could flourish. But to the immediate south were the concentrated Five Nations Iroquois, and to the west and south other more densely packed Amerindians. To the south-east were the swarming English colonists. So the canoe and beaver combination gave the French the means to gain vast interior territories but not the security of holding their ground in the long run.

With canoes, beaver, Amerindian corn and the Great Lakes waterways went interdependence between the French and most of the northern Amerindian people as well as hostility between this interdependent alliance and an influential minority of other Amerindians with inferior beaver supplies. Thus the early French traders were dependent on the northern Algonquian peoples, who quickly became equally or more dependent on French tools and weapons. Steel and matchlock guns gave Algonquians greater wealth and power than neighbouring nations, especially to the south of the Great Lakes. Steel axes also speeded up their beaver harvests, allowing them to chop their way rapidly into the beaver lodges in the winter. There was also much trade in brandy. To contemporaries, the Amerindian thirst for European alcohol seemed utterly unquenchable. The records abound with descriptions of innumerable drunken parties, ending, as often as not, in violence. Brandy barrels, however, were both very heavy and soon empty, and even big canoes had limited space. High-value long-lasting tools and weapons predominated in the canoe loads of Amerindian imports and it was on these things that the native cultures became increasingly dependent. As they competed for furs, steel and gunpowder weaponry became essential to survival itself.

When Champlain founded Quebec his little group of commercial colonists at once became allied with the Algonquian fur specialists in a mutually dependent relationship which demanded continuous expansion. The Hurons in the southern Ontario region were allied to Algonquians as food producers, so they too were pulled into the interdependence network. But the ethnic relatives of the Hurons, the Five Nations or Iroquois – Mohawks, Oneidas, Onondagas, Cayugas and Senecas – were Algonquian trade competitors and became the enemies of the alliance, threatening it from their position just south of lakes Ontario and Erie. From here the Iroquois, with a secure food base, could strike out against all the key Algonquian fur routes with the advantage of what military strategists call 'interior lines' (meaning a central position), much like the Aztecs had done from Tenochtitlan into all parts of the valley of Mexico. From the start French influence was expanded through the Algonquians and limited by the Iroquois. The Iroquois also pulled the French into conflict with other European colonizers. They had their own route to the Atlantic via the Hudson and Mohawk River system. It was not as good as the St Lawrence, nor were Iroquois canoes as good as Algonquian canoes, but if they could get beaver skins from Algonquian country, they too could import steel and guns from either English or Dutch traders. Guns were hard to get early, however. In fact, Champlain's shock application of firepower against the Mohawks is the accepted starting point of the long Iroquois effort to divert the fur trade to the Hudson River and destroy the French and Algonquian commercial and political alliance.

Of the many versions of Champlain's first blast against the Mohawks, Ian Steele's is the latest and among the very best. In July 1609 sixty Montagnais Algonquians and Hurons persuaded Champlain and two other Frenchmen, with arquebuses, to join them on a traditional raid against the Mohawks. This would be a French act of solidarity with their new trading partners. They met 200 Mohawks on the shore of the Lake Champlain (named after Samuel himself):

> The Mohawk landed and built a barricade, using what Champlain described as poor quality iron and stone axes. Champlain's companions spent the night in their canoes, anchored together offshore. After sending a legation to confirm Mohawk willingness to fight in the morning, both sides spent the night singing songs and shouting insults. Champlain and his allies landed unopposed in the morning, and the Mohawks came out of their barricade to fight. According to plan, the French remained hidden behind the Montagnais and Huron warriors until they were within thirty yards of the Mohawks, still without any arrows being shot. Champlain, supposedly the first white man seen by these Mohawk, then stepped forward and fired his overloaded matchlock arquebus at the three Mohawk chiefs. The Mohawk arrow-proof shields of wood and woven cotton proved worthless against musket balls; two chiefs were killed immediately, and the third was mortally wounded. As another French musketeer fired, the Mohawk fled with Huron and Algonquin in pursuit. When the skirmish had ended, Champlain's allies had reportedly killed numerous Mohawk and taken a dozen prisoners, while suffering fifteen wounded. In the subsequent victory celebration, one of the prisoners was subjected to the traditional Huron torture unto death.[4]

Jesuit missionaries attempting to convert the Hurons in the 1630s.

It is possible to load muskets with three or more undersize bullets and Champlain had done so. The Iroquois were therefore far more impressed by guns because of this first skirmish than was usually the case. In 1628, having been driven southward by the ascendant French-supported Algonquians, the Mohawks were still without their own guns. The Dutch were now at New Amsterdam (New York to be) and upstream at their fur-trading post at Fort Orange, later Albany. To get to them, however, the Mohawks had to get past the Mahican Algonquians initially allied to the Dutch. When a Mahican and Dutch war party tried the Champlain manoeuvre, against the Mohawks this time, European firepower no longer had its magic effect. The attackers were led by Dutch West India Company commissary Daniel van Krieckenbeeck:

> The Algonquian-speaking Mahican seemed likely to win and offered links to the hunters of the thicker furs of the north. Van Krieckenbeeck and six traders took muskets, but apparently no armor, and accompanied a Mahican war party. This venture proved to be the opposite of Champlain's successful intervention and subsequent prominence in a native alliance. Mohawk armed exclusively with bows and clubs ambushed the Mahican-Dutch war party. Van Krieckenbeeck and three of his companions were killed by arrows, and one of the dead Dutch was roasted and eaten by the victorious Mohawk warriors.[5]

Firepower was not always supreme. The Dutch were persuaded to bypass the Mahicans, whose fur sources were in fact inferior to the Iroquois anyway. A trade alliance with the Mohawks was reinstated and expanded. The Iroquois had further setbacks, losing half their population to an epidemic in 1633. The Mohawks alone were reduced from about 8,000 to 2,000 people, although their Huron enemies and the Algonquians also suffered heavy losses. But between 1643 and 1645 the Iroquois finally began to import hundreds of Dutch muskets, overcoming Dutch reluctance to supply them with guns.[6] With this growing firepower they were ready at least to avenge Champlain's lucky shot of 1609. The alliance structures and counterstructures of furs, canoes, the French and Algonquian link and the Iroquois and Dutch link were all in place. What accelerated both their cooperative interactions and their increasing conflicts were new forces from the French state itself. Cardinal Richelieu wanted to build an overseas empire.

THE EXPANSIONIST INITIATIVES OF CARDINAL RICHELIEU

Cardinal Richelieu became the first minister of the ineffectual King Louis XIII in 1624, serving as chief executive and in effect as acting monarch until his death in 1642. For the first half of his term France was distracted by great troubles at home and New France was almost lost entirely. But in his later years Richelieu strengthened both the home base and the colonial empire despite continuing weaknesses. He put state support behind colonization for the first time and set precedents for a much larger effort by the more powerful ministers of Louis XIV after 1661.

At home Richelieu had a king who was a minor, the Huguenot or Protestant parts of the country in periodic rebellion, and from 1635 a very expensive involvement in the fighting of the Thirty Years War. There was no overseas colonial empire worth mentioning in the early 1630s. In fact, in 1629 two English privateers, David and Lewis Kirke, actually captured Quebec itself for Charles I of England, and held it until 1632 as an English colony. Charles only gave it back under pressure from Richelieu while attempting to negotiate a royal bride for himself. Upon its return, Quebec had almost no French people. There were a few hundred in Acadia and some French settlers were moving into the West Indian island of St Kitts but that was all the French overseas empire there was. Richelieu now resolved to put whatever limited resources and influence he could spare from home affairs into a major effort to improve the colonial situation.

His main effort was in the West Indies. French settlement began there on St Kitts from 1623 and tobacco exports started in the 1630s but it took Richelieu until 1635 to reorganize the chartered company operating this project and to make sure, with some of his own money, that it was adequately funded. He insisted that at least 4,000 French Catholic settlers had to be sent out in the next twenty years. This number was exceeded and the French West Indian colonies began to grow, producing tobacco and cotton first and then turning to sugar grown with African slave labour after 1649. Carib Amerindians resisted French settlement on Guadalupe and Martinique until about 1660 but, like elsewhere in the West Indies, were eventually culturally as well as physically marginalized. These French sugar islands arguably produced even greater profits than those of the English, Barbados, Jamaica and the rest. By this time Richelieu was long deceased but he had helped to lay firm foundations. The only problem was that much of the French sugar trade was carried either in foreign ships or to foreign ports with less taxation on sugar and sugar products, or both.

Before 1642 Richelieu also turned to empire building in the Indian Ocean, where he helped to establish French control over the islands of Bourbon and Réunion (Mauritius). These islands produced no profits but did give France bases south of the Indian subcontinent for subsequent commercial and naval enterprises against principally English rivals. Richelieu's efforts to colonize Madagascar were not successful. But before all these endeavours, he had already started on Canada, his other main preoccupation.

In 1632 Richelieu reorganized the principal fur-trading company controlling the colony, improving its funding and increasing government control over it. The governor of the earlier fur companies, Samuel de Champlain, was now appointed as a royal official as well as a company director and sent to reclaim Quebec with three ships and a few dozen new settlers. About 100 became permanent residents. Richelieu also exerted his influence as head of the Roman Catholic establishment in his country. He sent and encouraged missionaries, especially the Jesuits, to civilize the Algonquians and the Hurons. By 1640 there were sixty-four French families at Quebec, mostly producing food to make the traders more self-sufficient. There were also the Jesuit fathers. The total permanent French population came to 211 men, 116 women and 29 Jesuits. From 1639 the Jesuits had four missions among the Hurons, winning converts steadily. In 1640 a church society set up a separate religious colonization project and settled the island of Montreal under Paul de Chomedy, Sieur de Maisonneuve in 1642. Montreal tightened French control over the main canoe route to the beaver country and the Hurons. By 1650 the combined populations of Quebec and Montreal were up to about 2,000 people.[7] This growth was still mainly the work of the private sector, aided by French religious societies, but the support of Richelieu up to 1642 was nevertheless most important in expanding the colony thus far.

This modest growth from 1632 generated growing Algonquian trade and Iroquois hostility. As the French trade expanded, the Iroquois increasingly raided the Algonquian and Huron fur flotillas coming to Montreal and Quebec. They raided and ambushed French settlers as well: New France was in an almost continuous state of Mohawk siege by 1642. There were never more than about 2,800 Iroquois warriors altogether, and they seldom fought as a unified force, but in the 1640s the French had even fewer men of fighting age and many of these were dispersed along the fur routes. From 1643, when the Dutch supplied the Mohawks, Senecas and others with more guns and ammunition than any of the French allies then possessed, the balance of power swung against New France. In 1649 the Mohawks and Senecas attacked the Hurons, some of whom were partly converted to Catholicism. By 1651 the Iroquois war parties, with their firepower advantage, dispersed the last of the numerically superior Hurons mostly westward and southward into the Ohio country. Here the fragments of the tribe interacted, conflicted and merged with the Algonquin and other people to become generally known as the Ottawas. Thus the Iroquois destroyed a main part of the French alliance structure and proceeded to divert great quantities of furs to the Dutch at Fort Orange. They also attacked Amerindians such as the Mahicans to the east and other nations to the west and south of their homeland to expand their domination. In 1653 they made peace with the French from a position of some superiority. The French fur companies suffered losses and rushed to arm the Algonquian allies.

By 1659 the Iroquois were no longer the best armed fighting force in the Great Lakes interior. They resumed their war against the French and their allies, attacking the fur flotillas going down to Montreal with great effect.[8] For the French it was again a desperate struggle for bare survival. In 1660, 17 Frenchmen led by Adam Dollard des Ormeaux, with 44 Amerindian allies, were attacked by 300 Iroquois at the Long Sault rapids. Below them Montreal was virtually undefended. They held their ground for five days. The Iroquois were reinforced by 500 more warriors and some of the French allies left. Dollard's men fought on for another three days from their hastily built defences but were overrun. Eleven were killed outright, five tortured to death. It was the biggest fight between the French and Iroquois so far. This last stand held off the Iroquois and Montreal was not attacked. But by 1661 it was obvious that the colony was not strong enough to survive such pressures for much longer. In a sense all that Richelieu's assistance to the private commercial colonizers had done was to stir up Iroquois attacks. While Virginia and New England were growing economically and demographically at amazing rates, New France was collapsing. In that year the Iroquois killed thirty-eight French settlers and took another sixty-one into captivity. These were the largest French casualties up to that time.[9]

THE NEW EMPIRE OF LOUIS XIV

The year 1661, however, was also the year in which the young Louis XIV took control of the French government away from his chief minister Mazarin, the successor of Richelieu. He was the first king to rule the nation directly since Henry IV and he had the capabilities, the advisers and the national resources to do an outstanding job. Louis rapidly transformed Europe's largest nation into its richest and most powerful one, though he did less well overseas. But whatever strength came to the French colonial empire by the end of his reign in 1715 was in very large part due to his and the state's direct interventions. The French empire was much more a state creation than the English or Spanish versions.

Louis centralized the power of the national government to its greatest degree. Perhaps he inherited most of the instruments and trends to do this and he certainly relied on the talents of a particularly brilliant set of state ministers, led by Jean-Baptiste Colbert, François Michel le Tellier, Marquis de Louvois, and Sébastien Le Prestre, Sieur de Vauban. Colbert consolidated state taxes and managed the economy; he also redesigned the empire and built a powerful navy. Together Louvois and Vauban gave Louis the most powerful land forces in Europe and arguably the world, outside Asia. Louis himself succeeded in unifying his people and getting their support as never before and in removing the political power of the French aristocracy by amusing them at Versailles or making the men officers in his expanding armies and navies. Jeremy Black has recently re-emphasised his argument that the most revolutionary military innovations of the modern era were those of Colbert, Louvois and Vauban:

> The principal changes in *c* 1660–*c* 1720 were both qualitative and quantitative. The replacement of the pike by the newly developed socket bayonet, the substitution of the matchlock musket by the flintlock, and the development of the pre-packed cartridge increased infantry firepower and manoeuvrability. It led also to a decline in the relative importance of cavalry in most European armies. The development of the socket bayonet, of the flintlock musket, and of improved warship design brought . . . a rise in the tactical importance of massed firepower in both land and naval warfare.[10]

France led in the application of these changes. Colbert's navy rose to be Europe's strongest, until it became second strongest in 1692. The French standing army grew to an unparalleled 400,000 men, organized into regiments in permanent garrison towns, all in uniforms, all marching in step to military music, and together setting the structures and styles of all European national armies until the French Revolution. The flintlock and bayonet combination remained the ultimate decider in land battles for a full 200 years, with no important modifications until the Crimean War. Thus Louis became Europe's leading warlord and drove the continent and its colonies into expanding military and naval competition. His generals won many battles but his main rivals, led by the English, countered his quantitative domination by building alliances against him and his qualitative advantages by imitation. In the colonies they had him outnumbered. He set the agenda but failed to conquer. The costs of war and empire were not balanced out by booty, territory or colonial revenues. The weight of tax on the French workers increased. The price of glory mounted as the quest for wealth went on.[11] Expenditures on New France were specifically designed to generate profits, even if indirectly. Colbert observed the growing prosperity of the English complex of West Indies plantation and mainland settlement colonies and determined to copy this success. He concluded that England made the money to sustain its naval superiority against his own fleets by running a triangular or multilateral trading system: the mainland colonies supplied ships, food and other necessities to the sugar islands, which supplied rum to buy African slaves, and all of which funnelled sugar into the European market and money into English pockets and armaments. He was wrong about the last part. England derived little government revenue from its colonies. Still, Colbert did have sugar islands of his own, growing on Martinique and Guadalupe at a faster rate than on the English islands. But they were supplied and serviced by foreigners. Why not make New France into a version of New England, producing ships and food for Martinique and Guadalupe? France would therefore have its own closed economic system, keeping all its wealth for itself. This was later called mercantilism, a form of aggressive state capitalism surrounded by a heavily armed tariff barrier.

Colbert's main effort to reconstruct New France on this basis began in 1663, with the appointment of Jean Talon as economic manager for the colony. The crown restructured the colonial government as a state rather than a trading enterprise and began to allocate funds for local improvements of various kinds. But the first job was to deal with the Iroquois threat, growing greater by each month. To boost the colonial population to the point that it could defend itself like the English colonists were doing would take time. Colbert could find very few voluntary settlers to face the freezing cold climate and the Amerindian terrors of New France. So, instead, he sent the first full professional regiment of European soldiers so far deployed in the colonies of any of the earlier European empires, the Carignan–Salières Regiment, in 1665. This was a veteran unit of twelve companies totalling 1,200 men under the Marquis de Tracy, with all their equipment and supplies. In fact, it was the best equipped regiment in the French army, the first to be fully armed with the advanced flintlock muskets, which were already the preferred weapon of the English colonists and the Amerindians.[12] Talon arrived with these soldiers and for the first time prime European troops in substantial numbers were applied against the Amerindians. For three years they were continuously supplied and reinforced over a range of 5,000 kilometres from bases in France, at costs greater than any colonizing government had yet undertaken. Even heavier military commitments came later but to begin with the French army went to the Iroquois because the colonists were too weak to do this job themselves.

This troop commitment worked adequately but not well. Within months of sighting their first soldiers from France on the peripheries of the colony, all the Five Nations Iroquois except the Mohawks asked for peace. They were impressed at such concentrated military personnel and so many disciplined muskets. The Mohawks, however, fought on. Early in 1666, 600 soldiers marched against the

Mohawk villages; 300 died of exposure. There was no combat, which was just as well because de Tracy and his officers proved to be unprepared in the special skills needed for North American tactics and travel. The survivors did manage to destroy some undefended Mohawk towns, however. Later in the year, advancing from an expanding network of French forts, 600 soldiers, 100 Amerindian allies and 600 colonists invaded Mohawk country again, with less trouble. They burned four Mohawk towns and destroyed Mohawk corn supplies. Again there were no battles and the following spring the Mohawks too made peace. A sustained demonstration of European military resources, if not skills, did the job.[13]

The regiment was now disbanded and the soldiers became colonists but in 1669 New France received a permanent professional garrison of six companies of *troupes de la marine*, 300 men recruited and trained in France specifically for Canadian service and officered by North American veterans. The government of France paid all the bills. These continued to go up as time went on.

With the Iroquois pacified, Colbert and Talon turned to colonial demographics and economy. Along with the demobilized professional soldiers, some 7,000 migrants were despatched from France, many of them recruited with difficulty from underemployed urban workers or minority groups. Marriageable women were also sent, along with shiploads of livestock, all at direct government expense. By 1680 the population of New France was boosted to about 10,000 Europeans. The population of the English colonies was already some twenty times greater, at no cost whatsoever to the English government, either for defence or assistance to migrants. Still, New France was now firmly colonized and a prosperous agriculture was developed in the valley of the St Lawrence River. The colony quickly became self-sufficient in food and the comforts of life. Because land was virtually free and there was limitless building material and fuel as well as wild game and fish, the Canadian *habitants*, or permanent settlers, rapidly attained a substantially higher level of material comfort than French peasants. State subsidies and development funds speeded this process quite considerably. Livestock expanded rapidly and horse ownership proliferated so much that government officials became alarmed, fearing that the peasantry was putting on too many of the airs and graces of their social betters. But by the 1680s the *habitants* were very firmly planted and beginning to multiply at a rate which, with no further migration from home, would increase their population by about five times in some seventy years.[14] The young men of this new society became militia soldiers and *couriers de bois*, that is, fur-traders, long-range inland canoe travellers, Amerindian contact people and negotiators, and French imperial agents. Colbert's costly demographic effort was a success – for the *habitants*.

The rest of his mercantilist plan was not a success, either for France or New France. The new settlers were supposed to produce food for export, barrels and ships. What surplus food they grew went instead to sustain the fur trade and French soldiers, and the shipbuilding programme failed despite the abundance of local Canadian timber. The French sugar islands grew richer and richer, with a population of 47,312 by 1687, of whom 27,000 were African slaves.[15] But they were supplied by foreigners, increasingly the English colonists, rather than by the *habitants*. Even the slaves were brought by

French explorer Father Jacques Marquette initiates the exploration of the Mississippi River from the Canadian end in 1673.

foreigners. Instead, the *habitants* preferred to put their spare energy and resources into the quicker profits of the fur trade, which for a time Colbert even tried to discourage. New France expanded inland, not out into the Atlantic trade routes. The government's expensive military apparatus was pulled inland as well. First the authorities had to build fortified outposts around the St Lawrence Valley itself to protect the settlers from Iroquois raids. Then posts were needed on the Great Lakes to protect the fur routes and the Algonquian and Ottawa allies. By 1682 René Robert Cavelier, Sieur de La Salle, with two French companions and some Amerindians, paddled all the way from the Great Lakes to the Gulf of Mexico via the Ohio and Mississippi rivers, claiming Louisiana for Louis XIV. His attempt to build a colony in 1684 failed, but only for the time being. From 1670 the English Hudson's Bay Company began to siphon furs away from the French Amerindians via Hudson Bay. The French traders therefore were also turning north to cut off this competition. After some delay small garrisons and forts supplied by the crown came with them. Instead of becoming a financial asset for Louis, New France just got more and more expensive.

This costly inward expansion was also generated by Amerindian demands which, in turn, resulted from earlier competition and conflict over fur sources. By the late 1660s the original Amerindian nations of the St Lawrence basin and Great Lakes were thoroughly broken up into refugee groups milling about in what became known as the Ohio and Illinois country of the continental centre, the region beyond the reach of the early European settlements. The big exceptions were tribal remnants such as the Abenaki in Acadia, who were relatively small in number, and the Five Nations Iroquois of upper New York. In fact, it was the trade-driven onslaughts of the Iroquois that broke up the Hurons and the eastern Algonquins and drove them westward as refugees. As such, they were cut off from secure food bases, became increasingly embroiled in fights with each other over basic survival issues, and therefore grew more and more dependent on the fur trade, both economically and politically. To survive in a new and hostile environment they needed the advantages of European tools and weapons more than ever. To get their furs to market past the Iroquois they looked increasingly to French military protection as well. As Richard White has so tellingly demonstrated, the mutual dependence of Algonquian Amerindians and French settlers on each other grew stronger as Amerindian communities became more disrupted by European influences and Iroquois reactions.[16]

Thus, after the Iroquois peace of 1666, the fur trade of the French and their allies expanded again, diverting furs from the Iroquois. When the French built their most western post at Fort Niagara in 1676, the Iroquois pushed more vigorously westward, at first without resorting to open war. Far from being subjugated by the French army in 1666, they were now even more dangerous because they were becoming the allies and military auxiliaries of the new English colony of New York, taken from the Dutch in 1664. The Dutch had been even weaker in numbers than the French settlers were before the Colbert migrations. The English colonists, beginning to coordinate their mutual interests at least at the elite and official government levels, were forming a solid block from the Carolinas to Acadia and filling up the coastal plain to the Appalachian Mountains. Already some were looking west to the Ohio Valley, the next logical expanse of 'free' land for English colonization. The Iroquois were a barrier between the English and New France. The French allies in the Ohio and Illinois country now faced pressure from prospective European settlement as well as armed Iroquois fur-trading competition. After 1664 the English authorities began to back Iroquois claims to the territories of the western Amerindians. In 1680 the wars were on again. Some 500 Iroquois attacked the Illinois people at Kaskaskia and dispersed them and the French traders. This was the start of a long series of intermittent raids and fights to 1701, when the Iroquois and the French finally agreed on a separate peace and the Iroquois agreed to stay neutral in any wars between the English and the French. In the course of these fur-trade wars the allies of the French in the west were further dispersed and fragmented and became even more dependent on French support, drawing the French further inland again. In 1689, 1,500 Iroquois destroyed 56 out of 77 houses at the town of Lachine just past Montreal, killing 24 *habitants* and 40 soldiers. This was the biggest blow against Colbert's strengthened colony, showing up its continued vulnerability even to hostile Amerindians and its continuing dependence on government protection from France.[17]

Louis XIV was now thoroughly entangled in the violent quarrels of his outnumbered settlers and their fragmented though more numerous Amerindian allies. These were on the brink of bigger conflicts with the multiplying thousands of English settlers, already looking for more lands to seize. North America was dragging France into expensive wars. But the wars that Louis was initiating in Europe itself were also dragging the North Americans into wars of no direct interest to themselves. The great war machine of Colbert, Louvois and Vauban, the strongest in Europe, was designed not only for national security but also for territorial gain. Louis wanted more lands, more workers, more taxes and more power. Colbert's colonies were supposed to raise funds predominantly for European territorial expansion, not to raise expenses and produce North American expansion. In any case, the French border wars began with the War of Devolution between 1667 and 1668 and with a concerted though unsuccessful effort, in alliance with England, to seize parts of the Netherlands in the Franco-Dutch war from 1672 to 1674. These aggressive efforts alarmed Louis' smaller neighbours to the point where England began to organize anti-French alliances, starting with the Dutch, in a pattern that was to become the strategy for maintaining a balance of power in Europe and the means to counter French power advantages. In the short run, Colbert also threatened England specifically by building a bigger and better navy.

In 1689 the first of the great Anglo-French wars, the War of the League of Augsburg, began in Germany, Ireland and the English Channel. French Admiral Tourville defeated the English navy at Beachy Head on 10 July 1690 and showed that France now had effective naval superiority in the Atlantic. But the English alliance balanced out French power. Two years later, eighty-eight English and Dutch battleships scattered forty-five French ships and regained the sea power advantage at La Hogue. In the European land fighting the two sides exchanged victories without major gains until a peace of stalemate was concluded in September 1697. In the West Indies French cruisers captured hundreds of enemy sugar transports and other trading ships, many of them belonging to the English colonists on the American mainland. These colonists were automatically at war with New France as well. The French colonists, more tightly directed from home, gathered their Amerindian allies and launched a series of nasty destructive raids against the frontiers of English settlements. The French and Abenaki from Acadia struck against northern New England, killing and capturing hundreds of colonists, and the governor, Count Frontenac, led the Algonquians, *habitants* and some regular soldiers against settlements in western New York, the Five Nations and western Pennsylvania, causing devastating damage. The French Iberville brothers led seaborne attacks against the English trading posts on Hudson Bay and cleared the English out completely. The counterattacks were weak, reflecting the still limited territorial ambitions and low hostility feelings of the English colonists. They were not nearly as interested in England's wars across the Atlantic as the colonists of New France had to be in the military fortunes of their mother country. And England sent neither frontline soldiers nor powerful naval units to help them against the French and Amerindians. But Acadia was weak: the Massachusetts colony collected a militia force and some armed transports under Sir William Phips and captured Port Royal in May 1690. A colonial force transported to Quebec later that year actually landed assault troops near this powerful Vauban-built fortress, but Phips' transports and warships were driven off by French artillery fire and the attack was a miserable failure. Still, for the first time, English and French colonists joined battle directly and the pattern of four more Anglo-French wars in both Europe and North America was set.

After all his efforts, the overseas empire of Louis XIV remained about as precarious as it had been when Colbert began his improvements. The main weakness was low person power. France, Europe's biggest country with 20 million people, sent proportionately the least number of settlers to her colonies. The Amerindian allies were thus a necessity to hold New France against its several enemies. Louis determined to use these numerically meagre and expensive but geographically spectacular North American assets as best he could, to counterbalance British sea power and to restrict the assumed growth of English wealth from the trade of English American colonists as much as possible. In 1701 his North American commanders received a new strategic directive from their king. He ordered them to colonize Louisiana, named after himself. The great French arc of interior trading posts, mostly generated by the fur trade, was now to be further fortified. It was to become an armed barrier against further English expansion, an extended battle station manned by professional soldiers, *habitants* and Amerindian allies.[18]

CHAPTER 8
The Rise of the Anglo-Americans

Overseas expansion slowed almost to a halt and in some places went into reverse for the whole of the eighteenth century. This was despite more activity and expenditure than ever. From England's Glorious Revolution of 1688 to the French Revolution of 1789, give or take a few years at either end for local variations, the main imperialist Europeans – and Americans as well – fought it out over the spoils of earlier European expansion. There were few territorial advances anywhere. Here and there the British and French made small gains at Portuguese, Spanish, Dutch or each other's expense. Up until the 1750s on the North American mainland the French and Canadians advanced west and south and the English colonists moved west but in neither case very far. Some Caribbean islands changed hands but sugar profits slowed. In 1760 the British and the Anglo-Americans drove France out of North America. In 1782 the Anglo-Americans and the French drove Britain up into Canada. Only in India from the 1750s did the British start a new advance, at mostly Indian expense, and only in Australia did they invade the lands of previously unaffected non-Europeans. Otherwise expansion ceased, to be resumed substantially only after 1815 when there were few unknown places and people left in any case. Thus the heroic age of European global integration was already over by the start of the eighteenth century. It took that century to work out which of the European imperialists would get to keep most of the benefits, whatever these really were.

This imperialist competition centred on North America north of Mexico and the players were the two leading European powers, France and Britain, and the no longer European Anglo-Americans. There were some Spanish and Dutch imperialists still struggling on the fringes and there were also remnants of the Amerindian people battling for survival, though now mainly as auxiliaries and clients of the European colonizers or colonists. The Iroquois kept up their struggle for independence longest. In terms of resources and effort, the main events were in what became the United States of America. The winners were the largely English-speaking Anglo-American ex-colonists. By driving out Britain they ended three centuries of entirely European control over overseas expansion. They did not end European expansion itself but they ended a European monopoly and signalled the beginning of the end for an exclusively European global domination.

It is still a popular belief that this monopoly brought vast booty and much power to Europeans while it lasted, and even after that. It is still widely seen as a cause of the Industrial Revolution, even by many academic experts. Thus, while millions of Asians, Africans and Amerindians were impoverished and driven to premature death, Europe grew stronger. But did Europe not also spend more and more of its total wealth on intereuropean competition and war over these overseas possessions? And what of the arguments of recent analysts who strenuously deny that Europeans gained more than a few percentage points – in Britain's case 4 per cent by 1815 – of their entire national incomes from overseas trade and colonies?[1] Were colonial empires really profitable necessities or the conspicuous consumption of the wealthiest, strongest west Europeans who generated so much energy at home that they had surpluses to spare overseas? There are all sorts of interpretive uncertainties here. Some of them change according to our latest cultural and political trends. Whatever the ultimate answers, all these imperialist efforts, whether necessary or frivolous, predatory or peripheral, still profoundly altered the global habitat.

ANGLO-FRENCH WARS

Overseas expansion after the 1680s and '90s slowed in part because all the attractive and easy conquests had mostly been used up and also because the strongest European powers became embroiled in increasingly hostile competition among themselves, much of it at home to begin with. There were other reasons but it was the Anglo-French wars that dominated European elite preoccupations. The War of the League of Augsburg, with its colonial consequences, was considered in the previous chapter as a culmination especially of French expansion in North America and also as the initiation of the aggressive border wars of Louis XIV. When it ended with the Treaty of Ryswick in 1697, after ten large battles at home and after the first clashes between colonists and Amerindian allies, neither Louis nor the opposition had any gains to show for the effort, but France was probably even stronger in military terms and England now had a small but important lead in naval power. In the main colonies the French had temporarily pacified the Iroquois by 1701, and were on their way to more expansion in Louisiana, but while they had terrified and enraged New England and New York settlements, they had not slowed Anglo-American population or economic growth. It was a stalemate but also a preview.

The next aggressions of Louis produced the War of the Spanish Succession between 1701 and 1714, with twenty-two great battles in Europe. Louis started the conflict by putting his grandson Philip of Anjou up as claimant to the Spanish throne, thus proposing to unite under the one Bourbon family Europe's greatest land power with what was still its largest American empire. For its day this was the equivalent of taking over the best part of the civilized world. England led the alliance to counter this destabilizing imbalance, bringing together the Netherlands, Austria, Prussia and Portugal, with Savoy as temporary member. France had Spain and Bavaria. In four big battles, John Churchill, Duke of Marlborough, won great victories against Louis. At Blenheim in 1704, Ramillies in 1706 and Oudenarde in 1708 he decisively halted major French drives. At

Malplaquet in 1709 he just barely beat the French in what was the world's largest battle to that time and for a century to come. Churchill led 100,000 allies against 90,000 French under Marshall Claude de Villars, losing 24,000 men and inflicting 12,000 casualties. The English were finally making a big impact in the land fighting. The French army, however, fought on. In the end, Louis had to pull back some of his frontier boundaries but the grandson became the recognized king of Spain.

At sea the English (or the British, from the Union with Scotland in 1707) maintained their small lead but had no great victories, and in America there was continuing stalemate. Enough French troops to hold all areas against the unassisted Anglo-Americans reduced the hostilities to a series of raids and counter-raids. The Abenakis and the Algonquians and Canadians struck at the New England and New York frontiers again, and this time there was combat with Spanish troops in Florida as well. But the relative strength of the sides remained much as before, as did their mutual hostility. Louis died in 1715 but his imperial vision was maintained by his successor Louis XV, as was Europe's most powerful army and the firm alliance of Spain.

The big gains were made by the British – indirectly. From Spain they gained the Asiento in 1714, a contract permitting them to trade a limited number of slaves and some manufactured goods to the Spanish colonies each year. From this small legal base after the war British traders broke further and further into both the Spanish-American and Portuguese-American colonial commerce, making more money than in any other area of economic growth until about the 1740s at least. According to D.W. Jones, national wealth and economic growth were stimulated more profoundly by these war gains in other people's trading zones than in any other enterprises.[2] Both Jones and Barbara Solow therefore argue that commerce built largely around African slavery was probably the most powerful element setting the preconditions for the Industrial Revolution. In any case, in the short run the Asiento helped British wealth creation considerably and so boosted British power.

The other advance growing out of the War of the Spanish Succession was the organization of the Bank of England and the 'funding' of the British national debt. As John Brewer has recently demonstrated, these measures marked the institutional foundations of the 'fiscal-military state' in Britain and enabled the British crown and parliament to raise funds for war together by borrowing on a larger and more efficient scale than any other world government.[3] Since the rise of the Portuguese and Spanish empires and the various 'military revolutions', starting at the end of the fifteenth century with the adoption of firepower weaponry, the biggest expenses of all the main European governments had been military and naval or national security costs. By the time Louis XIV took the throne, permanently maintained professional armies, numbering in his case 400,000 men, and permanent navies with an expensive new line of battleships and sailors, had pushed the security costs of governments up over the 60 per cent per annum mark. States provided few other public services and virtually nothing for social welfare, education or health. They collected tax, enforced the law and fought bigger and bigger wars. Since Philip II's time war costs were constantly outrunning tax incomes, even for Spain with its silver mines in America. Louis XIV and his fellow monarchs on the European mainland relied mostly on direct taxes levied on peasants and workers and these were never enough, forcing governments to borrow from the rising merchant banker communities in places like the Netherlands. There was therefore a direct link between the size and power of armies and the size of tax revenues and quality of royal credit ratings. In this revenue-raising competition, the British government, under its Hanoverian kings from 1714, did better than others. The Bank of England itself was founded in 1694 as a private corporation but it soon became a government agency providing the state with its essential war funding and underwriting state borrowings from citizens and overseas. In 1717 the British parliament added a Sinking Fund, whereby the national debt was consolidated into one amount automatically serviced by regular government interest and principal payments designed to ultimately pay the whole thing off. Up to the French Revolution and beyond, however, the national debt kept growing instead. For a century and more each of the big wars, mostly with France, just added to the fund which became rising not sinking. For example, in 1701, the unfunded government debt stood at just under £20 million. In 1748 the funded debt was just under £80 million, in 1760 it was around £140 million and in 1783 it stood at about £250 million.[4] In this period military and naval expenditure came to 74 per cent of total government expenditure in 1689–97, 64 per cent in 1739–48, 71 per cent in 1756–63 and 61 per cent in 1775–83. In 1780 this 60 per cent plus translated into 12.5 per cent of total national income, or about double that of the largest military budgets today.[5] The reason all this disastrous spending was more bearable in Britain than elsewhere, however, was that British tax revenues also rose at about the same rate as expenditures and borrowings. Britain relied more heavily on taxes from trade and commerce, indirect taxes, and her overseas trade expanded at a faster rate than the agricultural output of Britain itself or its continental rivals. The Asiento and its exploitation, the growth of the slave trade, and the growth of the American markets for British manufactures – including the Spanish and Portuguese and even part of the French colonial markets – were all critical elements here. As is the case today, the money market of Europe put its loans where it believed income was growing at a slightly faster rate than indebtedness. Whether this was actually correct is not entirely clear, though Brewer and other experts believe that it was because of this that Britain had a superior credit rating to that of France, Spain and lesser European powers. In the words of P.K. O'Brien and P.A. Hunt, who also argue that the Hanoverians were immensely better funded than any previous English monarchs or governments, 'It was indirect taxes which effectively underwrote the capacity of Hanoverian governments to service an irredeemable national debt and to borrow the huge amounts of money required to wage eight wars between 1689 and 1815'.[6] This was war by fiscal attrition. The costs were passed on to future generations. The British did not even win all the time but at least they won more often than their next strongest rival and, by 1815, stood ready to carve out the grandest European empire of them all.

In the meantime, in the 1720s and '30s, there were gradual continuations of these sorts of European and colonial power trends leading to yet another big war from 1739 to 1748. This began as a fight between Britain and Spain over Asiento abuse. Captain Robert Jenkins persuaded a parliamentary committee to declare war by waving his own pickled ear at them, which Spanish customs authorities had chopped off back in 1731. The navy sailed to capture Caribbean islands and ports but had little success. On the Georgia frontier Anglo-Americans under James Edward Oglethorpe, founder of that colony in 1733, prepared to defend themselves against Spanish attacks from Florida. There was, however, no major fighting until 1740 when Frederick II of Prussia invaded Silesia and started the much bigger War of the Austrian Succession (King George's War to the Anglo-Americans) which lasted until 1748. For a time Frederick joined France and Spain against Britain, Austria and a group of smaller countries. He himself won. Britain began to commit growing numbers of soldiers to the European front, in large part because King George II was also king of the German state of Hesse-Darmstadt, but additionally because, both here and in the colonies, and despite considerable combat, there was again stalemate.

There were, however, three important developments for the future, one in Europe and two in North America. These, along with the rise of the British 'fiscal military state', helped set the power balances for the next big fight. The most important of them was the military rise of Frederick II. From his rather mean-spirited but highly efficient father Frederick inherited the hardest hitting and fastest marching medium-size land army on the continent and in the world. His country was neither populous, well resourced, nor geographically united, and the best he could do was to put together a maximum field army of 65,000 or so troops, usually commanding only half of this number in battle, but he was his own field commander, the training and discipline of his men were almost always superior to rival armies, he fought his campaigns from a central position and so tended to outmanoeuvre opponents, and he concentrated his forces on the battlefield so as to achieve local numerical superiority against parts of the usually bigger enemy armies. He was the only eighteenth-century commander who could regularly, though not always, defeat numerically stronger foes and win against the demographic odds. In fact, he is arguably the most successful general in all of modern history in this respect.[7] The Prussian army was substantially bigger than the British army. Up to 1756 it allied with France against Britain but if it could be recruited into the British camp, it was formidable enough to tie down much of the preponderant French land force on the continent. In the next war Prime Minister William Pitt successfully recruited Frederick II and his excellent army into the British camp.

In North America there was intense fighting along the usual northern and western frontiers as well as in the Georgia area. Anglo-Americans from the Carolinas and their Amerindian allies also fought French and Amerindians from Louisiana, where the French empire now had its headquarters at New Orleans near the mouth of the Mississippi river. The British colonists carried more and more of their own land-fighting duties because, aside from some British navy units, the home government made it plain that there would be no regular soldiers to help them against French or Spanish professionals. For the first time Anglo-Americans volunteered to join overseas expeditions in their region as militia soldiers. Hundreds went with the British navy to attack Cartagena, which turned out to be a dismal failure. The survivors concluded that the British were militarily incompetent. Nevertheless some 3,000 volunteers from New England and beyond joined what was really the first colonial land army in an attack on the major French fortress of Louisbourg in 1745. Louisbourg was on Cape Breton Island, built entirely from French materials according to the latest fortification technology, and constructed to protect the Gulf of St Lawrence and the water entry to New France. It was considered just about impregnable, especially if French fleet units were also stationed under its guns. Neither French nor British experts considered that it was in any danger from the Anglo-American colonists, who had neither professional armies nor navies. But the New Englanders already hated Louisbourg as a nest of French and Spanish pirates, as the main North American base of armed commerce raiders preying on the Anglo-American Atlantic merchant fleet. In March 1745 William Pepperrell of Massachusetts collected a force of 2,800 Massachusetts and 200 New Hampshire and Connecticut volunteers and raised a squadron of colonial warships for a direct attack on the French fortress. The British navy agreed to send a squadron of warships under Commodore Warren, four ships of the line. Warren set up a naval blockade and Pepperrell's militia successfully landed near the fortress and surrounded it with artillery in April. The defenders had 600 regular soldiers and 900 militia but depended on resupply by sea, now blocked by Warren. By July they were out of ammunition, while the Anglo-Americans kept blazing away and Warren kept picking off French relief ships. Louisbourg surrendered. It was an incredible result to the European professionals. The Anglo-Americans were ecstatic.[8] They had shown a military independence matching their economic independence and were full of self-confidence. Thus their frustration and anger was all the greater in 1748 when the home government gave Louisbourg right back to the French. In India the French had captured Madras from the British East India Company. To get Madras back, British leaders returned Louisbourg. The Anglo-Americans protested loudly but in vain. At least they had demonstrated their military potential to everybody as a consolation. That potential would grow, as would their determination to deal with their own border threats from now on.

In western New York the Anglo-Americans made another power advance by winning Iroquois war support. In 1737 an Irish migrant named William Johnson had settled next to the Mohawks on an extensive land grant which he could only develop with Iroquois cooperation. This he gained brilliantly, in part by intermarriage, becoming in effect a recognized Iroquois chief. Between 1701 and 1740 these Amerindians, now called the Six Nations, had maintained a neutral position between their old French enemies and previous English allies. Frontenac's French regulars had intimidated them into passivity. Now Johnson persuaded most of the eastern Iroquois, and especially his Mohawk relations, that the English were strong enough to take on the garrisons of New France and eventually win. The Mohawks went on the warpath against the

French and western New York turned into a minor but quite vicious war zone of raids and counter-raids. In 1746 New York made Johnson its commissioner of Amerindian affairs as well as a colonel. Subsequently he was to lead his Iroquois again in the next war and his influence over them continued sufficiently after his death in 1774 to bring many of them over to the American side in the Revolution. The British knighted him and made him a baronet. In any case, he revitalized the Iroquois threat to New France by 1748 and thus strengthened the most critical western frontier of the Anglo-American colonies.

GROWTH OF THE ANGLO-AMERICAN COLONIES

With these military initiatives the Anglo-Americans were demonstrating their growing strength and community maturity. By 1750 there were already thirteen colonies, from Maine in the north to Georgia in the south, with hostile French frontiers at both ends and just to the west of Virginia, Pennsylvania and New York. The population was now up over the million mark and doubling about every twenty years. In 1750 there were 964,000 Europeans and 242,000 Africans in the colonies, for a total of 1,206,000. By 1770 these figures rose to 1,816,000, 467,000 and 2,283,000 respectively. By contrast, the British West Indies were already eclipsed by 1750, with only 35,000 white settlers and 295,000 Africans.[9] The proportional difference between the mainland colonies of Britain and France remained about the same as in the 1660s, about 20 to 1 in the British favour. In 1739 New France had 43,382 permanent settlers. Through natural increase these grew to over 70,000 by the time of the British conquest in 1760. Cape Breton Island, around Louisbourg, had another 5,845 in 1752 and French Louisiana had about 20,000 Europeans and an equal number of Africans by the 1760s.[10] The French *habitants* and other settlers produced food surpluses, especially wheat, and led prosperous and comfortable lives but they exported little and had a small commercial participation in Atlantic and European trade generally. Even the fur trade was moving too far north by now. For France, their main role was denying Britain control of North America. By contrast, the Anglo-Americans were now growing economically and commercially at an entirely unprecedented rate. In the words of J.J. McCosker and R.R. Menard:

> . . . though estimates of the growth rate are on the most tenuous of grounds, little more than guesses, it is clear that the colonial economy must have expanded at a faster rate than the population. Both productivity and the standard of living in the colonies got better during the colonial era, which argues quite forcefully for real per capita growth in the economy.[11]

The Anglo-American standard of living, widely spread over a dominant middle-type class, was an all-time historical record.[12] Of the dominant British merchant marine, probably one-third of the ships were Anglo-American owned and operated. Thus the colonists now had the third largest merchant fleet in the world, after Britain and the Dutch.

'Free' or very cheap land was not the only reason for this great economic success but it was important and the new American landholding and maritime trading elite regarded it as the prime cause. By the 1750s this elite was deeply involved in land speculation, in buying up western land titles for sale to new waves of migrants and the multiplying children of old settlers. The main target for the land speculators was the Ohio Valley across the Appalachian Mountains. From 1748 the Virginia and Pennsylvania elites organized a series of land companies, some backed by British money, and began to send traders and explorers west to make claims and scout out the opportunities. The governor of Virginia, Robert Dinwiddie, backing the Ohio Company, was the most energetic of these expansionists. In Canada and Paris the French were determined to move faster than the Anglo-Americans and from 1749 sent royal troops to the area where the Ohio River forks, which was the transportation key to the whole Ohio country, in order to announce officially their prior claim, to get the Amerindians on side, and to expel any Virginian or Pennsylvanian intruders. By 1753 a race between the French and the Virginians for the domination of the forks of the Ohio accelerated toward open combat. Dinwiddie sent George Washington, the young owner of the Mount Vernon estate, to tell French troops to get out. They were polite but insisted he had to go instead. In 1754 they sent reinforcements and constructed Fort Duquesne near the present-day site of Pittsburgh, Pennsylvania. Washington took a small force of thirty-three Virginians and some Amerindian allies to try to block this effort. He ambushed thirty-five regular French soldiers, killing a third of them, before realizing that the total Virginian force that he had, some 400 men, was heavily outnumbered by 500 French professionals and 400 Amerindians at the forks of the Ohio. The French now launched a pursuit of Washington's force, caught it in a makeshift fortification called Fort Necessity, killed about 100 Virginians, and then took the surrender of the rest. Washington's battered command was allowed to retreat back to Virginia and the French were now planted in force in the disputed land.[13] In effect, Washington had ordered the first shots in a new war between France and Virginia, now unofficially in progress. The trouble for the Anglo-Americans was that even with all their rapid expansion and growing strength they were still not a match for the full power of imperial France.

DRIVING OUT THE FRENCH

To clear the Ohio Valley for a profitable settlement to relieve population pressure, the Virginians and their fellow colonists north and south discovered that they had to defeat French power in North America as a whole. It would be necessary not just to capture Fort Duquesne but also to recapture a reinforced and strengthened Louisbourg, and then Quebec itself. In the process, it would be necessary to block the power of the world's second largest navy as well. Only the British government could provide the kind of military machine needed to conquer Canada and its outposts. William Pitt, the British Prime Minister, was persuaded by the Virginia elite and its London supporters to provide that necessary war machine, to wipe out the French empire in America entirely so that Britain's Atlantic colonies

The fall of Major General Edward Braddock at the hands of the French and Amerindians, 1775.

could expand their trade even more profitably for the mother country. He still believed that colonies brought wealth and power. This decision was a major turning point in British colonial policy. For the first time the home government would send full naval fleets and entire professional armies to fight the French, not in Europe as usual, but in North America. British regulars would now fight for the colonists.

They began badly. Pitt ordered two British regiments to attack the French in America, the Irish 44th and 48th Foot under Major General Edward Braddock, later to be reinforced by several regiments raised from the Anglo-Americans, and two naval squadrons under Admiral Edward Boscawen with nineteen ships of the line and two frigates. Both commands arrived early in 1755. Boscawen was to intercept French reinforcements. He missed the bulk of the French fleet because of fog and powerful French forces got through to Quebec. Braddock did worse still. There are many exciting versions of his defeat. William Eccles provides one of the most concise assessments:

> Braddock, at the head of 2,200 men, British regulars and colonial troops, got his army over the mountains and within a few miles of Fort Duquesne – by itself no mean feat. In an almost forlorn hope Captain Daniel de Beaujeu led 108 *troupes de la marine*, 146 Canadian militia, and 600 Indians to oppose him. The ensuing clash was a disaster for the British. The Canadian and Indian forces took cover on the forested flank of the enemy, encumbered by siege artillery and a vast wagon train. The measured British volleys had little effect against the concealed foe. The Canadians and Indians advanced close. Noting that the British ranks reloaded to ordered drumbeats, they picked off the officers and drummers. Confusion, then panic, spread through the British ranks. The battle became a slaughter. The troops broke and fled. More than two-thirds of the British force were killed or captured, along with the cannon and a vast store of supplies. This, at a cost to the French and their allies of twenty-three killed and twenty wounded.[14]

The French Amerindians and the Canadians were formidable foes – so were the French regulars from Europe. Pitt had to send more warships and more regiments because the Anglo-American militia troops and armed transports were clearly inadequate by themselves, despite unprecedented efforts on their parts. His measures did not at first prosper; 1756 and 1757 were bad years for British arms in North America as every one of their offensives was repelled and their naval blockades repeatedly failed. But from 1756 Pitt and the British leadership were much encouraged to persist when they recruited Frederick II and the Prussians, plus the Portuguese, onto their side against a French-led coalition including Austria, Spain and Russia. Frederick made the big difference. His reputation for winning against the odds by sheer qualitative superiority of both troops and command was no doubt exaggerated then and now. Of the seven main battles he fought against his main opponent Austria and its allies – to try to keep Silesia which he had invaded back in 1740 – he was victorious in five. Of the five, he actually outnumbered the opposition army in three battles.[15] Nevertheless,

Killing of an Indian scout in the Ohio Valley; an episode of irregular woodland warfare between American forces with Amerindian allies and French forces with Amerindian allies during the Seven Years War.

American and Amerindian raiders under Robert Rogers set out to attack the French during the Seven Years War.

Frederick kept vastly superior enemy forces occupied longer than any previous commander simply by continuing to manoeuvre with a bit more skill and speed with his limited forces. He pinned down most of the French ground troops in Europe and he freed Britain's relatively small numbers of redcoats for North American service entirely. He himself made few gains. He got to keep Silesia and he kept Brandenburg–Prussia intact but by 1762 he was actually close to disaster. He was only saved from being crushed by powerful allied armies converging from all sides by the sudden death of his archenemy the Empress Elizabeth of Russia. Her successor, Czar Peter, was an admirer of Frederick and he took the Russian armies out of the attack. While Frederick struggled heroically for survival, however, the British army triumphed in America.

In July 1758 the redcoats attacking Canada had one more unpleasant defeat at the hands of the reinforced French professionals under General Louis Joseph Marquis de Montcalm. With only 3,000 men Montcalm threw back a major British invasion force of 12,000 troops under James Abercromby at Ticonderoga. The turning point came in July. Generals Jeffrey Amherst and James Wolfe took 9,000 British regulars and 500 colonial militia in 40 ships and captured

Major General James Wolfe (1727–1759), conqueror of Louisbourg in 1758, and Quebec in 1759.

The death of Major General Wolfe on the plains of Abraham, 1759.

Louisbourg a second time. This war was now predominantly between professional European forces, paid for directly by home governments. The colonials and their respective Amerindian allies on both sides continued their habitual raiding activities against each other but only the European forces could now decide the final outcome in sieges and battles of a scale equivalent to, though smaller than, that of the war in Europe itself. To this degree the fate of the Anglo-Americans and their various local ambitions still rested in the hands of European governments, war machines and taxpayers.

At home in 1759 Frederick II was in full fighting mode and the British navy finally blocked all transatlantic supplies to Canada. In June Admiral Saunders sailed an unopposed battle fleet to Quebec itself, guided into the unfamiliar waters by a young naval officer named James Cook, of later Pacific exploration fame. With Saunders went General Wolfe with 9,000 men. Montcalm actually had more troops, though only 4,500 locally, including an officer named Louis Antoine de Bougainville, also of later Pacific exploration fame. The British and French infantry met in formal battle order, as in Europe. British volleys were better controlled. Both generals died in battle but Quebec fell. Early next year there was yet another battle at Quebec between French and British infantry. This time the French actually won but they were totally cut off and it was their last gesture. From 1760 the entire French empire on mainland North America, except for some small islands and New Orleans, went to the British. It was the most spectacular imperial triumph yet. The Treaty of Paris in 1763 confirmed all the gains.

DRIVING OUT THE BRITISH

For the British elite in parliament it was now time to collect just material rewards for this first unprecedented and vastly expensive commitment of government forces to North America. The Americans had only paid for their own militia but were now set to grab big territories in the Ohio Valley and beyond and take over the wealth and trade of the French Canadians as well. To add insult to injury, by 1763 they were already pressing the now defenceless Amerindians of the west so hard that a general uprising called Pontiac's Rebellion occurred, which had to be put down with British troops. The British ruling elite resolved to curb this Anglo-American expansionism and also to make the colonists pay some taxes for government services rendered. The results were a series of confrontations which escalated into the causes for the American Revolution.

These causes are as well covered by excellent scholarly literature as any topic in the English language and better than most. The details do not require repetition here, except in passing. In 1763 parliament imposed a Proclamation Line banning all further Anglo-American settlement beyond the Appalachians until such time as the British government was ready to sell western land to them. The official reason was the need to pacify the Amerindians. Next, in 1765, came a Quartering Act, which made colonists pay for garrison costs of redcoats, and the Stamp Act, the first important direct tax levied in British North America. The Anglo-Americans now began to become just plain Americans. Some lobbied and complained but others began to resist and plan

The Battle of Lexington, 19 April 1775, the first major clash of arms in the American Revolution.

rebellion. The British actually backed off and repealed the Stamp Act in 1766 but at the same time passed a Declaratory Act which said they could tax Americans whenever they chose to later on. In 1767 they imposed new duties under the Townshend Acts, driving the Americans to boycott British imports. The disputes again moved towards revolt and the British backed off again. But in 1770 violence flared between Americans and redcoats in Boston, which was called the Boston Massacre, and further violence occurred in North Carolina in 1771. In 1773 Parliament passed a Tea Act which wiped out all the American tea-traders by giving a monopoly of importation to the East India Company. Tea had become the most popular drink in the colonies but now it ceased to be drunk. At Boston and then elsewhere the Americans seized East India Company tea and held 'tea parties' by dumping it into the harbour. In 1774 Parliament passed the Quebec Act which largely excluded Americans from Canada and restored French laws and customs to the *habitants*, under British governors. It looked to the Americans that now the British were replicating and replacing the old French imperial barrier on their inland progress. Parliament, meanwhile, resolved to punish Americans who dared run around destroying valuable British tea. The Americans began to organize a joint government called a Congress.

Perhaps two-thirds of the colonists wanted to stay loyal to Britain. Most of these were country folk living inland. The wealthy urban east-coast elite wanted independence. The British government still thought it had sufficient popular support to crush the rebels. On 19 April 1775 at Lexington and

The Battle of Bunker Hill, 1775. British forces abandon Boston, and the American Revolution gains momentum.

Concord, 21 miles from Boston, 700 redcoats fought it out with about 4,000 American militia. The British had 73 killed, 174 wounded and 26 missing, the Americans lost 93 casualties in total. The war of the American Revolution was now on. Congress was organized and it, in turn, organized an American army and navy. The next year it formally issued the Declaration of Independence on 4 July. By then battles were in progress around New York and were building up elsewhere.

The war for independence that now ensued is as well reported in scholarly writing as are the causes, and it is here only necessary to note some of the general trends and forces shaping the outcome. The main point is that the rebels had neither the numbers, skills nor funds to guarantee success against an aroused if painfully expensive British war machine which was supported locally by between a third and a quarter of the colonists who chose to remain loyal, over 100,000 of whom later styled themselves United Empire Loyalists and left the country. So, while the British found it difficult to pacify the urban coastal areas, the Americans found it impossible to oust the British or to gain decisive victories. They won only two important battles against the redcoats, at Saratoga in New York in 1777 and at King's Mountain in North Carolina in 1780. At Saratoga General John Burgoyne and 6,000 regulars were decisively beaten by American militia and the rifles of the sharpshooting frontiersmen led by Dan Morgan. The victory impressed European observers and probably helped to convince the French Comte de Vergennes that his country should now help the Americans and get some revenge for the humiliation of the previous war. King's Mountain was a fight mostly between Carolina Loyalists and Patriots, of some moral significance but not much more. The war was at best drifting toward stalemate. What tipped the balance in the Americans' favour was undoubtedly the intervention of the French.

Vergennes had expected an American revolt and had planned for it. In 1778 he officially joined the Americans in a Franco-American alliance. In 1779 Spain came in on the American side as well, and later the Netherlands joined and Russia declared its sympathy. Thus, as Britain's armies and navies became bogged down in North America, her European rivals took the opportunity to cut her down to size. It was obvious she was getting too rich and powerful. France needed time to mount an attack but by 1781 a French army under Counts Rochambeau and Lafayette of 5,000 regulars and a full battle fleet under Admiral de Grasse were operational in the North American theatre. In September and October a Franco-American army of 9,000 men under Washington and Lafayette, with the French vastly outnumbering the Americans, besieged Britain's main field army at Yorktown, Virginia. The British had a force of 8,000 men under General Lord Cornwallis, dependent on supplies from the navy operating in Chesapeake Bay. For once de Grasse outfought the British fleet, cutting off those supplies. Cornwallis surrendered on 19 October and America was independent. He was beaten by the French army and the French navy, with a bit of American help. United Empire Loyalists numbering 7,000 marched to Upper Canada to join the French *habitants* in a new rump North American colony called British North America. Britain had to fight the Americans again between 1812 and 1814 over

The surrender of Lord Cornwallis at Yorktown, 1781.

this remnant, which was the core of a later Canadian nation. But from 1782, as confirmed in treaties the next year, the United States of America joined the European nations as the first and the strongest of the overseas countries created by the three formative centuries of forceable global integration since 1492.

From here the Americans went on to conquer their own western territorial empire. They failed to capture Canada in 1812–14 but they took Florida and New Orleans from Spain, the far west from Mexico, and vast territories in between from the Amerindians. By the turn of the next century they were all the way across the Pacific to the Philippines.

The French were not so fortunate. The American war of 1778–82 was their last imperialist success. The year after Yorktown Admiral Rodney smashed de Grasse's previously victorious fleet in the Caribbean at the battle of the Saints, and another French fleet was repelled from British possessions in India. The French monarchy itself just wound up deeper in debt. Revolution came in 1789, followed by Napoleon and a bid for European dictatorship. Again Britain led the coalitions that broke French power and France sank to a distinctly second-rate status, with only a fragmentary overseas colonial empire.

Britain, however, went on to a second and more glorious empire, the largest and richest of them all. In addition to Canada in 1788, Britain invaded and occupied the last separate continent on the planet and moved into key areas in the Pacific, Asia and Africa. But the core of the new empire was India and its millions of tax-paying agricultural peasants. While Pitt was preparing the armies and fleets needed to conquer the French empire in North America, an officer of the British East India Company, Robert Clive, joined battle with the army of the ruler of Bengal at a place called Plassy in April 1757. Despite odds of 17 to 1 against, with only a few hundred British troops, and against a Bengal army armed, advised and supported by the French, Clive won a resounding victory. It was the first in a series of triumphs that gave the company control of Bengal and a share of its taxes by the 1780s. The British government joined in and all of India was gradually conquered. Throughout the nineteenth century Britain ruled most of the world's colonies and all of the world's oceans. Yet these nineteenth-century gains were mostly the workings out of initiatives already concluded by the start of the eighteenth century. They were achieved inland inside North America, Asia and Africa, and they expanded by land rather than water. The seaborne part of European expansion was over by 1788, when the groups that seized control of oceanic communications also conquered the best overseas coasts and river valleys.

What were the gains to humanity of this European process of planetary integration? The incomplete statistics do not permit an accurate or reliable balance sheet. Was the world as a whole indeed richer because of the imperialist aggressions of a few specially energetic western Europeans between 1492 and about 1700? These expansionists made a series of short-term decisions in the quest for quick riches and almost always wound up with unexpected results. Many of these were unpleasant in the extreme. Millions of Amerindians and Africans suffered awfully and died early: thousands of European settlers and investors lost heavily. As usual, only a small minority gained wealth, power and glory. Nevertheless, whatever the costs and benefits, at least the linking together of just about all the people and places on the planet itself was by 1788 irreversible.

CHAPTER 9
Conclusion

SORTING OUT CAUSES

There is continuing disagreement about the events of colonial conquests as printed details lengthen while readership attention spans shorten. But there is even more disagreement about causes and consequences. Early European overseas imperialism did start off the process of 'continental connecting' which we rather inharmoniously call globalization. This planetary integration process is now absorbing public minds everywhere as something self-evidently momentous. Its progress is of necessity obscure because even the wisest humans seldom predict the future precisely. But what about the causes, in all their documented details and after generations of intellectually formidable analysis? Given the importance of the consequences and the acceptance of the general view that globalization did indeed begin – perhaps after an important medieval lead-up of expanding knowledge and interactivity – with Columbus and the traders and colonizers of the sixteenth century, a rise in the interest of clarifying the causes could be expected. But if the readership is interested, the interest is in shorter answers only. Fields of knowledge multiply, community interests diversify and interest in detailed historical explanations is declining in terms of book sales. Internally, historians battle against the temptations of political propagandizing on the one hand and postmodernist denials of the possibility of objective historical truthfulness on the other. In academe agreements about reality itself are debatable. So what can be said to clarify the start of globalization? Is there a middle ground between escalating academic complexity at the writing end and demand for evermore simplified answers at the reading end? What follows is an attempt to define one such middle ground. Academic historians can no longer communicate the complexities of their findings even to colleagues in related fields. They must simplify their findings to communicate at all, let alone to the all-powerful 'general reader'. But they must also resist the temptations of excessive popularization, when historical understanding is translated into ideological and political sloganeering. The assumption is that the clarification of causes is indeed a pursuit of some world community interest.

The popular interpretation of imperialistic colonial conquerors has gone from one extreme to another in not much over a generation, from the prevailing view that the European conquerors were mentally and culturally superior to the current conviction that they were more aggressively nasty than any other people on the planet. In the 1950s most English language historians still believed the colonizers were smarter than the rest. Now most say they believe these invaders were just nastier and most of the popular writing on causes is focused on the 'whose-fault-was-it' question, with the roles of perpetrators and victims predetermined. This result prevails despite – or perhaps because of – continuously high-quality historiographic analysis work by leading scholars since Helmuth Von Ranke.

Thus the main interpretations of the outbreak of European overseas imperialism have moved along from Enlightenment notions of civilizing and humanizing noble savages through liberalism, *laissez-faire* capitalism, Marxism, relativism, multi-causality and the acceptance of conflicting interpretations. For example, in the last century the European empires were each seen as manifestations of specific national energies and virtues, as very ethnic but very positive. Nationalist phenomena created new nations, such as the USA, in their own essential nationalist images. While they competed bitterly, the European imperialist nations could nevertheless agree that they all shared a superior civilization and that they brought the blessings of this culture to the lesser humans in their colonies. Indeed it was obvious to them, well into the twentieth century and as far as the 1950s and 1960s, that conquered native peoples in all the other continents were better off as a result of European rule. The main dissenting interpreters from the end of the nineteenth century were the Marxist and socialist writers. To them, overseas imperialism was ruthless capitalist exploitation of the materially weaker native peoples by the richer and stronger Europeans. Indeed, European capitalists rose to global political and cultural dominance by brutally exploiting and expropriating colonial subjects, using this extorted wealth, along with that squeezed from poor workers at home, to fund industrialization and political and economic monopoly.

Between the 1950s and 1990s there were indeed serious historiographic efforts to come to balanced assessments but usually at the risk of narrowing their thematic focus. Following on from Edward Gibbon's *Decline and Fall of the Roman Empire* theme in 1776, great scholars like J.H. Parry, C.R. Boxer, Geoffrey Scammell and many others turned to the detailed explanations for both the rises and the falls of the various European empires, stressing unique features and circumstances. National efforts, successes and failures were relativistic, as more recently on a broader front in Paul Kennedy's *Rise and Fall of the Great Powers* (1987). Some analysts attacked the Marxist interpreters, as did Patrick O'Brien with his argument that overseas empires were economically peripheral and did little to stimulate industrialization; others such as Barbara Solow, however, now urge that profits from slave-grown sugar did indeed fund some early industrialization efforts. Elsewhere, post-colonial or 'subaltern' interpretations have focused more on the effects of conquests and colonizations on the colonized people, especially in Asia. Out of these and other detailed interpretations have emerged the two dominant causal explanations of the 1990s, the technological and the biological, or the guns, ships, steel cause and the germs cause.[1] They stand historiographically apart from the superior smartness/superior nastiness dichotomy but perhaps tend to fit a bit better with nastiness, though they are seldom combined explicitly.

How can these interpretive varieties be integrated into a balanced view that on the one hand considers the complexities of the events and the participants, with their diverse capabilities and their various motivations, yet on the other includes the full range of European circumstances and characteristics enabling or driving early imperialism? And what about the grand simplifications of so-called Eurocentricism – Europe's civilizing inputs to the rest – or Marxism, or post-colonial guilt of the invader oppressors? In one sense the start of globalization was caused by everything at the time, which is an inscrutable notion. In another sense the strong beat up the weak, which is equally unsatisfying, if also nice and brief, even if some of the main strengths are listed. As a minimum starting point, it seems important to begin a clarification of causes by establishing exactly who it was among the Europeans who were directly involved in the foundations of overseas empires, and what kinds of trends and characteristics induced them to do this.

ENVIRONMENT, CLIMATE, AND POPULATION

Besides the famous leaders of the first colony building ventures, the main body of traders, conquerors and colonists were European multinational minority groups, but these were groups with specific common characteristics. All the main colonization initiatives were the work of people from the Atlantic coasts of Spain, Portugal, England, France and the Netherlands. Only these Europeans sailed the ships and manned the founding expeditions which began the so-called 'expansion of Europe'. Only they expanded in the sixteenth and seventeenth centuries. The rest of the Europeans stayed at home or moved about within their own continent, usually from country to town or from civilian to military life. Atlantic European expansion was more geographically specific than culturally or politically specific. By the time of Columbus their deep-water seafaring capabilities were the most effective on the planet and grew more effective over the next centuries. And they had perceptions of crowding – perhaps of being pressed up against their stormy Atlantic Ocean by multiplying inland neighbours – that drove them to migrate across the seas. Location itself was a basic cause. There were probably also strong climatic and population changes shaping these Atlantic Europeans and their expansionist inclinations, which are too often ignored.

The expert climate historians remain tentative because of reliable evidence problems. Despite the introduction of new scientific weather pattern investigations, such as various ice and soil core and tree ring examinations, the weather history for Western Europe, as for other places, has both many gaps due to heavy reliance on scattered contemporary comments and many local exceptions and complications. Nevertheless, experts like H.H. Lamb[2] can agree with colleagues that between *c.* 1300 and *c.* 1700 Western Europe was in the fairly moderate grip of the 'Little Ice Age', which had its coldest part probably between 1550 and 1600. Population growth was probably slowed overall, more in some regions such as Scandinavia than elsewhere, but the main population trend remained positive and Europeans multiplied gradually, after recovering from widespread disasters such as weather-driven crop failures and weather-related epidemics at the start of the Little Ice Age.

But for seafaring Atlantic communities the weather changes had more specific impacts. The Scandinavian Norse were Europe's most wide-ranging Atlantic mariners until about 1300, having reached Canada by about 1000 and colonized Greenland. They covered unequalled open-ocean distances with very basic technology but their sailors were especially proficient and possessed exceptional skills and toughness. Their small largely open ships had limited wind use capabilities and remained partly dependent on muscle-powered oar propulsion non-conducive to sustained oceanic travel. But in the warm period from 1000 to 1300, the Norsemen managed a small volume transport route in subarctic Atlantic waters, a great feat in many ways. With the onset of colder weather, however, Arctic ice moved southward and gradually blocked off Norse navigation not only in the North Atlantic but also the Baltic Sea, in which their sea transport system had been developed. By the time of Columbus they still sailed to Iceland but the Greenland communication was over.

Furthermore, the Scandinavians also lost their herring fishery, the support base for their sea transport system, again due to the advancing ice from the north. By early in the sixteenth century, as the Atlantic Europeans became seriously active on the oceans, the herring grounds of the Baltic shifted to the North Sea between England and the Netherlands, of great seafaring benefit to the Dutch in particular. A little earlier, other Atlantic Europeans, led by the Portuguese and West Country English, also discovered the Grand Banks cod fishery south of Newfoundland and expanded their Atlantic fishing fleets and crews substantially. The effect of weather pattern changes and fishing grounds on the Spanish mariner communities and Portuguese mariners prior to the late 1400s is not so clear. However, it does seem that during the critical start in the development of Spanish and Portuguese seafaring improvements, which in the late fourteenth and the fifteenth centuries gave them the first working fleets of the so-called full-rigged or Atlantic sailing ships – caravels, carracks and naos – they quite possibly benefited from somewhat easier Atlantic sailing conditions in their less stormy and less frigid coastal waters. But for all the Atlantic maritime Europeans south of the Scandinavians, the colder weather of the Little Ice Age meant the need for both tougher and more efficient ship technology and sailor proficiency if they were to sail from their coasts at all. Increasingly they felt the need to sail, to find seafood, to trade and then to emigrate. The rising populations of their inland hinterlands pushed them to make the extra efforts to master one of the most hostile waterways on the planet. In the 1490s the Atlantic Europeans began to discover that if they could now reliably (if uncomfortably) sail their coastal waters, they could sail anywhere where the waters did not freeze solid.

Along with the need to conquer their only communication medium, made more difficult by climate change, came the negative and positive stimuli from the population growth that the Little Ice Age was not cold enough to prevent. Here again the experts are necessarily vague due to the statistical shortcomings of largely innnumerate ancestors who kept birth, death and other population records. Best estimates, however, are largely accepted by most of the human geographers, demographers and population historians. Thus, Spanish and

Portuguese populations rose to a combined total of about 8.5 million by 1600 but then fell off to 7.5 million by 1700, after the expansionist lead went to northerners. The population of England, meanwhile, went from 2.5 to 4.1 million between 1520 and 1603, building up a potential for seafaring and colonization. From 1603 to 1700 English population grew to 5.8 million and by 1750 it grew to 6.2 million. The population of the Netherlands grew from 1.6 million in 1600 to 1.95 million in 1700. The population of France, on the other hand, actually declined between 1560 and 1600, and stayed static at around the 20 million mark for the next century or so.[3]

Tens of thousands of these Atlantic Europeans went to sea to sail, trade and colonize. Without them there would have been no 'expansion of Europe' at all. For most contemporaries the ocean travel that was indispensable to this expansion was a daunting barrier. Among other expert analysts such as Ian K. Steele, David Cressy points out the prevailing fears of Atlantic travel:

> English migrants to North America often approached their journey with apprehension and fear. Stories of storms and wrecks effectively dissuaded some prospective migrants from voyaging to America; others battled anxieties as they encountered the strange and terrifying world of the sea.[4]

Thus there are reasons to believe that the combination of European repulsions and New World attractions – the so-called 'push' and 'pull' factors – must have been strong to drive tens of thousands one way across the oceans. Exact figures are again scarce but the experts generally accept estimates such as the following:

(1) 280,000 Portuguese went overseas between 1500 and 1580 out of a population of 1.5 million, at an annual rate of 3,500. Most did not return.[5]

(2) 243,000 Spaniards went to 'the Indies' between 1506 and 1600, at a rate of 2,583 per annum, out of a population of 8 million. Most went as bosses, to take charge of Native American workers. Their conquests were of people as much as of territories.[6] Between 1600 and 1650 about 3,000 to 4,000 Spanish migrants moved to the Americas each year.[7]

(3) Half a million Dutch migrants moved to Asia between 1600 and 1700 out of a maximum population of 1.9 million.[8]

(4) The French had the lowest colonial migration rate of the Atlantic Europeans, perhaps in part because of stagnant population. Still, between 1609 and 1700, about 10,000 migrants went to New France, somewhat more to the West Indies.[9]

(5) The English sent the most early migrants to the Americas. Between 1630 and 1642 alone 21,200 Puritans settled in New England. Up to 150,000 migrants went to the Virginia-based Chesapeake area by 1700.[10] The English population of all the North American colonies together rose from 97,000 in 1650 to 266,000 in 1700 and to 999,000 in 1750, due to a combination of migrant influx and natural increase. In addition, the English caused the forceable importation, with its subsequent natural increase, of 117,000 Africans in 1650, 146,000 in 1700, and 537,000 in 1750, for a total British,

European and African population of 1,536,000 in that year.[11] In 1700 the average number of British sailors actively involved in all oceanic maritime enterprises was about 10,000.[12] These too participated throughout in the overseas colonization effort and can in part be added to the human resource totals of British seaborne imperialism each year.

Did these nevertheless quite small colonist and invader groups overcome the resistance of vast indigenous majorities, as prevailing impressions still suggest? Did the invaders overcome massive odds against them in their dispossession campaigns? After all, Cortés overthrew an Aztec empire of millions with never more than 1,500 Spanish fighters and he did it in a matter of months, between 1519 and 1521. Did not the 180 followers of Pizarro seize the entire Inca ruling elite in two hours of sword play at Cajamarca in 1532, and the entire Inca empire along with Atahualpa? Images of embattled handfuls of colonists driving off hordes of warriors continue through the colonization stories right up to Custer's Last Stand and Rorke's Drift. (Isandhlwana, where the Zulus won over substantial numbers of professional soldiers, is less often noted.) Of course, it is also obvious that Cortés beat an Aztec elite in a city of 200,000 and only with much help from significant portions of their Mexican subjects; that Pizarro never had to fight organized Inca military forces, and that small invader groups never actually engaged significant portions of the total Native American populations, or other indigenous populations in other continents. The invaders were seldom massively outnumbered. They overcame small segments of total indigenous populations who were as representative of the total defender populations as the invaders were equally representative of the total European population. In 1500 the invader groups represented the energetic colonizing migrant minority out of a population of 67 million, versus an estimated Native American population of 42 million. In 1600 the invaders came out of a European population of 89 million and the defender groups they confronted now represented only 13 million remaining Native Americans.[13] So, small as the mere thousands and tens of thousands who chose to invade and colonize were, in the context of the even smaller local and regional populations they mostly dispossessed, their numbers were a greater strength than customary impressions convey. The size of the migrant flow to overseas colonies was probably a main cause and among the strongest reasons for Atlantic European imperial expansionism. But it is still also true that we need more detailed quantification to underline this point. It is not a point strongly made by current leading historians and it probably should be. Atlantic Europeans had the person-power and chose to use it for overseas trading and invading, against usually more thinly manned communities, at least in the so-called settlement colonies.

BIOLOGICAL CAUSES

Instead of sorting out relative healthy and active invader and defender numbers, at least in the case of the American invasions, a leading group of colonial expansion interpreters concentrates on germs and epidemic diseases as main causes. Indigenous Native Americans, and later Australasians and Pacific Islanders, lacked immunities against common Eurasian epidemic diseases in the 1492 to 1788 invasion time. The Atlantic Europeans brought smallpox and other such epidemics with them. From their first contact with early precursor groups of explorers and traders, these Eurasian epidemic pathogens began to race through Native American and other populations, killing millions. The shattered remainder groups were too weak to offer serious resistance to colonial subjugation. This is the core of the argument first documented impressively by William H. McNeill in his *Plagues and Peoples* in 1977,[14] then expanded by Alfred Crosby in his *Ecological Imperialism* in 1986[15] and currently popularized by Jared Diamond in his *Guns, Germs and Steel*.[16] These authoritative scholars all point to instances of critical disease impact in the Aztec, Inca and New England invasions. The smallpox epidemic imported into Tenochtitlan in 1520, albeit unintentionally, so weakened the defending Aztecs as to give an unlikely victory to the besieging followers of Cortés. An epidemic brought by European reconnaissance parties prior to 1532 so disrupted the Inca state that the Pizarro coup at Cajamarca was sufficient to topple it. And because of the effects of two epidemics brought in by early European explorers and traders, the native people of New England were so reduced in population in 1620 and 1630 that the Pilgrims and Puritans were able to move into virtually empty lands, some with native cornfields cleared and ready for European planting. The other main foundation invasions, especially Hispaniola from 1493, Virginia from 1607 and New France from 1609, were not so obviously facilitated by disease but did experience high local Native American casualties from invading pathogens during and after the early settlement stages. By various estimates, half to over nine-tenths of the potential defender populations in these critical areas were thus terminated without the need for further European efforts.

But there are doubts about both the full impact and the timing of introduced pathogens as the main causes for successful colony planting, especially in the Americas. Francis Brooks has pointed out that in the case of the Aztec smallpox tragedy of 1520, the only detailed description of the full effects by the eyewitness historian Motolinia was almost certainly plagiarized from the Old Testament rather than based on close observation.[17] There is little doubt that the Aztecs were seriously weakened by the epidemic but were they devastated to the point of defeat? Was the pathogen impact the main cause of Spanish victory? Were the Mexican allies of Cortés not also reduced by this plague? And were the Aztecs of Tenochtitlan, 200,000 people among the millions they ruled, really strong enough to regain their power after becoming besieged largely by their own subjects before the plague struck? Such questions are yet to be examined in detail but historians continue to assess other causes for critical Aztec weakness besides disease. In the Inca case, we still have 180 Spanish swordsmen seizing an empire of millions of Native Americans in two hours, weakened and reduced by epidemics or not. Cajamarca remains a startling coup, with few parallels anywhere else in history. In the New England case, whether the Pilgrims and Puritans found untended cornfields because their owners were wiped out by earlier Eurasian pathogens or because of the slash and burn agricultural practice of these maize-growing people, which left exhausted cornfields scattered throughout New England, is just one general question about disease impact. There was no serious conflict between the settlers and old owners until 1637 in any case, so at least earlier epidemics did not seem to relate to defender fighting capabilities. In Hispaniola and Virginia, each in their way more fundamental settlements for permanent Europeanization than the three seemingly strongest disease examples, the invaders initially had much higher death rates than the defenders, in part from diseases generated by environmental peculiarities to which the Europeans were unaccustomed. Large-scale combat did not break out until well after there were more Europeans in the Santo Domingo and Jamestown regions than Native Americans, and serious epidemics did not devastate the defenders until well after their hopes of any kind of concerted counterattack against the invading communities were long gone. The Powhatans finally mounted serious attacks only in 1622 and 1644. The Taino/Arawaks never organized even modestly united armed resistance.[18] In New France the French invaders came mostly as allies of the Algonquian-Huron people, both commercially and territorially, in a sense becoming absorbed into Native American power politics as additional enemies of the Iroquois peoples. Whatever the effect of disease in specific invasions such as the Cortés attack may have been, overall pathogens do not appear to have been a major reason for invader success in planting foundation colonies.

TECHNOLOGY AND FIREPOWER

In the last decade or so, guns have been coming first as the main cause for the colonizing conquests. A main reason for this is the persuasiveness of the current 'war and society' scholars who argue the importance of the 'Military Revolution'. In the early modern period this made the Western European gun-based military system – already a clearly technocentric institutional, ideological and material structure – into the most combat effective system in the world. Thanks to the good efforts of Michael Roberts, W.H. McNeill, Geoffrey Parker, Jeremy Black, Frank Tallett and David Eltis,[19] a Military Revolution definition seems relatively easy. In the early modern period select Europeans developed and exported a combination of new gunpowder-based weapons and defences, new skills and martial institutions, and together the largest increase in per-person combat power in history. Among others McNeill and Parker link these military superiorities to European colonization successes. The gunpowder-based systems also laid the foundations for the industrialized militarism of the nineteenth century which made Europeans dominant over all other cultures. But since the Military Revolution supporters concentrate on internal European developments and provide few details about the application of the Revolution to outsiders, exactly how European firepower advantages were applied overseas still remains to be demonstrated in depth. Experts on colonization are divided on the importance of firepower in the early stages of colonizing invasions. It is clear that between the fifteenth and eighteenth centuries Europeans became more militarily potent than anybody else but it is not so clear how they projected this potency into invasion efforts on other continents. That projection came mostly after industrialization.

The second problem with the Military Revolution overseas is timing. Was this a revolution lasting for centuries and thus more of an evolution? Or did it actually have a tighter chronological core, for example at the time of the general adoption of guns prior to 1500, or at the time of Gustavus Adolphus, or of Louis XIV, or during some other key phase? The timing is important. If, for example, Michael Roberts and his 1955 version prevails, the Revolution comes too late to shape most of the critical overseas invasions. Thus the Revolution, despite its persuasive features, retains ambiguities relative to colonization.

But what about firepower advantages, with or without the rest of the Revolution? Did the invaders fight better than the defenders? As some Amerindians demonstrated repeatedly, man for man they were perfectly capable of outfighting the invaders. The Algonquian allies of the French did so again and again. The Iroquois defence of their homeland came close to substantial success. Individual Tainos, Caribs, Aztecs, Incas, Powhatans and others outfought better armed Europeans. From first contact the defending warriors recognized the superiority of European weapons and hastened to capture or buy them. From as early as the 1620s Amerindian warriors began to import advanced design flintlock, or snaphance, muskets and to evolve much more effective woodland combat tactics than European pike and volley methods so that by the second half of the century European settlers were in fact imitating the Native Americans. The Native Americans could fight better than they could concentrate numbers against invasion points. Indeed, the entire Native American woodland combat system was probably superior to the best Military Revolution methods and devices in the context of the North American environment.[20]

TECHNOLOGY AND TRANSPORT POWER

If it was not firepower technology that gave Europeans in America the main edge, was it their ship technology? They did have the efficient and reliable long-range vessels required for imperialism, but was it just the ships that made the critical difference? Did they really have a monopoly of good ships? Probably not. Aside from Arab watercraft of advanced capabilities, there were excellent ships in Asia. As Louise Levathes and others before her have argued, between 1405 and 1433 the Chinese under Admiral Zheng He had immensely better long-range ships than the Atlantic Europeans and could have outmatched the Portuguese fleets in the next century had they chosen to.[21] Nevertheless, the ship's cause has longstanding support, at least indirectly. Carlo Cipolla combined sails and guns as the main causes of European sea power superiority in Asian waters. J.H. Parry and C.R. Boxer portrayed the Spanish and Dutch empires as essentially 'seaborne' and Geoffrey Scammell called all the early European empires 'maritime'.[22] There are many other examples. From another ship-based perspective, navalist writers from A.T. Mahan through R.G. Albion, Gerald Graham and Paul Kennedy, to Modelski and Thompson and their 'global reach' concept, also stress sea power in empire building.[23] The problem is that some of these are better at explaining the start of the Asian empires than later colonization efforts and none of them separate out ship technology or transport systems from more generalized sea power factors, including big factors like capitalism and international politics. Finally, there are historians of transportation, with their research combining among other things economic history, technological history and human geography. Few of these, however, study European sea transport systems prior to industrialization. Those who do, like Ralph Davis, stress technical details and avoid broad contextual generalizations or relevance to big questions about historical change.[24]

Nevertheless, these ship-centered studies make up the most consistent theme within the post-1492 expansion of Europe story. In general terms more scholars believe that ships were involved in important ways than any other formative influence. And, after all, it was ships that delivered the guns and pathogens. So the case for ships is untidy and inconsistent but quantitatively more popular than the one for guns and diseases. The question here seems to be, can we pull enough consistent features out of the varieties of ship-based interpretation to produce a comprehensive definition that might work for the main episodes of empire and colony building? Can we then compare and contrast this with firepower superiority theories, to see which might explain more about the main causes?

Ship-based superiority over Asians, Africans, Native Americans and Native Australasians clearly comprised marine technology, knowledge and skills, economic and political means and wills, and indeed an Atlantic European maritime culture mostly concentrated in specific coastal regions of Portugal, Spain, the Netherlands, England and France. The full-rigged ocean ship, and all that created, operated and used it, was developed during the fifteenth century, perfected by 1492, and refined continuously up to industrialization and the application of steam power in the nineteenth century. What all this boils down to is a transport system for bulk goods and large numbers of people with virtually unlimited oceanic range (or 'global reach'), that travelled on regular, repeatable, predictable schedules, and all this at cheaper per ton and per person costs than for any other form of transportation. It was the first long-range heavy transport system powered by something other than human or animal muscles and so was the least labour-intensive transport system. It improved slowly in qualitative terms after Columbus but considerably in quantitative terms. It became so prevalent among the Atlantic Europeans who operated and exploited it as their special monopoly that it became commonplace to contemporaries. As Ian Steele has noted, their oceanic shipping was slow, exceedingly hazardous and very expensive. But it was also predictable, mostly reliable and thus taken for granted so much that contemporaries seldom commented on those aspects of it, the majority, which allowed the delivery of goods and people as expected.[25] And it was basic to the foundations of globalism.

There are plenty of good examples of the power exerted by sea transport superiority in the Atlantic European expansion process. The first one is the spectacular Portuguese seizure of an Asian trading empire in the short years between the Vasco da Gama and Affonso d'Albuquerque initiatives. Both earlier and later generations of experts agree sea power was central.

There were marine infantry triumphs – especially Albuquerque's successful assault against the elephant supported forces of the Sultan of Malacca in 1511 –

but for the most part it was sea transport superiority that enabled the Portuguese to get to key Asian trading centers, to stay for centuries, and to provide Asian land powers with better sea-trading services than they were getting from Asian shippers. Guns helped a great deal but rival Arab traders were not only driven off by heavier ordnance. They were also out-competed, as indicated by such developments as the extensive Portuguese 'country trader' networks. Along with Parry, Scammell and other pioneer interpreters, current writers such as B.W. Diffie and G.D. Winnius and Michael Pearson are all emphatic about the importance of Portuguese sea transport superiority.[26] Roger C. Smith points out that at the time of da Gama Portugal shared the qualitative lead in oceanic navigation with Spain and held the quantitative lead worldwide.[27] The Portuguese trading empire was a sea transport superiority empire throughout its period of prominence. When the Dutch, English and French joined in later, they began by imitating the Portuguese model. Until the 1750s none of the European imperialists in Asia – with the partial exception of the Dutch on Java – dominated anything much in terms of Asian territory. They only dominated the long-range maritime trade routes. At their ports they stayed on Asian sufferance.

OUTFIGHTING OR OUTNUMBERING?

But what about sea transport in the conquest of overseas inland territories? How could it be a dominant cause here? The short answer is, logistically, as a pipeline from a more numerous, wealthier and concentrated European region to American regions that were, in these sorts of terms, more thinly and weakly held. The popular assumption that the early colonization conquests were achieved against great Native American odds is inaccurate. The greater mobility of the invaders reversed this assumed numerical equation.

In the same decade as the start of the Portuguese trade empire a smaller Spanish maritime effort opened the communication to the West Indies in 1492 and from the following year proceeded to insinuate a permanent European community among the Amerindians of Hispaniola. During the critical months of securing a defensible lodgement in Taino/Arawak territory there was no serious violence between invaders and landowners. More Spanish settlers died of disease than Amerindians of imported Eurasian pathogens. The invaders were thoroughly outnumbered in the island as a whole but not very much at their main settlements, which were the terminals of the transport pipelines from their home ports. Not only did they replace losses from sickness and other hardships but they steadily reinforced their original numbers. Almost from the start their logistical system permitted a denser concentration of people in their base settlements than the Taino/Arawaks had in their main villages. Outnumbered generally, the colonist-invaders in turn outnumbered the indigenes locally. Since the latter were politically and geographically dispersed, and took many months to realize that the Spanish seaside villages were going to threaten all their territories, they failed to attack the invaders with sufficiently united and superior numbers early enough. When desultory warfare under leaders such as Caonabo did begin, there were already too many colonists to drive back into the sea. The Spanish did have military advantages such as some guns, armour, swords, horses and war dogs, but they also had enough manpower to maintain stronger forces than those of the defenders. The Spanish could outnumber the Taino/Arawaks at the points of violent contact between them. The violence of conquest went on but the European presence was already irreversible. The maritime transport pipeline from Spain swamped local Amerindian defences sequentially from the first landing places outward and inland. In essence this process was repeated from 1607 in Virginia by English invaders in Powhatan territory, and in later English foundation colonies.[28]

Before making additional comments on the English invasions, however, there are the Aztec and Inca conquests that need to be considered in terms of the sea transport superiority argument. Do they fit at all? C.H. Gardiner did argue that at the 1521 siege of Tenochtitlan the purpose-built brigantines of the conquistadors were a decisive application of naval power and the key to Spanish victory.[29] It is also obvious that Cortés could not have prevailed without seaborne reinforcements which got his combat strength up to an average of 1500 by the time of victory. Pizarro's 180-odd fighters, with all their combat necessities, also depended on sea transport to get to within striking distance of Atahualpa. But both the Aztec and Inca empires were far removed from ocean access alone. The few horses of both groups of conquistadors were probably not sufficient to give them much of a land transport advantage, and both groups relied on indigenous porters. If sea transport was thus indecisive, was superior fighting power more decisive against numerical odds in these two cases?

While there is no clear agreement about their firepower advantages, most historians do accept that both sets of invaders only overthrew relatively compact ruling elites, native governments unevenly supported by their subjects. In the Aztec case, where the battles of conquest were sustained and hard – though still small by contemporary European standards – Cortés relied heavily on large numbers of disaffected Aztec subjects who were his indispensable allies in the victory. The initial Spanish seizure of power over the Incas was facilitated by one small surprise massacre in Cajamarca in May 1532, when Pizarro's 180 or so armoured men wiped out Atahualpa's entire personal guard and bureaucracy in less than two hours, killing maybe up to thirty Incas each with their swords. The two conquests were more coups or rebellions than military campaigns.

But the Spanish invaders also appear to have outfought their opponents on a man-to-man basis and Military Revolution guns, cavalry and infantry firepower tactics were doubtless advantages. Neither group of conquistadors were full-time professional soldiers of the latest type, as led by innovative captains like Gonsalvo de Cordoba in battles against the French and others in Italy. Gonsalvo's infantry was a Military Revolution phenomenon. Some conquistadors had served with him in the Italian wars but most were amateurs with limited war experience or none. On the other hand, it is likely that the warriors they defeated were even less professional – at least in the European sense of being skilled to deal with a wide variety of combat experiences – than the conquistadors. Leading warriors were also often bureaucrats with demanding civil and sometimes religious duties. The invaders may have had the advantage of being full-time combatants opposed to part-time defenders. There is also the ongoing issue of exaggerated Aztec and Inca numbers. The numerical superiority of the defenders may in these terms be misleading and Military Revolution advantages might not have been so critical.[30] In any case, these two conquests are uniquely different among the founding colonization invasions of the Americas.

After Mexico and Peru the most decisive (or maybe more so) colonial foundations were in Virginia and New England. In Virginia the Powhatans resisted hard up to 1644, in New England Pequots, Wampanoags, Narragansetts and others kept up violent opposition until 1675. In neither case did the defenders strike back early enough, when the invaders were still few and insecure. By the time Opechancanough organized the local tribes to launch a general assault against Jamestown and its expanding hinterland in 1622, there were already too many English colonists too tightly concentrated. Later anti-invasion efforts in Virginia and elsewhere were all too late, too local and too outnumbered by the Europeans. Instead of driving out the invaders, by the second half of the seventeenth century the defenders themselves were being driven out, usually to the west.[31]

In the English invasion story there is a lot more migration than combat. The Native Americans were locally and regionally outnumbered in very short order. They continued to be outnumbered from the east right to the end of the nineteenth century. Swelling numbers of European migrants kept displacing shrinking numbers of Amerindian refugees. Initially and continuously, this invasive migration flow was mostly the product of the English phase of the European sea transport superiority. The new American colonies themselves became an integral part of this superiority. The tobacco colonies, with their vital tidewater export regions, were almost entirely dependent for life and growth on their water communications in the seventeenth century. The English settlements went only as far inland as the many rivers navigable from the ocean took them. As economic historians such as J.J. McCusker and R.R. Menard point out, all the early eastern seaboard colonies were essentially riverine, tied by water into the Atlantic transport system until the mid-eighteenth century.[32] From Virginia south the colonies lived on seaborne export earnings. Those in New England and surrounding areas ended up imitating and replicating England's own maritime regions and living substantially from their trade and transport services. By the 1750s their merchant fleet made up one-third of the entire British merchant fleet and was probably the second largest in the world. Their so-called 'triangular trade' dominated North Atlantic commerce. Thus the English colonies were very maritime and the Military Revolution arguments seem largely unnecessary to explain their foundations. None of these foundations required extensive or sustained military operations.

The first colonizers to deploy fully articulated European professional troops against Amerindians were the French in the St Lawrence Valley. From 1665 Jean Colbert, responding to colonial pleas, sent 1,200 men of the Carignan-Salières Regiment to New France to wipe out the Iroquois. They succeeded only in small part. Other professionals were sent but never in large enough numbers to secure the vast territories desired. Unlike the English, the French after 1608 did not send enough migrants to outnumber the Amerindians except around Quebec and Montreal, which were accessible to ocean transport ships. In the continental interior they placed outposts that encircled the English Atlantic settlements but never mustered the Europeans needed for effective occupation. Instead, they relied on Amerindian allies to help them hold their interior claims. The Algonquian-Ottawa alliances were essential to the French empire. Of all the Native American cultures, only these possessed birchbark canoes. Only by this birchbark technology was long-range inland transport beyond the headwaters of rivers flowing into the Atlantic made possible.[33]

It can be argued that birchbark canoe transport was the basis of the French empire in America because it gave the Algonquian-French mutual dependency alliance a monopoly over the movement of goods and people in the continental interior. It enabled the allies to gather the furs they needed for economic survival, to bypass and neutralize the Iroquois and to successfully contain the northward and westward expansion of the Anglo-Americans until 1759 to 1763. French and Indian inland defences held. New France was defeated at Louisbourg and Quebec by sea power and the maritime transport that ultimately brought Wolfe's redcoats to the plains of Abraham.

Thus the partial exceptions to the outnumbering powers of the sea-transport-driven Europeans were the birchbark canoe tribes. But birchbark trees only grew in the north-east and canoes could not cross oceans. There was little that most Amerindians could do to stop Europeans from carrying their goods and people wherever ocean ships could reach. In 1542 the Mississippi tribes were pursuing the last of de Soto's defeated gold-seeking conquistador aspirants out of their country. According to Ian Steele, one of the warriors shouted after the Spanish '. . . If we possessed such large canoes as yours . . . we would follow you to your land and conquer it, for we too are men like yourselves'.[34]

There is now an emerging interpretation pointing to maritime superiority as a main cause for industrialization itself. In 1966 Eric Williams argued that the capital for industrialization came from the African slave trade.[35] His minority view has now been elaborated more convincingly by Barbara Solow and others.[36] The sugar and slave trade central to Britain's domination of Atlantic maritime commerce substantially helped to accumulate capital for industrialization. D.W. Jones, meanwhile, has argued that it was Atlantic trade domination, won by naval sea power, which forced open Spanish colonial routes and by integrating them into the Anglo-American shipping system made Britain into a first-class power after 1713.[37] Patrick O'Brien, who earlier called the economic importance of empire and colonies 'peripheral' to Britain's rise, is now arguing that by means of John Brewer's 'fiscal-military state',[38] it was indeed the heavily defended British maritime transport system, with its one-third American component, which generated the capital for industrialization. Alterations in British agricultural practices or other internal changes were not as important.[39] Perhaps it was the alliance of the French navy with the American merchant fleet that really explains the success of the American Revolution, and the reabsorption of the American fleet into the British system afterward that explains the subsequent continuation of Britain's rise and France's decline.

CONSEQUENCES

What did these causes produce? The experts and non-experts have a wide variety of views but there is a general agreement that the consequences were most important. In the short term, the results were clear enough. In 1776 Adam Smith summed up the British experience with the economics of empire in his *Wealth of Nations*, laying down the doctrines of free trade, *laissez-faire* capitalism and the economic rationalism which is today's leading elite ideology. In 1782 James Watt patented the first of his two revolutionary steam engine designs, an action symbolizing the fact that industrialization began in the same decade as the United States of America, at the end of the first British overseas empire. In 1788 Britain colonized the last empty habitable continent on the globe, perhaps as part of Vincent Harlow's 'swing to the east' (in his *The Founding of the Second British Empire* (1952)), which began in the 1750s as British imperialists grew disenchanted with American colonists and sought better profits in Asia and beyond. In 1789 came the era of the French Revolution and the new nation-state system of nineteenth-century Europe, due in some part to the French monarchy bankrupting the nation in its many wars (both at home and overseas) and helping the Americans overthrow British rule.

More generally there is also agreement that the colonizing conquests caused nineteenth- and twentieth-century European imperialism directly and perhaps did much to cause industrialization as well. These in turn have driven human progress – and generated human disasters – towards the globally conscious world community of the 1990s. What seems clear today is that no nation or society on the planet can go forth to colonize rich new territories. All of the habitable spaces are occupied by societies more or less capable of holding on to them. There is now little scope for uninvited migration. There can be no repeat of the hoards of weakly held natural resources which were seized by a select but sizeable minority of Europeans between 1492 and 1914, and which perhaps elevated larger proportions of these groups into the relative prosperity and political power of the middle classes than ever before or since. During this age of empires the dominant human societies rose above the limitations of old hierarchical political and economic orders tyrannized by hereditary elites. So, did the imperialist despoliation of the lands and livelihoods of native tribal societies in other continents also bring improvements in egalitarianism and more equitable modes of resource sharing? In the end the remnants of original owner societies were themselves given the kinds of equalities first demanded by the aggressive migrant groups of the early empires. Multiculturalism grew out of migrant invasions and finally included the invaded remnant peoples also. But basic to migrant rights has been the right to larger shares of space and resources. For many, there are no more larger shares. Unless technology based ingenuity intervenes to redefine the relationships between people and environment, the planet is full up. But at the start of the globalization process, maritime and other technologies, themselves driven by climate and population changes, worked mainly to replace slower growth populations in the Americas and Australasia with faster growth populations, without altering the demographies of Asia and Africa. We are living with the consequences.

Maps

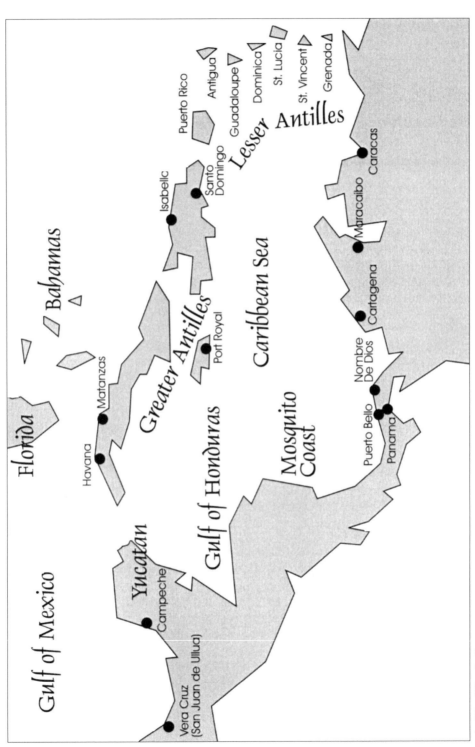

A. *The West Indies*

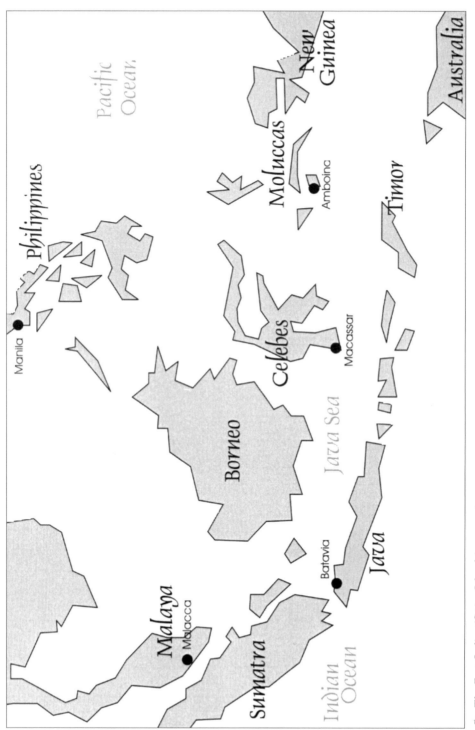

B. *The East Indies (Spice Islands)*

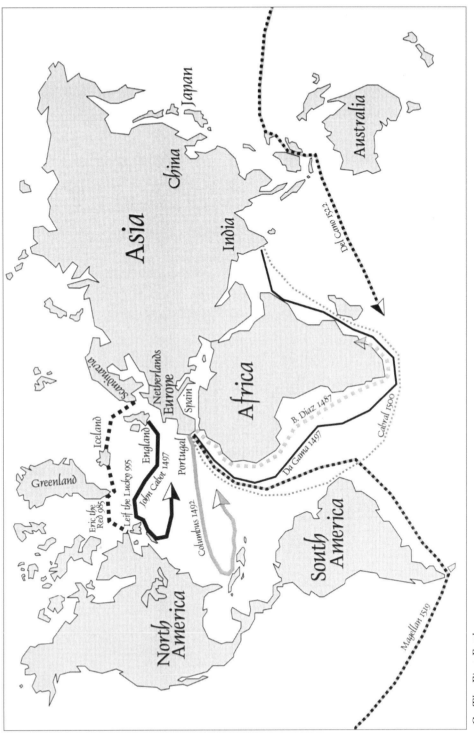

C. *The First Explorers*

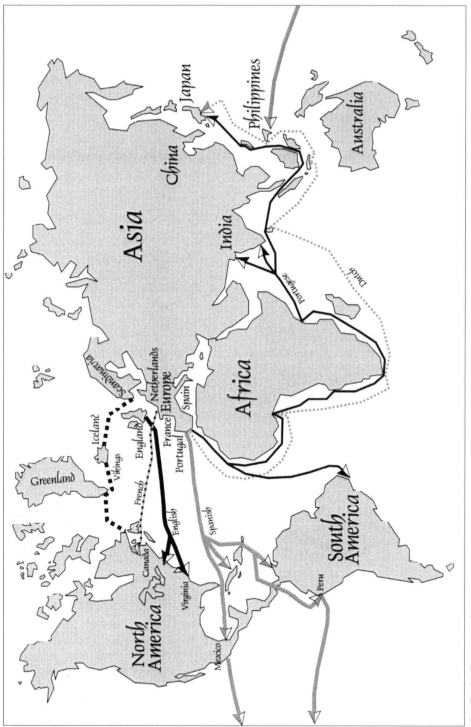

D. Early European Outposts

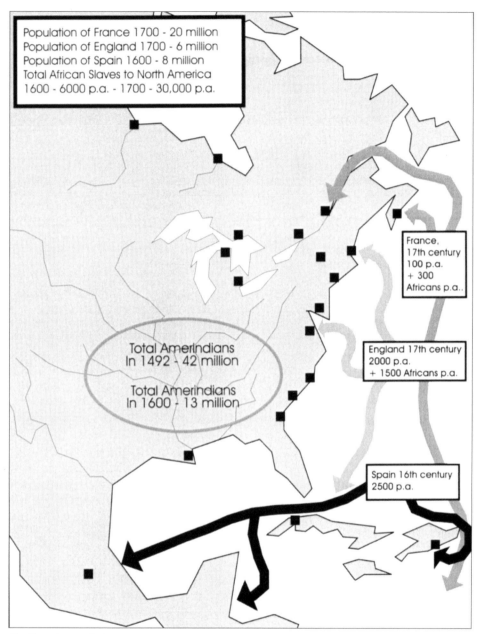

Population of France 1700 - 20 million
Population of England 1700 - 6 million
Population of Spain 1600 - 8 million
Total African Slaves to North America
1600 - 6000 p.a. - 1700 - 30,000 p.a.

France,
17th century
100 p.a.
+ 300
Africans p.a..

England 17th century
2000 p.a.
+ 1500 Africans p.a.

Spain 16th century
2500 p.a.

Total Amerindians
In 1492 - 42 million

Total Amerindians
In 1600 - 13 million

E. Foundation Colony Migration Flows, first century of colonisation

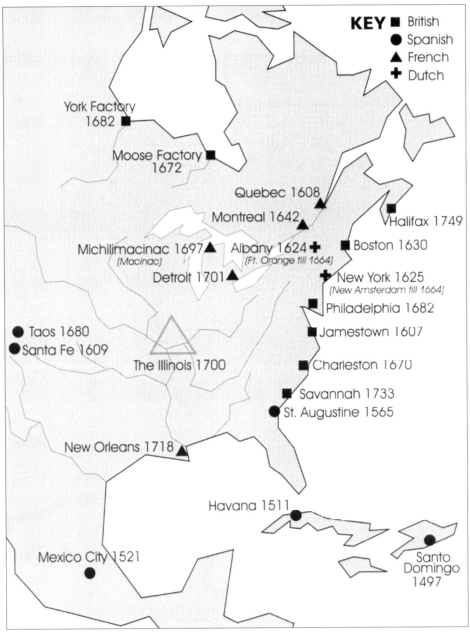

KEY
■ British
● Spanish
▲ French
✚ Dutch

York Factory 1682 ■

Moose Factory 1672 ■

Quebec 1608 ▲

Montreal 1642 ▲

■ Halifax 1749

Michilimacinac 1697 ▲
(Macinac)

Albany 1624 ✚
(Ft. Orange till 1664)

■ Boston 1630

Detroit 1701 ▲

✚ New York 1625
(New Amsterdam till 1664)

■ Philadelphia 1682

● Taos 1680
● Santa Fe 1609

The Illinois 1700

■ Jamestown 1607

■ Charleston 1670

■ Savannah 1733
● St. Augustine 1565

New Orleans 1718 ▲

Havana 1511 ●

Mexico City 1521 ●

Santo Domingo 1497 ●

F. *Early Colonial Outposts in North America*

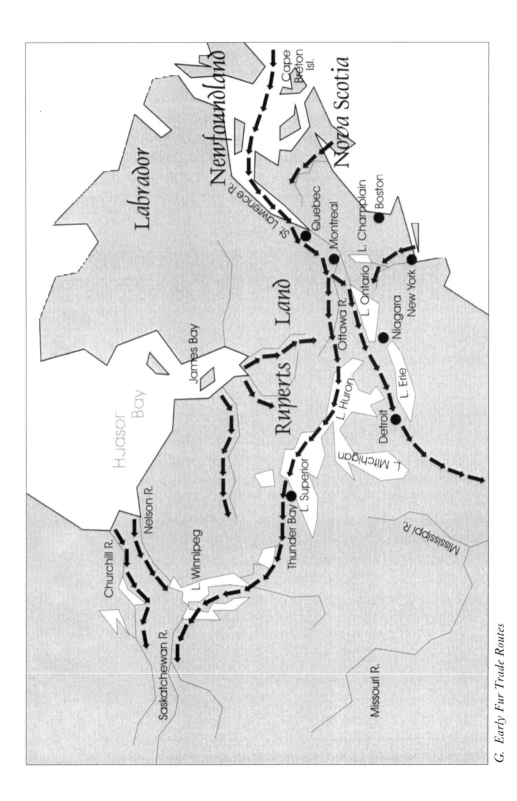

G. *Early Fur Trade Routes*

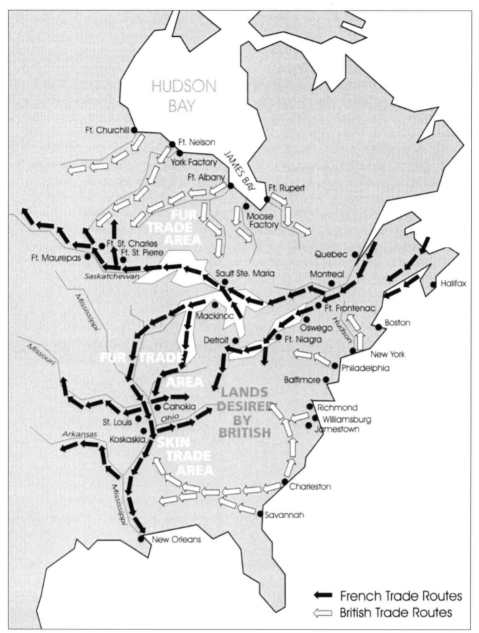

H. *Anglo-French Continental Rivalry 1700–1750*

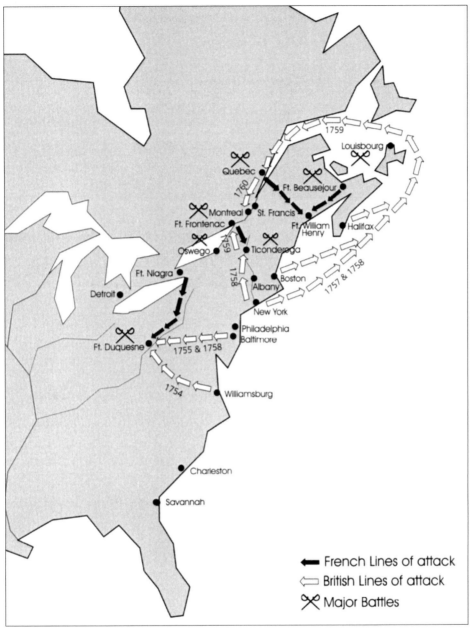

I. *French & Indian War 1754–1760*

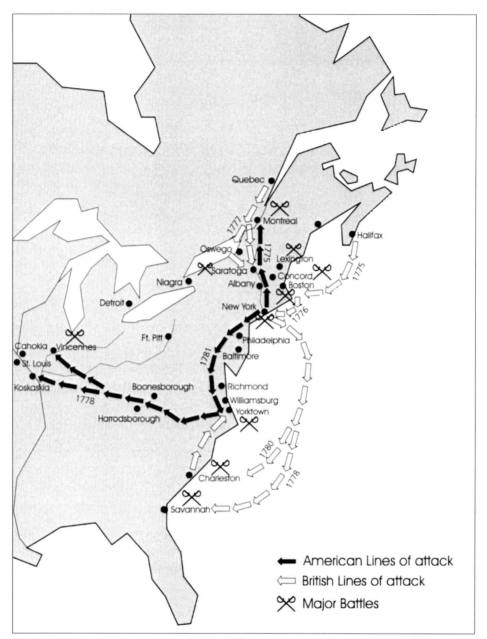

Quebec

1777

Montreal

1775

Halifax

Oswego

Lexington

Saratoga

Concord

Niagra

Albany

Boston

Detroit

New York

1776

Ft. Pitt

Cahokia   Vincennes

Philadelphia

1781

St. Louis

Baltimore

Koskaskia

Boonesborough

Richmond

1778

Williamsburg

Harrodsborough

Yorktown

1780

Charleston

1778

Savannah

◀━━ American Lines of attack

⇐ British Lines of attack

✖ Major Battles

J. War of the American Revolution 1775–1782

Notes

Chapter 1

1. For additional details see Else Roesdahl, *The Vikings* (Harmondsworth, Penguin, 1991) and F. Donald Logan, *The Vikings in History* (London, Routledge, 1991)
2. Logan, *op. cit.*, pp. 24–5
3. *Ibid.*, p. 28
4. Roesdahl, *op. cit.*, p. 83
5. *Ibid.*, p. 192
6. M. Magnusson and H. Palsson, trans. and intro., *The Vinland Sagas. The Norse Discovery of America* (Harmondsworth, Penguin, 1985), p. 100
7. *Ibid.*
8. G.J. Marcus, *The Conquest of the North Atlantic* (New York, Oxford University Press, 1981), p. 76
9. *Ibid.*, p. 5–15, 24, and elsewhere
10. *Ibid.*, p. 39
11. Dennis O. Flynn, 'Comparing the Tokagawa Shogunate with Habsburg Spain: Two Silver-Based Empires in a Global Setting', in James D. Tracy (ed.), *The Political Economy of Merchants Empires* (Cambridge, Cambridge University Press, 1991), p. 358
12. Roesdahl, *op. cit.*, pp. 86–7
13. *Ibid.*, pp. 89–91
14. *Ibid.*, p. 92
15. Logan, *op. cit.*, p. 33

Chapter 2

1. Richard W. Unger, *The Ship in the Medieval Economy, 600–1600* (Montreal, McGill-Queen's Press, 1980), *Dutch Shipbuilding Before 1800* (Amsterdam, Van Gorcum, 1978), and *Cogs, Caravels and Galleons: The Sailing Ship 1000–1650* (Annapolis, Naval Institute Press, 1993)
2. Carla Rahn Phillips, *Six Galleons for the King of Spain. Imperial Defence in the Early Seventeenth Century* (Baltimore, Johns Hopkins University Press, 1986)
3. Oscar H.K. Spate, *The Spanish Lake* (Canberra, ANU, 1979)
4. Unger, *The Ship in the Medieval Economy*, pp. 259–60
5. J.F. Guilmartin, *Gunpowder and Galleys. Changing Technology and Mediterranean Warfare at Sea in the Sixteenth Century* (Cambridge, Cambridge University Press, 1974), pp. 157–8
6. *Ibid.*, pp. 135–75
7. George Modelski and W.R. Thompson, *Seapower in Global Politics, 1494–1993* (Seattle, University of Washington Press, 1988), p. 161
8. Unger, *The Ship in the Medieval Economy*, p. 234
9. Carlo M. Cipolla, *Guns and Sails in the Early Phase of European Expansion 1400–1700* (London, Collins, 1965)

10. William H. McNeill, *The Pursuit of Power. Technology, Armed Forces, and Society since AD 1000* (Chicago, University of Chicago Press, 1982)

11. Guilmartin, *op. cit.*, p. 257

12. For example, in-depth studies of conquistadors do not now suggest that firearms were a major cause of their conquests. See George Raudzens, 'So Why Were the Aztecs Conquered, and What Were the Wider Implications?' in *War in History*, II, no. 1, 1995, pp. 87–104

13. Geoffrey Parker, *The Military Revolution. Military Innovation and the Rise of the West, 1500–1800* (Cambridge, Cambridge University Press, 1988)

14. Frank Tallett, *War and Society in Early Modern Europe, 1495–1715* (London, Routledge, 1929)

15. Modelski and Thompson, *op. cit.*, especially pp. 166–9

16. *Ibid.*, pp. 152–3 and 166

17. Phillips, *op. cit.*, p. 8

18. Louise Levathes, *When China Ruled the Seas. The Treasure Fleet of the Dragon Throne, 1405–1433* (New York, Simon & Schuster, 1994)

19. Pearson, M.N., *The New Cambridge History of India. The Portuguese in India* (Cambridge, Cambridge University Press, 1987), pp. 29–31

20. Jaap R. Bruijn, *The Dutch Navy. The Seventeenth and Eighteenth Centuries* (Columbia, South Carolina, University of South Carolina Press, 1993), pp. 72–3

21. Unger, *The Ship in the Medieval Economy*, pp. 262–7, and *Dutch Shipbuilding Before 1800*, pp. 24–40

22. Modelski and Thompson, *op. cit.*, p. 105

23. E.D.S. Bradford, *The Story of the* Mary Rose (London, Hamish Hamilton, 1982)

24. Philip D. Curtin, *Cross-cultural Trade in World History* (Cambridge, Cambridge University Press, 1984), p. 7

25. R.I. Rotberg and T.K. Rabb, *Population and History. From the Traditional to the Modern World* (Cambridge, Cambridge University Press, 1986) p. 108

Chapter 3

1. B.W. Diffie and G.D. Winius, *Foundations of the Portuguese Empire 1415–1580* (Oxford, Oxford University Press, 1977), p. 212

2. Anthony M. Stevens-Arroyo, 'The Inter-Atlantic Paradigm: The Failure of Spanish Medieval Colonization of the Canarie and Caribbean Islands', in *Journal of Comparative Studies in Society and History*, vol. 35/3, July 1993, 515–43. More comments about this early Spanish colonization effort follow in Chapter 4.

3. M.N. Pearson, *The Portuguese in India* in *The New Cambridge History of India* (Cambridge, Cambridge University Press, 1987), p. 8; and P.D. Curtin, *Cross-cultural Trade in World History* (Cambridge, Cambridge University Press, 1984), pp. 138–9

4. Curtin, *op. cit.*, p. 139

5. Pearson, *op. cit.*, p. 6

6. John Thornton, *Africa and Africans in the Making of the Atlantic World, 1400–1680* (Cambridge, Cambridge University Press, 1992)

7. *Ibid.*, pp. 74–9, 97, 125

8. Ivana Elbl, 'Cross-Cultural Trade and Diplomacy: Portuguese Relations with West Africa, 1441–1521', in *Journal of World History*, vol. 3, no. 2, 1992, 165–204, pp. 177–8

9. Diffie and Winius, *op. cit.*, p. 214

10. Pearson, *op. cit.*, p. 58

11. Peter Padfield, *Tides of Empire. Decisive Naval Campaigns in the Rise of the West*, vol. I, 1481–1654 (London, Routledge and Kegan Paul, 1979), pp. 49–52

12. Diffie and Winius, *op. cit.*, p. 241

13. *Ibid.*, p. 248

14. *Ibid.*, p. 258

15. Pearson, *op. cit.*, p. 31

16. Sanjay Subrahmanyam, *The Portuguese Empire in Asia 1500–1700. A Political and Economic History* (London, Longman, 1993), pp. 74, 217

17. Curtin, *op. cit.*

18. Subrahmanyam, *op. cit.*, pp. 166, 189

19. *Ibid.*, pp. 61, 86, 142, 163, 183

20. Curtin, *op. cit.*, pp. 142–3

21. Subrahmanyam, *op. cit.* p. 217

22. Pearson, *op. cit.*, p. 34

23. H.B. Johnson, 'The Portuguese Settlement in Brazil, 1500–80', in Leslie Bethell (ed.), *The Cambridge History of Latin America, Vol. I, Colonial Latin America* (Cambridge, Cambridge University Press, 1984)

Chapter 4

1. The most recent analytical biography of Isabella in English is Peggy Liss, *Isabel the Queen. Life and Times* (New York, Oxford University Press, 1992). A standard analysis of Ferdinand and Isabella is that of Felipe Fernàndez-Armesto, *Ferdinand and Isabella* (New York, Dorset, 1991)

2. Anthony Stevens-Arroyo, 'The Inter-Atlantic Paradigm: The Failure of Spanish Medieval Colonization of the Canary and Caribbean Islands', in *Journal of Comparative Studies in Society and History*, vol. 35/3, July 1993, 515–43; and Elena Lourie, 'A Society Organized for War: Medieval Spain', in *Past and Present*, no. 35, December 1966, 54–76

   Note that Stevens-Arroyo considers that Spanish colonization of the Canaries and Hispaniola was a failure because it did not meet the high expectations of the colonizers for wealth and for Christian and Hispanicized converts and workers; far too many conquered workers died. But on the other hand colonial conquest succeeded only too well, and too permanently. At no time did it look like the Guanches or Tainos could reverse the process by armed or other forms of resistance.

3. Mascarenhas Barreto, *The Portuguese Columbus. Secret Agent of King John II* (London, Macmillan, 1992)

4. John Larner, 'The Certainty of Columbus: Some Recent Studies', *History*, 73, no. 237, February 1988, 3–23, p. 15

5. Felipe Fernàndez-Armesto, *Columbus* (Oxford, Oxford University Press, 1991), p. 32

6. *Ibid.* This outline of the New World activities of Columbus follows Fernàndez-Armesto. There is a chronology on pp. xvii–xx. Details and interpretations on the early Caribbean settlements come below.

7. Carl O. Sauer, *The Early Spanish Main* (Los Angeles, University of California Press, 1966. 1992 reprint edition), p. 86

8. George Raudzens, 'Why Did Amerindian Defences Fail', in *War in History*, III, no. 3, 1996, pp. 16–17, 331–52. See Appendix A

9. *Ibid.*, p. 20. The following pages are based on this article, which is reproduced in full in Appendix A.

10. *Ibid.*, p. 17, and elsewhere

11. For the post-Hispaniola pre-Mexican colonization, see in particular Carl O. Sauer above. See also D.J.R. Walker, *Columbus and the Golden World of the Island Arawaks* (Kingston, Jamaica, 1992) and Irving Rouse, *The Tainos. The Rise and Decline of the People Who Greeted Columbus* (New Haven, Yale University Press, 1992)

12. Ross Hassig, *Mexico and the Spanish Conquest* (London, Longman, 1994), pp. 36–52
13. Ross Hassig, *War and Society in Ancient Mesoamerica* (Berkeley, University of California Press, 1992), pp. 21, 141–5
14. R.C. Padden, *The Hummingbird and the Hawk: Conquest and Sovereignty in the Valley of Mexico, 1503–1541* (New York, 1967), pp. 72–4
15. Bernard Grunberg, 'The Origins of the Conquistadores of Mexico City', *Hispanic American Historical Review*, 74:2, May 1994, 259–83, p. 261
16. Francis J. Brooks, 'Revising the Conquest of Mexico; Smallpox, Sources and Populations', *Journal of Interdisciplinary History*, 24, no. 1, Summer, 1993, 1–29
17. Hernan Cortés, *Letters from Mexico* (New Haven, Yale University Press, 1986), pp. 215–32
18. Bernal Diaz, *The Conquest of New Spain* (Harmondsworth, Penguin, 1963), p. 149
19. Fray Bernardino de Sahagun, *Florentine Codex. General History of the Things of New Spain. Book 12 – The Conquest of Mexico* (Santa Fe, New Mexico, 1975), p. 62
20. George Raudzens, 'So Why Were the Aztecs Conquered, and What Were the Wider Implications? Testing Military Superiority as a Cause of Europe's Pre-industrial Colonial Conquests'. This article is reproduced in full in Appendix B
21. Ross Hassig, in *Mexico and the Spanish Conquest*, provides the following specific chronology of conquest events on pp. 159–60

SHORT CHRONOLOGY OF THE CONQUEST

1492	Columbus reaches the New World
1502	King Ahuitzotl dies and Moteuczoma Xocoyotl becomes the ninth Aztec king
1515	King Nezahualpilli of Tetzcoco dies and is succeeded by Cacama
1517	
8 February	Córdoba sails from Cuba
Late February	Córdoba reaches Yucatan
29 March	Córdoba reaches Campeche
20 April	Córdoba returns to Cuba
1518	
3 May	Grijalva reaches Cozumel
31 May	Grijalva reaches Laguna de Términos
11 June	Grijalva reaches Coatzacualco
15 November	Grijalva returns to Cuba
1519	
10 February	Cortés sails for Yucatan
21 April	Cortés reaches San Juan de Ulua
12 May	Aztecs decamp, abandoning Cortés
3 June	Cortés reaches Cempohuallan
Mid-June	Cortés leaves Cempohuallan on his march inland
26 July	Cortés dispatches a ship to Spain
2 September	Cortés fights first battle with Tlaxcaltecs
23 September	Cortés enters city of Tlaxcallan
10 October	Cortés leaves Tlaxcallan for Cholollan
c. 25 October	Cortés leaves Cholollan for Tenochtitlan

| 8 November | Cortés enters Tenochtitlan |
| 14 November | Cortés seizes Moteuczoma |

1520

20 April	Narváes lands at San Juan de Ulua
Feast of	Alvarado massacres the Aztec
Toxcatl	nobles
c. 27 May	Cortés reaches Narváez's camp at Cempohuallan
c. 28 May	Cortés attacks and defeats Narváez
24 June	Cortés reaches Tenochtitlan
29 June	Moteuczoma killed
30 June	Cortés and the Spaniards flee Tenochtitlan
11 July	Cortés and the Spaniards reach City of Tlaxcallan
1 August	Cortés marches against Tepeyacac
16 September	Cuitlahua becomes the tenth Aztec king
Mid-October	Smallpox epidemic begins in Tenochtitlan
Early	Smallpox epidemic ends in
December	Tenochtitlan
4 December	King Cuitlahua dies of smallpox
28 December	Cortés begins his return to Tenochtitlan

1521

February	Cuauhtemoc becomes the eleventh Aztec king
3 February	Cortés marches on Xaltocan
18 February	Cortés returns to Tetzcoco
5 April	Cortés begins march against Yauhtepec
11 April	Cortés reaches Yauhtepec
13 April	Cortés conquers Cuauhnahuac
16 April	Cortés reaches Xochimilco
18 April	Cortés is forced to withdraw from Xochimilco
22 April	Cortés returns to Tetzcoco
28 April	Cortés launches his brigantines
22 May	Alvarado, Olid and Sandoval are dispatched with three armies to begin the battle for Tenochtitlan
31 May	Sandoval and Olid link up at Coyohuacan
30 June	Sixty-eight Spaniards are captured in battle and sacrificed
Mid-July	Fresh munitions arrive from Vera Cruz
1 August	Spaniards reach the great market in Tlatelolco
13 August	Cuauhtemoc is captured and the Aztecs surrender

22. Hassig, *War and Society in Ancient Mesoamerica*, pp. 163–4
23. John C. Super, *Food, Conquest and Colonization in Sixteenth-Century Spanish America* (Albuquerque, New Mexico, University of New Mexico Press, 1988), p. 88
24. James Lockhart, *The Nahuas After the Conquest. A Social and Cultural History of the Indians of Central Mexico, Sixteenth Through Eighteenth Centuries* (Stanford, California, Stanford University Press, 1992), pp. 4–5
25. For a standard narration of the Inca conquest, see John Hemming, *The Conquest of the Incas*, (London, Macmillan, 1970)
26. Massimo Livi-Bacci, *A Concise History of World Population* (Oxford, Blackwell, 1992), p. 51

27. Carla Rahn Phillips, 'Trade in the Iberian empires, 1450–1750', in James D. Tracy, *The Rise of Merchant Empires* (Cambridge, Cambridge University Press, 1990), pp. 83–4
28. *Ibid.*, pp. 100–1. See also John Lynch, *Spain 1516–1598. From Nation to World Empire* (Oxford, Blackwell, 1991), pp. 174–105
29. *Ibid.*, p. 78
30. Peter Padfield, *Tide of Empires. Decisive Naval Campaigns in the Rise of the West* (London, Routledge, 1979), pp. 129–30
31. Most of the details about the early raiders of the Spanish empire can be found in Padfield, above, or in standard reference works. See also John Lynch, *Spain, 1516–1598. From Nation State to World Empire* (Oxford, Blackwell, 1991)
32. For details and bibliography on the Dutch economy and revolt, see Chapter V below
33. I have no idea why Hawkins, Drake and the other Elizabethan captains were called Seadogs either by contemporaries or later historians.
34. This English Armada interpretation appears in standard histories up to the late 1980s throughout the literature. Just one authoritative version comes in Peter Kemp (ed.), *The Oxford Companion to Ships and the Sea* (Oxford, Oxford University Press, 1976), pp. 38–9
35. José Luis Casado Soto, 'Atlantic Shipping in Sixteenth-Century Spain and the 1588 Armada', in M.J. Rodriguez-Salgado and Simon Adams (eds), *England, Spain and the Gran Armada, 1585–1604* (Savage, Maryland, Barnes and Noble, 1991), p. 125
36. *Ibid.*, pp. 114–22
37. I.A.A. Thompson, 'The Spanish Armada: Naval Warfare Between the Mediterranean and the Atlantic', in M.J. Rodriguez-Salgao, *op. cit.*, pp. 70–1
38. David C. Goodman, *Power and Penury. Government, Technology and Science in Philip II's Spain* (Cambridge, Cambridge University Press, 1988), pp. 88–9, 173

Chapter 5

1. Jonathan I. Israel, *Dutch Primacy in World Trade, 1585–1740* (Oxford, Clarendon, 1989) pp. 12–13
2. Pieter Geyl, *The Revolt of the Netherlands, 1555–1609* (London, 1962)
3. Richard W. Unger, *Dutch Shipbuilding Before 1800. Ships and Guilds* (Amsterdam, Van Gorcum, 1978), p. 118
4. *Ibid.*, p. 11
5. *Ibid.*
6. *Ibid.*, especially p. 25. See also Jaap R. Bruijn, *The Dutch Navy at the Seventeenth and Eighteenth Centuries* (Columbia, South Carolina, University of South Carolina Press, 1993), pp. 43–74
7. Bruijn, *op. cit.*, p. 73
8. Frank Tallett, *War and Society in Early Modern Europe, 1495–1715* (London, Routledge, 1992), pp. 24–6
9. *Ibid.*, p. 24
10. Israel, *op. cit.*, p. 412
11. *Ibid.*, p. 413
12. This section on the Dutch overseas efforts is based on Israel, *op. cit.*, on Holden Furber, *Rival Empires of Trade in the Orient, 1600–1800* (Minneapolis, University of Minnesota Press, 1976), and on C.R. Boxer, *The Dutch Seaborne Empire, 1600–1800* (London, Hutchinson, 1966). There are no major recent reinterpretations in English
13. C.R. Boxer, *op. cit.*, p. 99
14. *Ibid.* and Geoffrey Scammell, *The World Encompassed. The First European Maritime Empires* c. *800–1650* (Berkeley, University of California Press, 1981), pp. 401–10

15. Jonathan I. Israel, *The Dutch Republic and the Hispanic World, 1606–1661* (Oxford, Clarendon, 1986), p. 117

16. For some of the most recent interpretations of key WIC activities see Johannes Menne Postma, *The Dutch in the Atlantic Slave Trade, 1600–1815* (Cambridge, Cambridge University Press, 1990)

17. Israel, *Dutch Primacy in World Trade*, p. 411

Chapter 6

1. Patrick O'Brien, 'European Economic Development: The Contribution of the Periphery', in *The Economic History Review*, 2nd series, XXXV, no. 1, February 1982, 1–18, p. 18

2. P.K. O'Brien and S.L. Engerman, 'Exports and the growth of the British economy from the Glorious Revolution to the Peace of Amiens' in Barbara L. Solow (ed.), *Slavery and the Rise of the Atlantic System* (Cambridge, Cambridge University Press, 1991), p. 179

3. Massimo Livi-Bacci, *A Concise History of World Population* (Oxford, Blackwell, 1992)

4. George Modelski and William R. Thompson, *Seapower in Global Politics, 1494–1993* (Seattle, University of Washington Press, 1988), p. 215

5. *Ibid.*, p. 218

6. J.J. McCusker and R.R. Menard, *The Economy of British America, 1607–1789* (Chapel Hill, University of North Carolina Press, 1985), p. 118

7. This summary of early Virginia Amerindian wars is based on the article by George Raudzens, 'Why did Amerindian defences fail?', in Appendix B

8. McCusker and Menard, *op. cit.*, pp. 118–19. For details on early Virginia see also Carl Bridenbaugh, *Jamestown 1544–1699* (New York, Ocford University Press, 1980)

9. Michael Williams, *Americans and Their Forests. A Historical Geography* (Cambridge, Cambridge University Press, 1989), p. 67. But see also other sections for the benefits the poorer colonists derived from the natural flora and fauna of the early colonies

10. These figures come from McCusker and Menard, *op. cit.*, p. 136

11. Neal Salisbury, *Manitou and Providence. Indians, Europeans, and the Making of New England* (Oxford, Oxford University Press, 1982), pp. 110–40

12. For details of the cost of migration and settlement see David Cressy, *Coming Over. Migration and Communication between England and New England* (Cambridge, Cambridge University Press, 1987)

13. McCusker and Menard, *op. cit.*, p. 103

14. William L. Shea, *The Virginia Militia in the Seventeenth Century* (London, Louisiana State University Press, 1983), pp. 16, 31, and elsewhere

15. Patrick M. Malone, *The Skulking Way of War. Technology and Tactics Among the New England Indians* (Baltimore, Johns Hopkins University Press, 1991)

16. Ralph Davis, *The Rise of the Atlantic Economies* (London, Weidenfeld and Nicholson, 1982), p. 265

17. Philip D. Curtin, *The Rise and Fall of the Plantation Complex* (Cambridge, Cambridge University Press, 1990), and Barbara L. Solow, *op. cit.*

18. McCusker and Menard, *op. cit.*, p. 54

19. Barbara L. Solow, *op. cit.*, p. 1

20. *Ibid.*, p. 28

21. Ralph Davis, *op. cit.*, p. 252

22. *Ibid.*, p. 257

23. Barbara L. Solow, *op. cit.*, p. 27

24. *Ibid.*, p. 29

25. Modelski and Thompson, *op. cit.*, pp. 217–18

26. For details of the Anglo-Dutch naval wars, see Paul Kennedy, *The Rise and Fall of British Naval Mastery* (London, 1976), J.R. Bruijn, *op. cit.*, Peter Padfield, *op. cit.*, and Helmut Pemsel, *Atlas of Naval Warfare* (London, Arms and Armour Press, 1977)
27. Jeremy Black, *European Warfare, 1660–1815* (London, UCL Press, 1994)
28. Modelski and Thompson, *op. cit.*, pp. 197 and 218
29. Modelski and Thompson, *op. cit.*, pp. 197, 218 and 257
30. *Ibid.*, pp. 198, 219 and 258
31. See Padfield, *op. cit.*, and Pemsel, *op. cit.*

Chapter 7

1. Harold A. Innis, *The Fur Trade in Canada* (New Haven, Yale University Press, 1930)
2. William Eccles, *Essays on New France* (Toronto, Oxford University Press, 1987). See also his other works, such as *The Canadian Frontier 1534–1760* (New York, Holt, Rinehart, 1969) and *France in America* (New York, Harper and Row, 1972). The political and economic details in this chapter are derived in large part from the Eccles interpretation.
3. Eric R. Wolf, *Europe and the People Without History* (Berkeley, University of California Press, 1962), p. 163
4. Ian K. Steele, *Warpaths. Invasions of North America* (New York, Oxford University Press, 1994), pp. 64–5
5. *Ibid.*, p. 114
6. *Ibid.*, p. 115
7. William Eccles, *France in America*, pp. 34–51
8. Steele, *op. cit.*, pp. 117–18
9. *Ibid.*, p. 73
10. Jeremy Black, *European Warfare, 1660–1815* (London, UCL Press, 1994), p. 7. See also Russell F. Weigley, *The Age of Battles* (Bloomington, Indiana University Press, 1991), pp. 45–58
11. For general information on the kingship of Louis XIV see Pierre Goubert, *Louis XIV and Twenty Million Frenchmen* (London, Alan Lane, 1970) and Roger Mettam, *Power and Faction in Louis XIV's France* (Oxford, Blackwell, 1988)
12. Steele, *op. cit.*, p. 73. See also Patrick M. Malone, *The Skulking Way of War*, *op. cit.*
13. Steele, *op. cit.*, pp. 74–5. See also Jack Verney, *The Good Regiment. The Carignan-Salières Regiment in Canada, 1665–1668* (Montreal, McGill-Queen's University Press, 1991)
14. Up to 1760 a total of just under 30,000 French people went to New France but most left again and only 8,000 or so settled. See Bernard Bailyn, *The Peopling of the British Peripheries in the Eighteenth Century* (Canberra, The Australian Academy of Science, 1988), p. 4
15. Eccles, *France in America*, p. 151
16. Richard White, *The Middle Ground. Indians, Empires and Republics in the Great Lakes Region, 1650–1815* (Cambridge, Cambridge University Press, 1991). See Chapter 1
17. Steele, *op. cit.*, pp. 137–43
18. Eccles, *Essays on New France*, pp. 80–3

Chapter 8

1. Patrick O'Brien, 'European Economic Development: The Contribution of the Periphery', *op. cit.*, p. 5, and elsewhere
2. D.W. Jones, *War and Economy in the Age of William III and Marlborough* (Oxford, Blackwell, 1988), pp. 311–17
3. John Brewer, *The Sinews of Power. War, Money and the English State, 1688–1783* (New York, Alfred A. Knopf, 1989)

4. *Ibid.*, p. 115, and elsewhere
5. *Ibid.*, pp. 40–1
6. P.K. O'Brien and P.A. Hunt, 'The Rise of the Fiscal State in England, 1485–1815', in *Historical Research*, 66, no. 160, June 1993, 129–176, p. 163
7. There are many good works on Frederick II but see for example Russell F. Weigley, *The Age of Battles. The Quest for Decisive Warfare from Breitenfeld to Waterloo* (Bloomington, Indiana University Press, 1991), pp. 167–95
8. Douglas Edward Leach, *Arms for Empire. A Military History of the British Colonies in North America, 1607–1763* (New York, Macmillan, 1973), pp. 230–41
9. McCosker and Menard, *op. cit.*, p. 54
10. W.J. Eccles, *France in America*, pp. 120, 180, 243, 246
11. McCosker and Menard, *op. cit.*, p. 55
12. *Ibid.*, p. 55
13. See Leach, *op. cit.*, pp. 334–41
14. Eccles, *France in America*, p. 184
15. Christopher Duffy, *The Army of Maria Theresa. The Armed Forces of Imperial Austria, 1740–1780* (London, David and Charles, 1977), pp. 147, 171–2, 173–5, 184–7, 190–1, 194–5, 199–200. See also Gerhard Ritter, *Frederick the Great. A Historical Profile* (Berkeley, University of California Press, 1970)

Chapter 9

1. Jared Diamond, *Guns, Germs and Steel. The Fates of Human Societies* (New York, W.W. Norton, 1997)
2. H.H. Lamb, *Climate, History and the Modern world* (New York, Routledge, 1995), pp. 288–9 and elsewhere
3. David Grigg, *Population Growth and Agricultural Change. An Historical Perspective* (Cambridge, Cambridge University Press, 1980), pp. 55–7
4. David Cressy, *Coming Over. Migration and Communication Between England and New England in the Seventeenth Century* (Cambridge, Cambridge University Press, 1987), p. 146. See also Ian K. Steele, *The English Atlantic, 1675–1740. An Exploration of Communication and Community* (Oxford, Oxford University Press, 1986), pp. 5–13
5. Sanjay Subrahmanyan, *The Portuguese Empire in Asia, 1500–1700: A Political and Economic History* (Harlow, Essex, Longman Group, 1983), p. 217
6. Nicolas Sanchez-Albornos, 'The First Transatlantic Transfer: Spanish Migration to the New world, 1493–1810', in Nicholas Canny, *Europeans on the Move. Studies on European Migration, 1500–1800*, (Oxford, Clarendon Press, 1994), pp. 27–8.
7. J.H. Parry, *The Spanish Seaborne Empire* (London, Hutchinson, 1966), pp. 234–5
8. *Ibid.*, p. 240
9. W.J. Eccles, *The Canadian Frontier 1534–1760* (New York, Holt Rinehart & Winston, 1969), p. 85
10. Bernard Bailyn, *The Peopling of British North America* (New York, Alfred A. Knopf, 1986), pp. 25–6. See also Nicholas Canny, *op. cit.*, p. 49
11. J.J. McCusker and R.R. Menard, *The Economy of British America, 1607–1789* (Chapel Hill, University of North Carolina Press, 1985), p. 54
12. Steele, *op. cit.*, p. 13
13. Massimo Livi-Bacci, *A Concise History of World Population* (Oxford, Blackwell, 1992), p. 31
14. William H. McNeill, *Plagues and Peoples* (New York, Doubleday, 1977)
15. Alfred W. Crosby, *Ecological Imperialism. The Biological Expansion of Europe, 900–1900* (Cambridge, Cambridge University Press, 1986)

16. Diamond, *op. cit.*

17. Francis Brooks, 'Revising the Conquest of Mexico: Smallpox, Sources, and Populations', *Journal of Interdisciplinary History* XXIV:I, Summer 1993, 1–29

18. George Raudzens, 'So Why Were the Aztecs Conquered, and What Were the Wider Implications?', *War in History*, II, no. 1, 1995, 87–104, and 'Why Did Amerindian Defences Fail?', *War in History* III, no. 3, 1996, 331–52

19. See especially W.H. McNeill, *The Pursuit of Power. Technology, Armed Forces, and Society Since AD 1000* (Chicago, University of Chicago Press, 1982) for the statement of 'gunpowder revolution' and 'gunpowder empires' argument. For the Military Revolution as currently argued, see Geoffrey Parker, *The Military Revolution* (Cambridge, Cambridge University Press, 1988); Jeremy Black, *European Warfare 1660–1815* (London, UCL Press, 1994); Frank Tallett, *War and Society in Early Modern Europe, 1495–1715* (London, Routledge, 1992); and David Eltis, *The Military Revolution in Sixteenth-Century Europe* (New York, I.B. Tauris, 1995)

20. See Patrick M. Malone, *The Skulking Way of War. Technology and Tactics Among the New England Indians* (Baltimore, Johns Hopkins University Press, 1991); Raudzens, 'Why Did Amerindian Defences Fail?'; and Leroy V. Eid, '"A Kind of Running Fight": Indian Battlefield Tactics in the Late Eighteenth Century', *The Western Pennsylvania Historical Magazine*, vol. 71, no. 2, April 1988, 147–71

21. Louise Levathes, *When China Ruled the Seas. The Treasure Fleet of the Dragon Throne 1405–1433* (New York, Simon and Schuster, 1994). Levathes concentrates on Chinese politics rather than maritime technology and institutions. But she is emphatic that the cancellation of China's seafaring enterprises was a deliberate political and cultural act by the central government, not any sort of technological or institutional decline.

22. See Carlo M. Cipolla, *Guns and Sails in the Early Phase of European Expansion, 1400–1700* (London, Collins, 1965); J.H. Parry, *The Spanish Seaborne Empire* (London, Hutchinson, 1966); C.R. Boxer, *The Dutch Seaborne Empire, 1600–1800* (London, Hutchinson, 1966); and G.V. Scammell, *The World Encompassed. The First European Maritime Empires, c. 800–1650* (Berkeley, University of California Press, 1981)

23. See A.T. Mahan, *The Influence of Seapower Upon History, 1660–1783* (London, 1890); R.G. Albion, *Forests and Sea Power. The Timber Problem of the Royal Navy, 1652–1862* (Hamden, Connecticut, Harvard University Press, 1926); Gerald Graham, *Empire of the North Atlantic* (Toronto, University of Toronto Press, 1950); Paul Kennedy, *The Rise and Fall of British Naval Mastery* (London, Ashfield Press, 1976); and George Modelski and William P. Thompson, *Seapower in Global Politics, 1494–1993* (Seattle, University of Washington Press, 1988)

24. Ralph Davis, *The Rise of the English Shipping Industry in the Seventeenth and Eighteenth Centuries* (Newbolt Abbot, David and Charles, 1962). While Davis is still the most thorough analyst of the growth of English shipping, he makes little attempt to assess its impact on European shipping or the European economy. He does not credit shipping expansion by itself with much contribution to English wealth and power

25. Ian K. Steele, *The English Atlantic 1675–1740* (Oxford, Oxford University Press, 1986). See especially pp. 5–17

26. See B.W. Diffie and G.D. Winnius, *Foundations of the Portuguese Empire, 1415–1580* (Oxford, Oxford University Press, 1977), and M.N. Pearson, *The Portuguese in India* (Cambridge, Cambridge University Press, 1987)

27. Roger C. Smith, *Vanguard of Empire. Ships of Exploration in the Age of Columbus* (Oxford, Oxford University Press, 1993). See also Richard W. Unger, *The Ship in the Medieval Economy, 600–1600* (London, Croom Helm, 1980). For an assessment of the qualitative superiority of Spanish ships, see Carla Rahn Phillips, *Six Galleons for the King of Spain. Imperial Defence in the Early Seventeenth Century* (Baltimore, Johns Hopkins University Press, 1986)

28. Raudzens, 'Why Did Amerindian Defences Fail?'

29. C. Harvey Gardiner, *Naval Power in the Conquest of Mexico* (Austin, University of Texas Press, 1956). See especially pp. 186–203

30. Raudzens, 'So Why Were the Aztecs Conquered, and What Were the Wider Implications?'

31. Raudzens, 'Why Did Amerindian Defences Fail?'

32. See J.J. McCusker and R.R. Menard, *The Economy of British America, 1607–1789* (Chapel Hill, University of North Carolina Press, 1985)

33. While birchbark canoe determinism is not a big feature of the histories of Algonquian-European relations, for general background the best surveys are those of W.J. Eccles, especially his *Essays on New France* (Toronto, Oxford University Press, 1987), of Ian K. Steele in *Warpaths. Invasions of North America* (Oxford, Oxford University Press, 1994), and of Bruce G. Trigger in *Natives and Newcomers: Canada's 'Heroic Age' Reconsidered* (Kingston, Ontario, McGill-Queen's University Press, 1985)

34. Quoted in Ian K. Steele, *Warpaths*, p. 16

35. Eric Williams, *Capitalism and Slavery* (New York, 1966)

36. See Barbara L. Solow and Stanley L. Engerman (eds), *British Capitalism and Caribbean Slavery. The Legacy of Eric Williams* (Cambridge, Cambridge University Press, 1987), and Barbara L. Solow (ed.), *Slavery and the Rise of the Atlantic System* (Cambridge, Cambridge University Press, 1991)

37. D.W. Jones, *War and Economy in the Age of William III and Marlborough* (London, Blackwell, 1988)

38. John Brewer, *The Sinews of Power. War, Money and the English State, 1688–1783* (New York, Alfred A. Knopf, 1989)

39. P.K. O'Brien and R. Quinault, *The Industrial Revolution and British Society* (Cambridge, Cambridge University Press, 1993)

Bibliography

Chapter 1

Logan, F. Donald, *The Vikings in History* (London, Routledge, 1991)

Magnusson, M. and H. Palsson, trans. and intro., *The Vinland Sagas. The Norse Discovery of America* (Harmondsworth, Penguin, 1985)

Marcus, G.J., *The Conquest of the North Atlantic* (New York, Oxford University Press, 1981)

Roesdahl, Else, *The Vikings* (Harmondsworth, Penguin, 1991)

Sawyer, P.H., *Kings and Vikings* (London, Methuen, 1982)

Tracy, James D. (ed.), *The Political Economy of Merchant Empires* (Cambridge, Cambridge University Press, 1991)

Chapter 2

Bradford, E.D.S., *The Story of the* Mary Rose (London, Hamilton 1982)

Bruijn, Jaap R., *The Dutch Navy. The Seventeenth and Eighteenth Centuries* (Columbia, South Carolina, University of South Carolina Press, 1993)

Curtin, Philip D., *Cross-cultural Trade in World History* (Cambridge, Cambridge University Press, 1984)

Cipolla, Carlo M., *Guns and Sails in the Early Phase of European Expansion 1400–1700* (London, Collins, 1965)

Guilmartin, J.F., *Gunpowder and Galleys. Changing Technology and Mediterranean Warfare at Sea in the Sixteenth Century* (Cambridge, Cambridge University Press, 1974)

Levathes, Louise, *When China Ruled the Seas. The Treasure Fleet of the Dragon Throne, 1405–1433* (New York, Simon and Schuster, 1994)

McNeill, William H., *The Pursuit of Power. Technology, Armed Forces and Society Since AD 1000* (Chicago, University of Chicago Press, 1982)

Modelski, George and W.R. Thompson, *Seapower in Global Politics, 1494–1993* (Seattle, University of Washington Press, 1988)

Parker, Geoffrey, *The Military Revolution. Military Innovation and the Rise of the West, 1500–1800* (Cambridge, Cambridge University Press, 1988)

Pearson, M.N., *The Portuguese in India* in *The New Cambridge History of India* series (Cambridge, Cambridge University Press, 1987)

Phillips, Carla Rahn, *Six Galleons for the King of Spain. Imperial Defence in the Early Seventeenth Century* (Baltimore, Johns Hopkins University Press, 1986)

Rotberg, R.I. and T.K. Rabb, *Population and History. From the Traditional to the Modern World* (Cambridge, Cambridge University Press, 1986)

Spate, Oscar H.K., *The Spanish Lake* (Canberra, ANU Press, 1979)

Tallett, Frank, *War and Society in Early Modern Europe, 1495–1715* (London, Routledge, 1989)

Unger, Richard W., *The Ship in the Medieval Economy 600–1600* (Montreal, McGill-Queen's University Press, 1980)

——, *Dutch Shipbuilding Before 1800* (Amsterdam, Van Gorcum, 1978)

——, *Cogs, Caravels and Galleons. The Sailing Ship 1000–1650* (Annapolis, Naval Institute Press, 1993)

Chapter 3

Chaunu, Pierre, *European Expansion in the Later Middle Ages* (Oxford, Oxford University Press, 1979)

Curtin, Philip D., *Cross-cultural Trade in World History* (Cambridge, Cambridge University Press, 1984)

Diffie, B.W. and Winius, G.D., *Foundations of the Portuguese Empire 1415–1580* (Oxford, Oxford University Press, 1977)

Johnson, H.B., *Colonial Latin America*, vol. I in Leslie Bethell (ed.), *The Cambridge History of Latin America* (Cambridge, Cambridge University Press, 1984)

Padfield, Peter, *Tide of Empires. Decisive Naval Campaigns in the Rise of the West* (London, Routledge, 1979)

Pearson, M.N., *The Portuguese in India*, vol. ? in ?? (ed.), *The New Cambridge History of India* (Cambridge, Cambridge University Press, 1987)

Reid, Anthony, *South-east Asia in the Age of Commerce, 1450–1680*, vol. I, *The Lands Below the Winds* (New Haven, Yale University Press, 1988)

Russell-Wood, A.J.R., *A World on the Move. The Portuguese in Africa, Asia, and America, 1415–1808* (Manchester, Carcanet Press, 1992)

Souza, George B., *The Survival of Empire. Portuguese Trade and Society in China and the South China Sea, 1630–1754* (Cambridge, Cambridge University Press, 1986)

Thornton, John, *Africa and Africans in the Making of the Atlantic World, 1400–1680* (Cambridge, Cambridge University Press, 1992)

Chapter 4

Barreto, Mascarenhas, *The Portuguese Columbus. Secret Agent of King John II* (London, Macmillan, 1992)

Cortés, Hernan, *Letters from Mexico* (New Haven, Yale University Press, 1986)

Diaz, Bernal, *The Conquest of New Spain* (Harmondsworth, Penguin, 1963)

Fernàndez-Armesto, Felipe, *Ferdinand and Isabella* (New York, Dorset, 1991)

——, *Columbus* (Oxford, Oxford University Press, 1991)

Goodman, David C., *Power and Penury. Government, Technology and Science in Philip II's Spain* (Cambridge, Cambridge University Press, 1988)

Hassig, Ross, *War and Society in Ancient Mesoamerica* (Berkeley, University of California Press, 1992)

——, *Mexico and the Spanish Conquest* (London, Longmans, 1994)

Hemming, John, *The Conquest of the Incas* (London, Macmillan, 1970)

Liss, Peggy, *Isabel the Queen. Life and Times* (New York, Oxford University Press, 1992)

Livi-Bacci, Massimo, *A Concise History of World Population* (Oxford, Blackwell, 1992)

Lockhart, James, *The Nahuas After the Conquest. A Social and Cultural History of the Indians of Central Mexico, Sixteenth Through Eighteenth Centuries* (Stanford, California, Stanford University Press, 1992)

Lynch, John, *Spain 1516–1598. From Nation to World Empire* (Oxford, Blackwell, 1991)

Padden, R.C., *The Hummingbird and the Hawk: Conquest and Sovereignty in the Valley of Mexico, 1503–1541* (New York, Harper, 1967)

Rodriguez-Salgado, M.J. and Simon Adams (eds), *England, Spain and the Gran Armada, 1585–1604* (Savage, Maryland, Barnes and Noble, 1991)

Rouse, Irving, *The Tainos. The Rise and Decline of the People Who Greeted Columbus* (New Haven, Yale University Press, 1992)

Sahagun, Fray Bernardino de, *Florentine Codex. General History of the Things of New Spain. Book 12 – The Conquest of Mexico* (Santa Fe, New Mexico, University of New Mexico Press, 1975)

Sauer, Carl O., *The Early Spanish Main* (Los Angeles, University of California Press, 1992)

Super, John C., *Food, Conquest and Colonization in Sixteenth-Century Spanish America* (Albuquerque, University of New Mexico Press, 1988)

Tracy, James D., *The Rise of Merchant Empires* (Cambridge, Cambridge University Press, 1991)

Walker, D.J.R., *Columbus and the Golden World of the Island Arawaks* (Kingston, Jamaica, 1992)

Chapter 5

Boxer, C.R., *The Dutch Seaborne Empire, 1600–1800* (London, Hutchinson, 1966)

Bruijn, Jaap R., *The Dutch Navy in the Seventeenth and Eighteenth Centuries* (Columbia, South Carolina, University of South Carolina Press, 1993)

Furber, Holden, *Rival Empires of Trade in the Orient, 1600–1800* (Minneapolis, University of Minnesota Press, 1976)

Geyl, Pieter, *The Revolt of the Netherlands, 1555–1609* (London, 1962)

Israel, Jonathan I., *The Dutch Republic and the Hispanic World, 1606–1661* (Oxford, Clarendon, 1986)

——, *Dutch Primacy in World Trade, 1585–1740* (Oxford, Clarendon, 1989)

Postma, J.M., *The Dutch in the Atlantic Slave Trade, 1600–1815* (Cambridge, Cambridge University Press, 1990)

Scammell, Geoffrey, *The World Encompassed. The First European Maritime Empires* c. *800–1650* (Berkeley, University of California Press, 1981)

Tallett, Frank, *War and Society in Early Modern Europe* (London, Routledge, 1989)

Unger, R.W., *Dutch Shipbuilding Before 1800. Ships and Guilds* (Amsterdam, Van Gorcum, 1978)

Chapter 6

Black, Jeremy, *European Warfare, 1660–1815* (London, UCL Press, 1994)

Bridenbaugh, Carl, *Jamestown 1544–1699* (New York, Oxford University Press, 1980)

Cressy, David, *Coming Over. Migration and Communication between England and New England* (Cambridge, Cambridge University Press, 1987)

Curtin, Philip D., *The Rise and Fall of the Plantation Complex* (Cambridge, Cambridge University Press, 1990)

Davis, Ralph, *The Rise of the Atlantic Economies* (London, Weidenfeld and Nicholson, 1982)

Kennedy, Paul, *The Rise and Fall of British Naval Mastery* (London, Ashfield Press, 1976)

Livi-Bacci, Massimo, *A Concise History of World Population* (Oxford, Blackwell, 1992)

McCusker, J.J. and R.R. Menard, *The Economy of British America, 1607–1789* (Chapel Hill, University of North Carolina Press, 1985)

Malone, Patrick M., *The Skulking Way of War. Technology and Tactics Among the New England Indians* (Baltimore, Johns Hopkins University Press, 1991)

Modelski, George and W.R. Thompson, *Seapower in Global Politics, 1494–1993* (Seattle, University of Washington Press, 1988)

Padfield, Peter, *Tide of Empires. Decisive Naval Campaigns in the Rise of the West* (London, Routledge, 1979)

Pemsel, Helmut, *Atlas of Naval Warfare* (London, Arms and Armour Press, 1977)

Salisbury, Neal, *Manitou and Providence. Indians, Europeans, and the Making of New England* (Oxford, Oxford University Press, 1982)

Shea, William L., *The Virginia Militia in the Seventeenth Century* (London, Louisiana State University Press, 1983)

Solow, Barbara L. (ed.), *Slavery and the Rise of the Atlantic System* (Cambridge, Cambridge University Press, 1991)

Williams, Michael, *Americans and Their Forests. A Historical Geography* (Cambridge, Cambridge University Press, 1989)

Chapter 7

Bailyn, Bernard, *The Peopling of the British Peripheries in the Eighteenth Century* (Canberra, The Australian Academy of Science, 1988)

Black, Jeremy, *European Warfare 1660–1815* (London, UCL Press, 1994)

Eccles, William, *Essays on New France* (Toronto, Oxford University Press, 1987)

——, *The Canadian Frontier 1534–1760* (New York, Holt, Rinehart, 1969)

——, *France in America* (New York, Harper and Row, 1972)

Goubert, Pierre, *Louis XIV and Twenty Million Frenchmen* (London, Alan Lane, 1970)

Innis, Harold A., *The Fur Trade in Canada* (New Haven, Yale University Press, 1930)

Malone, Patrick M., *The Skulking Way of War. Technology and Tactics Among the New England Indians* (Baltimore, Johns Hopkins University Press, 1991)

Mettam, Roger, *Power and Faction in Louis XIV's France* (Oxford, Blackwell, 1988)

Steele, Ian K., *Warpaths. Invasions of North America* (Oxford, Oxford University Press, 1994)

Varney, Jack, *The Good Regiment. The Carignan-Salierès Regiment in Canada, 1665–1668* (Montreal, McGill-Queen's University Press, 1991)

Weigley, Russell F., *The Age of Battles. The Quest for Decisive Warfare from Breitenfeld to Waterloo* (Bloomington, Indiana University Press, 1991)

White, Richard, *The Middle Ground. Indians, Empires and Republics in the Great Lakes Region, 1650–1815* (Cambridge, Cambridge University Press, 1991)

Wolf, Eric R., *Europe and the People Without History* (Berkeley, University of California Press, 1962)

Chapter 8

Brewer, John, *The Sinews of Power. War, Money and the English State, 1688–1783* (New York, Alfred A. Knopf, 1989)

Duffy, Christopher, *The Army of Maria Theresa. The Armed Forces of Imperial Austria, 1740–1780* (London, David and Charles, 1977)

Jones, D.W., *War and Economy in the Age of William III and Marlborough* (Oxford, Blackwell, 1988)

Leach, Douglas Edward, *Arms for Empire. A Military History of the British Colonies in North America, 1607–1763* (New York, Macmillan, 1973)

Ritter, Gerhard, *Frederick the Great. A Historical Profile* (Berkeley, University of California Press, 1970)

Weigley, Russell F., *The Age of Battles. The Quest for Decisive Warfare from Breitenfeld to Waterloo* (Bloomington, Indiana University Press, 1991)

Chapter 9

Albion, R.G., *Forests and Sea Power. The Timber Problem of the Royal Navy 1652–1862* (Hamden, Connecticut, Harvard University Press, 1926)

Bailyn, Bernard, *The Peopling of British North America* (New York, Alfred A. Knopf, 1986)

Black, Jeremy, *European Warfare 1660–1815* (London, UCL Press, 1994)

Boxer, C.R., *The Dutch Seaborne Empire, 1600–1800* (London, Hutchinson, 1966)

Brewer, John, *The Sinews of Power. War, Money and the English State, 1688–1783* (New York, Alfred A. Knopf, 1989)

Brooks, Francis, 'Revising the Conquest of Mexico: Smallpox, Sources, and Populations', in *Journal of Interdisciplinary History* XXIV:1, Summer 1993, 1–29

Canny, Nicholas, *Europeans on the Move. Studies on European Migration, 1500–1800* (Oxford, Clarendon Press, 1994)

Cipolla, Carlo M., *Guns and Sails in the Early Phase of European Expansion, 1400–1700* (London, Collins, 1965)

Cressy, David, *Coming Over. Migration and Communication between England and New England in the Seventeenth Century* (Cambridge, Cambridge University Press, 1987)

Crosby, Alfred W., *Ecological Imperialism. The Biological Expansion of Europe, 900–1900* (Cambridge, Cambridge University Press, 1986)

Davis, Ralph, *The Rise of the English Shipping Industry in the Seventeenth and Eighteenth Centuries* (Newbolt Abbot, David and Charles, 1962)

Diamond, Jared, *Guns, Germs, and Steel. The Fates of Human Societies* (New York, W.W. Norton, 1997)

Diffie, B.W. and G.D. Winnius, *Foundations of the Portuguese Empire, 1415–1580* (Oxford, Oxford University Press, 1977)

Eccles, W.J., *The Canadian Frontier 1534–1760* (New York, Holt Rinehart & Winston, 1969)

Eid, Leroy V, '"A Kind of Running Fight": Indian Battlefield Tactics in the Late Eighteenth Century', in *The Western Pennsylvania Historical Magazine*, vol. 71, no. 2, April 1988, 147–71

Eltis, David, *The Military Revolution in Sixteenth-Century Europe* (New York, I.B. Tauris, 1995)

Gardiner, C. Harvey, *Naval Power in the Conquest of Mexico* (Austin, University of Texas Press, 1956)

Graham, Gerald, *Empire of the North Atlantic* (Toronto, University of Toronto Press, 1950)

Grigg, David, *Population Growth and Agricultural Change. An Historical Perspective* (Cambridge, Cambridge University Press, 1980)

Jones, D.W., *War and Economy in the Age of William III and Marlborough* (London, Blackwell, 1988)

Kennedy, Paul, *The Rise and Fall of British Naval Mastery* (London, Ashfield Press, 1976)

Lamb, H.H., *Climate, History and the Modern World* (New York, Routledge, 1995)

Levathes, Louise, *When China Ruled the Seas. The Treasure Fleet of the Dragon Throne 1405–1433* (New York, Simon and Schuster, 1994)

Livi-Bacci, Massimo, *A Concise History of World Population* (Oxford, Blackwell, 1992)

McCusker, J.J. and R.R. Menard, *The Economy of British America 1607–1789* (Chapel Hill, University of North Carolina Press, 1985)

McNeill, W.H., *Plagues and Peoples* (New York, Doubleday, 1977)

McNeill, W.H., *The Pursuit of Power. Technology, Armed Forces, and Society Since AD 1000* (Chicago, University of Chicago Press, 1982)

Mahan, A.T., *The Influence of Seapower Upon History, 1660–1783* (London, 1890)

Malone, Patrick M., *The Skulking Way of War. Technology and Tactics Among the New England Indians* (Baltimore, Johns Hopkins University Press, 1991)

Modelski, George, and William P. Thompson, *Seapower in Global Politics 1494–1993* (Seattle, University of Washington Press, 1988)

O'Brien, Patrick K. and R. Quinault, *The Industrial Revolution and British Society* (Cambridge, Cambridge University Press, 1993)

Parker, Geoffrey, *The Military Revolution* (Cambridge, Cambridge University Press, 1988)

Parry, J.H., *The Spanish Seaborne Empire* (London, Hutchinson, 1966)

Pearson, M.N., *The Portuguese in India* in *The New Cambridge History of India* series (Cambridge, Cambridge University Press, 1987)

Phillips, Carla Rahn, *Six Galleons for the King of Spain. Imperial Defence in the Early Seventeenth Century* (Baltimore, Johns Hopkins University Press, 1986)

Raudzens, George, 'So Why Were the Aztecs Conquered, and What Were the Wider Implications?', in *War in History*, II, no. 1, 1995, pp. 87–104

——, 'Why Did Amerindian Defences Fail?', in *War in History*, III, no. 3, 1996, pp. 331–52

Scammell, G.V., *The World Encompassed. The First European Maritime Empires,* c. *800–1650* (Berkeley, University of California Press, 1981)

Smith, Roger C., *Vanguard of Empire. Ships of Exploration in the Age of Columbus* (Oxford, Oxford University Press, 1993)

Solow, Barbara L. and Stanley L. Engerman (eds), *British Capitalism and Caribbean Slavery. The Legacy of Eric Williams* (Cambridge, Cambridge University Press, 1987)

Solow, Barbara L. (ed.), *Slavery and the Rise of the Atlantic System* (Cambridge, Cambridge University Press, 1991)

Steele, Ian K., *The English Atlantic 1675–1740. An Exploration of Communication and Community* (Oxford, Oxford University Press, 1986)

Subrahmanyam, Sanjay, *The Portuguese Empire in Asia 1500–1700. A Political and Economic History* (Harrow, Essex, Longman Group, 1983)

Tallett, Frank, *War and Society in Early Modern Europe 1495–1715* (London, Routledge, 1992)

Trigger, Bruce G., *Natives and Newcomers: Canada's 'Heroic Age' Reconsidered* (Kingston, Ontario, McGill-Queen's University Press, 1985)

Unger, Richard W., *The Ship in the Medieval Economy 600–1600* (London, Croom Helm, 1980)

Index

References to illustrations are given in bold